FEMINISM, ADULT EDUC[...] [...]
CREATIVE POSSIBILITY

FEMINISM, ADULT EDUCATION AND CREATIVE POSSIBILITY

Imaginative Responses

Edited by
Darlene E. Clover, Kathy Sanford and Kerry Harman

BLOOMSBURY ACADEMIC
LONDON • NEW YORK • OXFORD • NEW DELHI • SYDNEY

BLOOMSBURY ACADEMIC
Bloomsbury Publishing Plc
50 Bedford Square, London, WC1B 3DP, UK
1385 Broadway, New York, NY 10018, USA
29 Earlsfort Terrace, Dublin 2, Ireland

BLOOMSBURY, BLOOMSBURY ACADEMIC and the Diana logo are
trademarks of Bloomsbury Publishing Plc

First published in Great Britain 2022
This paperback edition published 2023

Series design by Catherine Wood
Cover image © Studiojumpee/Shutterstock

A catalogue record for this book is available from the British Library.

A catalog record for this book is available from the Library of Congress.

Library of Congress Control Number: 2022932622

ISBN: HB: 978-1-3502-3104-7
         PB: 978-1-3502-3108-5
       ePDF: 978-1-3502-3105-4
      eBook: 978-1-3502-3106-1

Series: Bloomsbury Critical Education

Typeset by Integra Software Services Pvt. Ltd.

To find out more about our authors and books visit www.bloomsbury.com
and sign up for our newsletters.

CONTENTS

Part I
VISUALIZING AND THE FEMINIST IMAGINARY

Part IV
CARING AND THE FEMINIST IMAGINARY

FIGURES

Chapter 1

Chapter 2

Chapter 3

Chapter 5

Chapter 6 (All photos by Nancy Taber)

Chapter 7

Chapter 8

Chapter 10

Chapter 12

Chapter 13

CONTRIBUTORS

Salsabel Almanssori is a doctoral candidate, teacher educator and instructor at the University of Windsor, Ontario, Canada. She is also a registered and practising school teacher. Her interdisciplinary research is focused in the intersections between teacher education and feminist understandings of gender-based and sexual violence.

Darlene E. Clover is Professor of Adult Education in Leadership Studies, University of Victoria, Canada. Her areas of research and teaching include cultural leadership and education, feminist adult education and leadership, and arts-based adult education and research methods. Darlene's current international research focuses on art galleries and museums, and she is Co-President of the Board of the Society of Friends of St Ann's Academy (SFSAA), a heritage site that facilitates critical conversations on women's and feminist issues.

Eve Cobain is Research Officer at AONTAS, the Irish National Adult Learning Organisation, Ireland. She supports the delivery of the organization's research initiatives, with a particular focus on community education. Eve received a PhD from the School of English Trinity College, Dublin, in 2017.

Sondra Cuban's research focuses on mapping migration, gender and care labour using a feminist perspective. She has received numerous grants and published two books: *Deskilling Migrant Women in the Global Care Industry* (2013) and *Transnational Family Communication: Immigrants and ICTs* (2017). Her forthcoming book focuses on migrant women in the Latin American & Caribbean region, *Mapping Southern Migration Routes of Women: A Case Study of Chile*. See: https://wce.wwu.edu/user/cubans

Edna TŦE NE SNÁ, ĆSE LÁ,E SEN EȾ W̱JOȽEȽP. My name is Edna Ellsworth, I am from the W̱JOȽEȽP First Nation. I am a Camosun College student who aspires to become a doctor to be able to create change and provide a sense of comfort to all. I believe that art is an impactful way to provoke thought in people, and is a beautiful way to represent the experiences and perceptions of others. I believe that through art people, especially women, are able to create change through sharing their stories in hopes that others will begin to understand what needs to be changed in the world.

Gaia Del Negro was awarded a PhD in Education from Canterbury Christ Church University, UK. Currently, she is an independent researcher collaborating with Milano-Bicocca University. Gaian explores auto/biographical transformative methodologies for researching knowing in professional lives, studies ecosomatic artistic movement and teaches Italian as a foreign language.

Leah Dowdall is Head of Research at AONTAS, the Irish National Adult Learning Organisation, Ireland. She is responsible for the development and implementation of AONTAS' research agenda and has published on learner voice and community education in Ireland. She holds a PhD and MPhil in history from Trinity College Dublin, Ireland and a Master of Education degree from Framingham State University, USA. Leah has worked as an educator in both the United States and Ireland.

Suriani Dzulkifli is a Malaysian PhD candidate at the University of Victoria (UVic), Canada. Her research focuses on adult education in higher education, social justice, decolonizing discourses, using an arts-based approach. She is Research Coordinator of the UVic Gender Justice, Creative Pedagogies and Arts-Based Research Group and the programme manager and co-instructor of the Knowledge for Change training programme in community-based participatory research with the UNESCO Chair in Community-Based Research and Social Responsibility in Higher Education.

Catherine Etmanski is a descendant of immigrants from mixed European heritage. She currently serves as Professor and Director of the School of Leadership Studies at Royal Roads University, British Columbia, Canada. She is a passionate educator who incorporates creative, experiential approaches into her scholarship, leadership practice and work toward social-ecological justice and the ongoing process of decolonization.

Claudia Firth is currently Associate Lecturer at Ravensbourne University, UK and Birkbeck College, University of London, UK. She recently completed a PhD in Cultural and Critical Studies. Her study examined informal adult education within a non-linear history of three moments of post-economic crises, situating small group learning within social and political movements of each era. Recent publications include *The Force of Listening* co-written with Lucia Farinati, which explores the role of listening at the intersection of contemporary art and activism. Claudia is also a facilitator and consultant working with groups and organizations such as the Precarious Workers Brigade and the London Renters Union.

Laura Formenti is Professor at Milano Bicocca University, Italy, President of the Italian Universities' Network for Lifelong Learning and Joint Convenor of ESREA's Life History and Biography Network. Her work focuses on developing a compositional approach in adult education research, mixing participatory and arts-based methods with biographical writing, embodied experience and critical reflection. Her book, *Transforming Perspectives in Lifelong Learning and Adult Education: A Dialogue*, co-written with Linden West received the 2019 Cyril O. Houle Award.

Kerry Harman is Director of the Research Centre for Social Change and Transformation in Higher Education, at Birkbeck, University of London, UK. She also leads the MSc in Education, Power and Social Change, in the Department of Psychosocial Studies. Kerry is a founding member of the Decolonising the Academy Collective (Birkbeck) and the Feminist Aesthetic Research and Pedagogies of Possibility network, an international network of activist scholars using feminist aesthetics approaches. Kerry is interested in approaches for producing knowledge that take the knowledges of marginalized groups seriously. She is currently working with homecare workers in the UK through New imaginaries of care.

Bev Hayward is Associate Lecturer at Birkbeck College, University of London, UK, within the Psychosocial Department. She teaches in the master's programme in Education, Power and Social Change. Having a learning disability, she was often marginalized in the UK educational system; accordingly, by exposing this vulnerability she hopes to foster a transformative and democratic pedagogical student experience. Bev was awarded the Tilda Gaskell prize for the best student paper (PhD) and the Laurel Brake award for her master's thesis. She is a poet, writer and embroider.

Kaye Hare is an SSHRC-funded PhD Candidate and Public Scholar at the University of British Columbia (UBC), Canada, in the Department of Language and Literacy Education. She has also taught as a sessional faculty member at UBC and University Canada West. Her research interests include bodies and embodiment, sexuality education and qualitative and arts-based research methods. Her work can be found in journals such as *Culture, Health & Sexuality*, *The International Journal of Qualitative Methods*, and *Emotion, Space and Society*. She loves documentary films and writing small stories. Email: hare.kathleen@gmail.com

Dorothea Harris' family is from Snuneymuxw First Nation, and she is a grateful visitor on the Lekwungen, W̱SÁNEĆ and Sc'ianew territories in Victoria, British Columbia. Dorothea is Indigenous Initiatives Coordinator at the University of Victoria, Canada, and holds a BSW (Indigenous Specialization) from UVic. She is currently PhD student in Leadership Studies, Adult Education and Community Engagement and was recently awarded the prestigious Vanier Award. Her research focus is the impacts of post-secondary education on Coast Salish students.

Ivan Kirchgaesser is a transgender writer, researcher and performer based in Berlin, Germany, and Puebla, Mexico. In 2020 he received a PhD from Oxford Brookes University. Living life as art is an interest he has been following for many years so his research takes place anytime and anywhere – from kitchen tables and drag shows to academic conferences and gardens. Ivan draws on creativity research; transformative learning theory; phenomenology; adult education; queer and feminist studies as well as psychoanalysis. Ivan has begun to write about his transgender experiences, and his blog, artistsofsociety.com, takes up multifaceted question of how people can become creative co-shapers of society.

Silvia Luraschi earned a PhD from Milano-Bicocca University, Italy, and is an educator, Feldenkrais method practitioner and researcher in Adult Education collaborating now with Milano-Bicocca University. Her research interests include embodied narratives, aesthetic practices and walking methodologies. In 2020 she won the Canada-Italy Innovation Award from the Canadian Embassy in Italy for her project entitled *Changing Gendered Patterns of Power through Creative Dialogic Pedagogies*.

Amber Moore is an SSHRC-funded PhD Candidate and Killam Laureate at The University of British Columbia (UBC), Canada. Her research interests include adolescent literacies, feminist pedagogies, teacher education, arts-based research, rape culture and trauma literature, particularly YA sexual assault narratives. Her work can be found in journals such as *Cultural Studies ↔ Critical Methodologies, Feminist Media Studies, Journal of Adolescent and Adult Literacy* and *Qualitative Inquiry*, among others. Amber is an incoming Banting Postdoctoral Fellow at Simon Fraser University.

Tracey Murphy is a PhD candidate in Equity Studies at Simon Fraser University, Canada. Her research has examined the potential of art-based research, pedagogy and activism to disrupt colonial narratives and create platforms for alternative voices for truth telling. Tracey's current research focus includes decolonizing land-based environmental restoration through an Indigenous feminist lens, embodied listening and disruption/dismantlement of the ongoing patriarch colonial structures in education.

Hayałkangame'– Carey Newman is a multi-disciplinary artist and master carver of Kwakwaka'wakw, Coast Salish, and Settler ancestry. He is Audain Professor of Contemporary Art Practice of the Pacific Northwest at the University of Victoria, Canada. Through his work, he strives to highlight Indigenous, social and environmental issues, examine the impacts of colonialism and capitalism, and harness the power of material truth to trigger the necessary emotion to drive positive change.

Kathy Sanford is Professor in Curriculum & Instruction at the University of Victoria, Canada. Her research interests include feminist pedagogy, critical adult education, community-engaged learning, teacher education and assessment practices. Her teaching includes multiliteracies, transdisciplinary learning and qualitative feminist research methodologies. She also focuses on museums and art galleries, and her most recent co-edited volume is entitled *Feminist Critique and the Museum: Educating for a Critical Consciousness* (Brill, 2020).

Lauren Spring completed her PhD in the Adult Education and Community Development, University of Toronto, Canada. She holds an MA in International Development and has also attended various theatre schools in both Canada and Europe. Lauren has written and published scholarly and creative work about gender, madness, art history, theatre, museum pedagogy, critical disability and arts-based research. She is a sessional course instructor at the University of Toronto where she teaches in the Sociology and Equity Studies departments as well as with the School of the Environment and the Interdisciplinary Centre for Health and Society.

Nancy Taber is Professor in the Department of Educational Studies at Brock University, Canada. She teaches in the areas of critical adult education and sociocultural learning, with a focus on gender and militarism. Her research explores the ways in which learning, gender and militarism interact in daily life, popular culture, museums, academic institutions and military organizations. Her publications include *Gendered Militarism in Canada: Learning Conformity and Resistance* (2015). Nancy is currently conducting fiction-based research to explore the complexities of women's lives as relates to war and militarism.

SERIES EDITOR'S FOREWORD

This new book series was introduced against an international background that comprised and continues to comprise situations that are disturbing and intriguing. The onset of Covid-19 has thrown into sharp relief arguably the major casualty of this pandemic, an unprepared, failed state. We have been left with a state shorn of the facilities and provisions one would expect of a purportedly 'democratic' entity that dances not only to the tune of capital accumulation but also to that reflecting the concerns of all people under its jurisdiction. The latter is certainly not the case as, with regard to the provision of social safeguards, the state has, in many places, almost been rendered threadbare by its accommodation of nefarious neoliberal policies which leaves everything outside the demands of capital to the market and voluntary organizations. While wealth is concentrated, as a result, in the hands of a few, there are those who are left to struggle for survival in a Darwinian contest that rewards the 'winners' and renders others disposable. Questionable wealth is concentrated in the hands of a few, who take advantage of their network of spin-doctors and 'fake news' soothsayers, to play the victim with regard to the pandemic. They and the many policymakers who accommodate them deflect their responsibility onto ordinary citizens and further justify curtailing the state's social spending, to the detriment of the many, 'the multitudes', as referred to by Michael Hart and Toni Negri.

The series was launched at a time when the 'social contract', ideally one which transcends the capitalist framework (as Henry Giroux astutely remarks), is continuously being shredded as several people are removed from the index of human concerns. Many are led to live in a precarious state. Contract work has become the norm, a situation that renders one's life less secure. There is also criticism targeted at the very nature of production and consumption with their effects on people and their relationship to other social beings and the rest of the planet, hence 'questionable wealth'.

They are also difficult times because the initial enthusiasm for the popular quest for democracy in various parts of the world has been tempered by eventual realism based on the fact that strategically entrenched forces are not removed simply by overthrowing a dictator. Far from ushering in a 'spring', the uprisings in certain countries have left political vacuums – fertile terrain for religiously motivated terrorism that presents a real global security threat. This threat, though having to be controlled in many ways, not least tackling the relevant social issues at their root, presents many with a carte blanche to trample on hard-earned democratic freedoms and rights. The situation is said to further spread the 'culture of militarization' that engulfs youth, about which much has been written in critical education. Terrorist attacks or aborted coups allow scope for analyses on these grounds, including analyses that draw out the implications for education.

The security issue, part of the 'global war on terror', is availed of by those who seek curtailment of human beings' right to asylum seeking and who render impoverished migrants as scapegoats for the host country's economic ills. The issue of migration would be an important contemporary theme in the large domain of critical education. This phenomenon and that of Covid-19, as with any other pretext, are availed of by powers acting exclusively in the interest of capital. This leads to a further siege mentality marked by increasing otherizing, scapegoating, surveillance and incarceration. Security extends beyond the culture of fear generated through terrorism to include health issues such as the pandemic, the latter said to be spread by those who, in reality, are the least equipped to work and live safely in their homes, including rejected asylum seekers and other migrants denied citizenship, those who live in restricted and overcrowded spaces or ... who do not have a home – period. They face a stark choice: exposure or starvation. Barbarism, in Rosa Luxemburg's sense of the term, is a key feature of this choice and the society in which many live.

The series was introduced at a time when an attempt was made for politics to be rescued from the exclusive clutches of politicians and bankers. A more grassroots kind of politics has been constantly played out in globalized public arenas such as the squares and streets of Athens, Madrid, Istanbul (Gezi Park), Cairo, Tunis and New York City. A groundswell of dissent, indignation and tenacity was manifest and projected throughout all corners of the globe, albeit, as just indicated, not always leading to developments hoped for by those involved. Yet hope springs eternal. Some of these manifestations have provided pockets for alternative social action to the mainstream, including educational action. Authors writing on critical education have found, in these pockets, seeds for a truly and genuinely democratic pedagogy that will hopefully be explored and developed, theoretically and empirically, in this series.

It is in these contexts, and partly as a response to the challenges they pose, that this new series on Critical Education was conceived and brought into being. Education, though not to be attributed powers it does not have (it cannot change things on its own), surely has a role to play in this scenario; from exposing and redressing class politics to confronting the cultures of militarization, consumerism, individualism and ethnic supremacy. The call among critical educators is for a pedagogy of social solidarity that emphasizes the collective and communal in addition to the ecologically sustainable.

Critical educators have for years been exploring, advocating and organizing ways of seeing, learning and living that constitute alternatives to the mainstream. They have been striving to make their contribution to changing the situation for the better, governed by a vision or visions of systems that are socially more just. The ranks of the oppressed are swelling. Hopefully, it is the concerns of these people that are foremost in the minds and hearts of those committed to a social-justice-oriented critical education. I would be the first to admit that even a professed commitment to a critical education can degenerate into another form of radical chic or academic sterility. We need to be ever so vigilant towards not only others but also ourselves, coming to terms with our own contradictions, therefore seeking, in Paulo Freire's words, to become less incoherent.

This series offers a platform for genuinely socially committed critical educators to express their ideas in a systematic manner. It seeks to offer signposts for an alternative approach to education and cultural work, constantly bearing in mind the United Nations Sustainable Development Goals that, albeit difficult to realize, serve as important points of reference when critiquing current policies in different sectors, including education. The series' focus on critical education, comprising the movement known as critical pedagogy, is intended to contribute to maintaining the steady flow of ideas that can inspire and allow for an education that eschews the 'taken for granted'.

In this particular volume, Darlene Clover, Kerry Harman and Kathy Sanford assemble a team of feminist activists and scholars to indicate, internationally, how the creative arts can serve to rupture narratives of patriarchy and domination in general and steer skilfully a meandering route through complexity especially with regard to the seemingly opposites they highlight in the first chapter which, however, existed in relation with each other and therefore dialectically. The creative arts, in which the editors have long been engaging in their critical analyses, help one to capture the tensions involved bringing to light the relational elements which are not easily perceived in our readiness to dismiss concepts and actions as simply binary opposites. 'Without contraries is no progression', an English artist and bard, albeit male, once declared. The authors in this volume create progressive feminist pathways from the contraries explored, showing, given their feminist acumen, that we live in a relational world where the so-called contraries often exist in a delicate tension with each other. This is a boon for those who believe in the creative arts and products of the imagination as vehicles for learning and partaking of social justice. The connections identified between critical education and different forms of creative practice, the focus of a Master's degree programme in the department in which I teach (Social Practice Arts & Critical Education), are teased out in the various chapters in this well-crafted volume that is genuinely international.

Peter Mayo
Series Editor,
University of Malta,
Msida, Malta

Introduction: Opposites, Intersections, Turns and Other Imaginative Possibilities

Darlene E. Clover, Kathy Sanford and Kerry Harman

But danger and possibilities are sisters.

Solnit, 2004, p. 12

When we trace the decades of feminist thought and activism, what emerges is a complex story of opposites, of losses and victories, declines and upsurges, setbacks and groundswells. The global context in which feminists work is too composed of dangers and possibilities, separations and commonalities, fragmentations and solidarities, distortions and alignments, dominations and rebellions, oppressions and liberations, rationalities and creativities, objective forces and subjective forces, helping and hindering, invisibilities and visibilities, silence and voice, caring and indifference, fake news and truth telling, despair and hope, and the ever resilient notions of masculinity and femininity (Cocks, 1989; Moraga & Anzaldua, 1981; Rowbotham et al., 2013; Solnit, 2004/2014). For Cocks (1989) opposites are problematic but they should not be seen as simply dichotomies. Too, Indigenous feminists such as Archibald (2004) and Atleo (2016) ask us to see opposites not merely as separations but rather as 'two-eyed seeing … a perceptual shift between two grounds' (p. 36).

Feminism, adult education and creative possibility: Imaginative responses emerges at the intersections of these opposites, recognizing them as dynamic tensions, neither easily reconcilable nor completely dissolvable, using them as resources for theorizing, teaching, learning, investigating, performing, caring, collaborating, painting, recycling, visualizing, representing, exhibiting and storying. In this volume, we propose the broad term 'feminist imaginary' as the ability to think what was unthinkable, to hear voices previously dismissed as noise, to rupture and unsettle, to act upon the unactionable, to anchor with pragmatism yet roam with imagination. The feminist imaginary is an aesthetic rupture with the prevailing relations of power, a shaking loose of normative perspectives, the generation of new knowledges, histories and possibilities and senses of hope in and with the uncertainties arising from an oppositional world. More specifically, the feminist imaginary in this volume is the arts-based and aesthetic practices of a group of feminist adult educators, teacher educators, researchers, scholars and activists from Canada, England, Italy, Malaysia, Germany and Chile/United States, who in diverse ways work to change what Solnit (2004) calls the 'imagination of change' (p. 57). We use the term 'aesthetic practices' broadly and understand these as practices that are associated with art and creativity but also, a feminist imaginary aesthetic rupture, where cultural materials and artefacts as well as experiences are reconfigured into what is able to be known, sensed and acted upon.

Foundational to the creation of *Feminism, Adult Education and Creative Possibility: Imaginative Responses* was a series of critical questions: How do feminist adult educators, researchers and activists encourage an imagination adequate to our current dangers and possibilities? What is the feminist imagination and how is it activated in the interests of gender justice and social change? How does an emphasis on the aesthetic disrupt the epistemologies of mastery and practices of 'common sense' making that exclude, silence and marginalize? What creative feminist practices are being wielded to encourage new knowledge and creative action? How do feminist decolonizing strategies imagine and galvanize hope and change? What types of feminist representations and stories evoke a sense of care and the spirit of possibility?

This volume is a celebration of our responses to the work of creative feminist adult educators, researchers and activists who came before and upon whom we draw. It is a collection of aesthetic methods, strategies, explorations and approaches aimed at a deeply troubled gendered, colonial, unjust and unsustainable world. It is centred in a belief of the powerful role that art, creative practices, the imagination and aesthetic rupture can play to change history, the present and the future. We, the authors, believe that feminist imaginary, enacted through feminist adult education and research, has a transformative potential to encourage people to think critically as well as creatively, to critique and tackle oppressions yet remain caring and optimistic, and to learn and act collectively to disrupt and destabilize continuing gender inequity and its intersection with other forms of injustice by attending to what is often not named, seen, heard, felt and making other stories, visualizations, and ways of knowing count.

The 'turns': Aesthetics and feminisms

Feminism, Adult Education and Creative Possibility is animated by two critical turns towards creativity, hope, vitality and possibility. The first turn is in the field of adult education, what Wildermeesch (2019) characterized as the 'aesthetic turn'. This turn is marked on one hand by an increase in a cultural politics of imaginative and creative thought and practice. Particularly amongst women and feminist adult education scholars, activists and researchers, this is manifested as an increase in the use of artistic and creative mediums ranging from theatre to textiles, photography to documentary films, storytelling to graphic novels to address ongoing gender, social, cultural and ecological injustices and inequities (e.g., Bishop, Etmanski & Page, 2019; Butterwick & Roy, 2018; Clover & Sanford, 2013; Yang & Lawrence, 2017). To borrow from Greene (1995, p. 123), at the very least, arts-based and aesthetic practices 'enable us to see more in our experience, to hear more on normally unheard frequencies'. In other words, to reconfigure common sense and the conventional. Experience, knowledge and politics all contain an aesthetic dimension, and this is a much broader notion of aesthetics than the focus on art, beauty and the sublime that came to dominate Western philosophy in the eighteenth century (Chanter, 2018). As Shotwell (2011) notes, aesthetics is the 'pursuit of a politics within which people can live with our whole selves – as political, social, emotional, physical beings who need to be able to find dignity and delight in many different dimensions of our being' (p. 119). Feminist politics attends to the plural experiences of women and the varied ways they, and others who have been excluded and marginalized, make sense of the worlds they inhabit by attending to pluralities of sensations and the ways these are made meaning. In this book, feminist sense and meaning making revolve most specifically, around the aesthetic, around a new feminist imaginary of vision, story, decolonization and caring.

For the feminist adult educators, researchers and activists who have contributed to this edited volume, the possibility of tackling the complex opposites of being multidimensional; of reconfiguring perspective, the conventional and the common; rests upon our ability to see, attend to and reimagine problematic patriarchal and prejudicial underpinnings and the impact these have on what can be seen, heard, known and imagined and by whom. Patriarchy's constructions of gender superiority and inferiority and its promotion and maintenance of white privilege, colonialism, neoliberalism, classism, authoritarianism and an array of other fundamentalisms have proved to be far more intractable than imagined. So prevalent and so embedded in the collective social imaginary, this patriarchal, classed and colonial conception of the world is often taken as simply how things are rather than as constructions developed in the interests of a few (e.g., Ahmed, 2017; Criado Perez, 2019). And this narrow way of conceiving the world has had very real, material effects. In its 2019 report, the United Nations reminded us that gender equality remains 'unfinished business *in every country in the world*' (p. 1, emphasis ours). Violence against women 'in its many manifestations continues in epidemic proportions in both South and North' (Baksh & Harcourt, 2015, p. 13). The global pandemic has revealed that women are 'far more affected … by the social and economic effects of infectious-disease outbreaks' (Wenham et al., 2020, p. 1). Hundreds of Indigenous women and girls have been murdered or gone missing under the radar of the justice system that purports to protect (see Etmanski & Newman and Murphy & Ellsworth this volume). In the UK, feminist histories are being removed from school curricula. 'When you erase women from the curriculum, you teach boys and girls that women's work is not important, that the contributions they made are not as valuable. If you start this drip-feeding early then you invite the sexism, inequality and misogyny that women are still experiencing today' (Speller, 2015, n/p). Controls continue to be wielded over people's bodies and identities, limiting choices and actions, obstructing rights and agency and even threatening lives (see Kirkgaesser this volume).

Patriarchal relations of power are re-enforced into the collective consciousness on a daily basis through language, stories and representations that consciously and unconsciously delineate the world along traditional gender lines as well as other lines that teach us who and what is important. Collectively, words, narratives and visualizations exercise a powerful force over our sense of perspective, in particular what people can, are able or are allowed to see and thus to know or to imagine as possible (Rose, 2001; see also Sanford & Clover this volume). When people's capacities as knowers are discounted, belittled or silenced, their ability to function 'fully as subjects' is weakened and they 'participate unequally in the practices through which social meanings are generated' (Fricker, 2007, p. 2; see also Harman this volume).

As patriarchal power reasserts itself in new ways, particularly through social media, new meanings and ways of seeing hearing and doing need to be developed, and collective political actions mobilized. This brings us to the second 'turn' that animates *Feminism, adult education and creative possibility: Imaginative responses,* a turning to feminism in new and exciting ways. Feminism has a complex history and there have been problems created by some feminists themselves, in particular the failure to attend to white privilege (see Dzulkifli this volume). From the outside, feminists have faced decades of vilification, allegations of being bra-burning, man hating, ugly, angry old hags who are irrelevant to young 'modern' women (e.g., McRobbie, 2009). Yet we are now in the midst of a resurgence of new feminist thought, including greater contributions by trans and Indigenous feminists that are made material through new social movements such as #MeToo, Black Lives Matter and women leading Indigenous movements such as Idle No More. To borrow from Nazneen and Sultan (2014), this turn is a 'critical motor that gives women the greatest possibility of being seen and heard' (p. 5). Feminism is being reclaimed by both young and old as a hopeful, richly complicated and promising political project of transformation and change that is, as hooks (2007) reminds us, for everyone.

For trans feminist Scott-Dixon (2006), coming to feminism is an '"aha" moment of abruptly punctuated reality, a mixture of anger at social injustice, feelings of doubt and wanting to know more, to gobble up ideas and experiences that speak to a budding consciousness' (p. 11). She also frames it in opposites, noting how sometimes feminism 'is painful; sometimes it is freeing' (p. 11). When Ahmed (2017) hears the term feminism it fills her with a sense of hope and a new energy. For Indigenous feminist scholar Green (2017) reclaiming feminism offers us a means to address 'issues ranging from colonialism, racism and sexism, sexuality, environmental integrity, and infrastructure, to identity … and political liberation' (p. 17). It enables us to address prejudice, problematic common sense, systemic racism and the gender injustice that is built into all institutions and structures of society. For the contributors to this volume, feminism is also about asking ourselves how we can most creatively disrupt, unsettle and destabilize patriarchal power and privilege using alternative forms and means to see, know, hear, speak and imagine other possibilities.

Feminist adult education

To borrow from Manicom and Walters (2012), feminist adult education in this volume is a standpoint, a political process and a pedagogical intent through a variety of methods, approaches and strategies. While there is not one overarching definition of feminist adult education, feminist adult educators work with 'women' as a constituency and a political category because this category still very much exists. The world is still divided along traditional gender lines of masculinity and femininity that align with the opposites of superiority and inferiority, making it easy 'to ignore, dismiss, reject and even hurt one another' (hooks, 1984, p. i). Yet feminist adult educators also recognize that 'women' is not a unified social group; we are not all the same and we do not see or experience the world similarly. The category of 'women' consists of intersectionalities of race, sexuality, class, ethnicity, age and ability that influence how feminists educate and understand change. The aim, therefore, is to acknowledge differences whilst forging connections and alliances that expand the horizons of intelligibility. This is an expansive notion of knowledge production and learning.

The chapters in *Feminism, Adult Education and Creative Possibility: Imaginative Responses* contribute to an understanding of feminist adult education as a process of producing aesthetic rupture and reconfiguring what and who is able to be sensed and made sense of. In this sense feminist adult education is about 'unsettling' problematic assumptions and common-sense perspectives that have been instilled through traditional gendered or colonial narratives as well as expanding experiences, understandings and capacities (see Walters & Von Kotze, 2021). Learning as aesthetic rupture is when we can sense and make sense of sense in ways that were previously not possible. Feminist adult educators work to create learning environments that begin with and respect people's knowledge by providing the opportunity for learners to share their experiences. Through the process of sharing experiences existing experiences can be expanded. As feminist adult education is action-orientated, this might include engaging in public actions. At times collective public action can attract fierce and abusive backlash and critique. This brings us to a set of tensions in feminist adult education: the personal and collective.

Heng (1996) reminds feminist adult educators that we need to focus on the personal and individual needs of women, and others who have experienced systemic oppression. For Heng, this means attending to women's personal lack of power and the unique 'disempowering experiences that have disabled them' (p. 204) by shaping learning around individual needs and concerns in ways that validate and build confidence and self-esteem. Yet to change this deeply problematic patriarchal world requires a collective response, an overtly political pedagogy of knowledge production that constructs a collective political subjectivity with the power to speak uncomfortable truths through collective public action. Ahmed's figure of 'the feminist killjoy' (2017) captures this ambition.

On one hand, feminist adult education is about the cognitive, the recognition and creation of knowledge as a response to what Fricker (2007) calls the epistemic injustices that silence, belittle and undermine individuals and entire groups of people such as women in their capacities as holders, speakers and 'givers of knowledge' (p. 7). Yet equally critical is a focus on other dimensions of knowing. Feminist adult educators have long realized the important role emotions play in daily life and the learning process. Passions such as fear, wonder, love, sadness and happiness are powerful tools. Anger, what Freire (2004) once called 'just ire', about issues such as pollution and social injustice stimulates actions and projects for change (see Cobain and Dowdall this volume). To talk about the cognitive and the emotional as separate is problematic because together they enable us 'to discuss multiple oppression and discrimination processes' without losing sight of the power of the human emotional dimension to produce alternatives (Akkent & Kovar, 2019, p. 3).

Other dimensions of feminist adult education, raised in this volume particularly by Firth and Harris, are speaking and hearing, storytelling and listening. Creating space for dialogue, conversation and storytelling sharpens both our 'language of critique and language of possibility' (Butterwick, 2016, p. 12). But feminist adult educators also need to inspire what Fricker (2007) calls 'responsible hearers', people with the ability to listen deeply because 'deep listening is an embodied and active standpoint' (Butterwick & Selman, 2003, p. 7). Building on this are questions of invisibility and visibility and how feminist adult educators render visible practices that make some histories, experiences and needs invisible.

The feminist imaginary

Although the imagination is often presumed to be light, ephemeral and 'not real', the effects of the imagination are not inconsequential and therefore the imagination is not neutral (Helmore, 2021). The 'imagination is highly consequential because control over it is control over ... the future. Imagining what could be is a very powerful tool' (n/p). In a world where imperialist, white capitalist patriarchy prevails, the imagination has a deeply problematic side because the imagination is what has enabled humanity to build bombs, to control natural forces, and to lie, not just little lies but 'massive collective lies such as racism, sexism, classism, and fascism' (p. n/p). Writing about the current environmental crisis, Solnit (2014) argues that one of the problems is in fact 'a failure of the imagination' (p. 24).

The imagination, like feminism and feminist adult education, has no single definition. It is, however, a driving force of individual expression as well as a collective process that enables us to navigate the contours of a troubled yet promising world. To exercise the imagination through arts and other aesthetic practices is to explore possibilities. The feminist imaginary in *Feminism, Adult Education and Creative Possibility: Imaginative Responses* is a conscious creative political project that rests on the notion that the imagination is one of the most subversive things people can have (Mohanty, 2012). It is the capacity to see what is not there, to sit in discomfort as well as to take risks, to tell our stories and to listen to the stories of others, to be logical and reasonable yet creative and playful. In the hands of the contributors of this volume, the feminist imaginary reflects the challenges and possibilities of intersections so while some curate exhibitions, others write love letters; while some unearth white privilege others encourage ecological consciousness; as some script fictions others physically map their environments; while some paint murals others reimagine care; as some employ theatre others compose poetry; as some wield cameras others weave blankets; while some ask us to listen others show us how to speak; as some tackle racism others blog women's power; while some produce documentaries others embroider identity; and as some share stories of trauma and pain, others paint rose gardens. Despite differences of emphasis, context, genre or intent, *Feminism, Adult Education and Creative Possibility: Imaginative Responses* is a celebration of intersections and the challenges and potential for hope and change these intersections make possible.

Visualizing and the feminist imaginary

The explosion of new visualizations today is not only illuminating but vital to change. To visualize is to form an image of something and to create a representation. Equally, to represent is to visualize through portrayal, to show something. Visualizations and representation are signs and symbols that aim to instil something in the mind but equally, to challenge something that may have become 'common sense'. Visualizing and representing are acts of imagination and as such they are never neutral. Our visualizations can express experiences, and they can also contribute to reimagining the world. Representations can envision the past and show a way forward.

Whenever 'people create representations of the world there are agendas at play', and particular sets of ideas, values, attitudes and identities assumed and normalised. There are thus issues of power, ownership, authenticity, and meaning at stake' (Kidd, 2015, p. 3). For Kidd (2015), representations are nothing less than what comes 'to be seen as common sense, and is accepted about the world' (p. 3). For this reason, Hall (2013) position representation as the most powerful socially educative force of our time. Representations have the capacity to reinforce ideas and beliefs (what Kidd called common sense) by reaffirming cultural and gender stereotypes. But they can also open new ways of imagining the world. Visualizing is a powerful form of knowledge and of knowing and knowledge is always saturated with power. In addition, as authors in this section point out in their diverse ways, representations are about visualizing the complexities of power and using those visualizations to engage in struggles for power. What we come to see through the contributions to this book is how representations have been used to solidify power relations, in particular, superiorities and inferiorities such as masculinities and femininities, whiteness and 'not' whiteness, humans and nature. However, as the authors also illustrate, the power of representation does not only reside with the powerful – representations can also be used to instil very different images, understandings and meanings of the world and ourselves; representations can disrupt the normative, render visible and reconfigure the way we know and understand the world.

Darlene Clover and Kathy Sanford start off in the world of visualizing and representation by recounting a disruptive pedagogical process they call *Curating Visibility: The Disobedient Women Exhibition as a Representational Feminist Imaginary of Possibility*. Designed as an intervention into the problematic patriarchal and colonizing public narratives of the Sesquicentenary of Canada, the authors take us on a visual and curatorial journey into the feminist multimedia research and pedagogical exhibition entitled *Disobedient Women: Defiance, Resilience and Creativity Past and Present*. Positioning the chapter in feminist discourses of vision, visibility, representation and imagination, Clover and Sanford outline the pedagogical elements behind the design and construction of their exhibition and how, through paintings and posters, poetry and puppets, videos and newspaper clippings, textiles and dioramas, *Disobedient Women* represented and shared the diversity of women's historical and contemporary defiance, resistance and resilience creativities. Interweaving comments from exhibition visitors, the chapter describes the impacts this exhibition had on the many visitors as it encouraged other ways of seeing, knowing and acting.

In Chapter 3, *Migrant Women Drawing Themselves in to Their Homes and Communities*, Sondra Cuban turns to the role that maps play as representational understanding of how women navigate space. The chapter is focused around a feminist ethnographic study through which migrant women from various Latin American and Caribbean (LAC) countries represented their im/mobilities within their new homes and communities through hand-drawn maps. Harkening back to a world of dichotomies we see in particular how differently two study participants experienced the worlds they inhabited despite their similarly marginalized positions. For Cuban, maps are powerful representational practices because they illuminate feelings, perceptions, subjective positionings, as well as the geographical imaginations of marginalized women in their new places of settlement. As the migrant women walked and waited for work opportunities, their maps capture their inner or outer worlds of anxiety on one hand, and courage on the other. For Cuban, mapping is not only a cartography of reality, experience, emotion and a person's sense of observation but a critical pedagogy that enables us to see and rethink colonization along gendered lines.

Through *Conversations from Creative Toolboxes: Journeys as Artists, Educators and Curators*, in Chapter 4 Bev Hayward introduces us to the important and creative, yet side-lined and subjugated work, of Learning Support Workers (LSAs) employed at a UK higher education institution. Interwoven with poetry and revolving particularly around two self-portraits, the chapter focusses specifically on the stories of two female support workers – the author herself and Luna – and how they (re)represented their own dichotomies of work and the aesthetic. Sidelined by the university from exhibiting their works in a public gallery, Hayward finds a way to exhibit publicly the works of LSAs in order to challenge masculine, elitist norms in both the academies of art and higher learning and celebrate the LSAs as artists and as artist-educators. In conversation with Luna, Hayward takes us on a journey of representational opposites, of oppression and exclusion, of power and courage, of setbacks and norms, and of the liberation that she proposes comes from seeing and being seen as artists.

The next two chapters are situated in feminist ecological imaginaries. They take up the current environmental crisis as in the context of a global path of destruction. We begin with Chapter 5, *The Feminist Aesthetic and Climate Action: A Case Study on Roscommon Women's Network,* where Eve Cobain and Leah Dowdall introduce us to the Roscommon Women's Network and its CycleUp group. Arguing that feminist community education groups are at the forefront of consciousness-raising and action around climate change in Ireland, the authors illustrate through the work of CycleUp how a material representative aesthetic works as a form of feminist-inspired environmental action. Central to the work of this is an imaginative repurposing of discarded items from the group's charity shop into diverse reusable and decorative household items. For the authors, feminist aesthetic practices not only challenge modern consumer culture, they also encourage women to envision a different world, to represent what the future can and needs to be from a feminist perspective. Artefacts in this case stimulate the critical feminist dialogues necessary to imagine a new practice of sustainability. Despite the challenges of being a small, underfunded women's group, Cobain and Dowdall illustrate the far-reaching benefits of participation in CycleUp as a transformative learning experience for both participants and the local community.

In the final chapter entitled *WASTELAND: A Feminist Public Pedagogical Response to Climate Anxiety,* Kathy Sanford and Darlene Clover describe a public pedagogical arts-based installation – in this case a pre-demolition house – called *Wasteland Climate Anxiety Haunted House* that was imagined into being by three feminist activist artist-educators. Working in collaboration with Indigenous and non-Indigenous artists, the installation provided a visual voice of visceral responses to concerns about today's most threatening challenge to our collective well-being. Sanford and Clover explore how the feminist artist-educators mobilized creativity, imagination and aesthetic practice, working in collaboration with youth from local secondary schools and a variety of other community artists to design and curate this powerful and provocative representative act of protest and pedagogy. Through its powerful representations this installation imagined previously unexpressed anxieties into being; through eerie murals, images, dioramas, plastic sculptures, paper mâché figures, music and lighting it gave hundreds of visitors' insights into very real fears that haunt so many.

Storying and the feminist imaginary

Harvey (2017) reminds us that 'we are all, every one of us, tellers and consumers of stories' (p. 1). The act of storytelling is in essence a social activity because stories are created, told and heard in social contexts. Stories are in fact crucial to our social interactions and are remarkable in their sheer generativity, flexibility and changeability. Stories are powerful in and of themselves; they are a struggle for the power to be told, how, where and by whom they get told and who really 'hears' them. For Archibald (2004) and Okri (1997) we both 'live by our stories [and] we live in them' (p. 46). These stories are planted in us but we also seed them 'knowingly or unknowingly – in ourselves' (p. 46).

Living by and in stories can be problematic because we are all positioned in particular ways in and through the circulation of prevailing metanarratives. And metanarratives often ignore the experiences of marginalized groups, making particular people and things invisible (hooks, 1984). Some stories have been silenced and ignored which constrains the development as a speaking and thus knowing subject. Yet as Solnit (2004) reminds us, there are always 'other ways of telling' (p. 13). The success of feminist social movements indicates that people have the power to change the stories that attempt to confine them and in so doing have the possibility to change their lives and those of others.

Feminist adult educators have long employed, honoured and celebrated storytelling as a pedagogical and methodological practice to challenge the powerful narratives that have had a stranglehold over the voices of women, those most central to this volume, as well as all who have been silenced and excluded. Telling our own stories matters because it shows us how our lives 'intersect with wider institutionalisations of gendered meaning' (Hemmings, 2011, p. 1). Stories and counter-stories can also be disrupting when they narrate 'uncomfortable truths about ongoing gender inequalities' (p. 1) in the form of a challenge to the masculine gaze through which so many lives have been refracted. Stories can bring experience to life, to make it present and real; they can be healing or empowering as people forge, through self-authored accounts, senses of self and society that articulate their own experience through their own words. Using different forms and mediums, and giving new and different life to past, the present and even the future, feminist storytelling speaks to that which is imaginable and what has been unimaginable. For this reason, Andrews (2014) positions 'narrative and imagination [as] integrally tied' (p. 1) to broader thoughts about what the world is or might be as well as an imagination of the minutiae of daily lives lived in and through our stories.

Nancy Taber begins the journey into the power of feminist storytelling in Chapter 6, *Feminist Fiction-based Research in the Context of War and Military Museums: Fostering Imagination, Engagement, and Empathy*. She focuses on the power of history and historical storytelling, sharing the tenets of fiction-based approaches to research that transform data into a creative pedagogical narrative. Framing her work through a feminist anti-military lens and drawing from the images and objects in war and military museum exhibitions and a heritage site as well as a historical text of a novel about Acadian women across different centuries, Taber shares two created fictional short stories that tell a tale of the past and the present. The first is about the First World War nurse haunted by war dead and the second recounts the story of a woman who believed her astronaut mother's death was the result of a conspiratorial cover-up. Taber argues that fictional storytelling is a creative feminist aesthetic of political possibility due to its power to engage readers' imaginations, challenge assumptions about women in the past, and generate empathy and connection in the interests of socio-gender change.

In Chapter 7, *Dark Realism: An Auto/Biographical Enquiry into Creative Strategies of Queer Resilience,* Ivan Kirckgaesser invites us into a piece of creative nonfiction told in three parts about how queer people make life worth living. One part is an auto/biographical narrative from the perspective of the author as a transgender feminist life researcher. The second part features personal case studies of their positive and negative experiences in Portugal, Berlin and Mexico. In part three, storytelling, reflection, analysis and images are woven together to explore the role of community and artistic life practices for LGBTQIA+ people's growth, learning and healing. Throughout the chapter, Kirckgaesser draws on the notion of aesthetics as 'enlivened being' and how this informs the shape of queer resilience and creativity, enabling us to think in spectrums rather than binaries to build building bridges across divisions of 'otherness'.

In the same genre, but writing as a collective, Laura Formenti, Silvia Luraschi and Gaia Del Negro present their disruptive practice of auto/biographical storytelling inspired by a Melandri, a Milanese feminist educator, in *Bringing Research into Life: An Experience of Feminist Practice with Artists.* Using what they call a 'mineralogy of thought' the authors illustrate how they 'mined' experience as a challenge to normative structures of the European academy and traditional forms of education that have excluded and othered experience as a form of knowing. To create the stories, Formenti, Luraschi and Del Negro interviewed two artists, a dancer and a pianist, as co-researchers. The result was the composition of a theatre script, written from and through the various embodied narratives. This was then presented as a performance at an international adult education conference. For the authors, writing, storying and performing experiential lives is an important feminist, embodied and imaginative pedagogy of possibility.

In Chapter 10, Salsabel Almansorri tells us a story of the alternative visions of the possibility of public sexual violence pedagogy happening at the colourful intersections of the #MeToo movement and the world of digital political activism. Using discourse analysis and situating her work in feminist theory, *#MeToo and the Feminist Digital Imaginary: Public Pedagogy on Sexual Consent and Violence* draws attention to the complexities and epistemological significances of storytelling as a pedagogical process in the online, virtual feminist world of YouTube vlogs. Almansorri's chapter begins with a critical review of the key concepts involved in understanding feminist sexual violence prevention, then positions #MeToo as a form of public pedagogy on consent and sexual violence and gives us critical look into the discursive representations, conversations and collective social understandings of sexual violence by women who speak out in the virtual world.

Centred particularly in opposites of thoughtfulness and thoughtlessness is the final chapter in this section, written by Suriani Dzulkifli. *We Are here and We Are Not a 'Minority': Co-creating a Decolonizing Feminist Space and Narrative for Non-white Women through Photography* begins with her own story of feeling dismissed and disrespected when it is announced by her colleague that her surname is deemed too difficult to learn. Despite her shock, no one comes to her defence. Based in issues of white privilege and racism, Dzulkifli introduces us to two other storytellers, Layla and Rae, who through photography are able to narrate and visualize their experiences of racism, specifically of abusive encounters on buses on their way to study at the university, and the lack of support they received from fellow riders, both male and female. This chapter reminds us of the power of images to help women to tell their stories of pain and trauma, of the reality and impact of racism on non-white women and of the need for white women to do better.

Decolonizing and the feminist imaginary

Decolonizing, as Tuck and Yang (2012) remind us, is not a metaphor. Rather, decolonizing serves to redress colonial injustices and repatriate Indigenous lands and life. Decolonization is intended to disrupt settler colonialism and bring to light both the wrongs perpetrated on Indigenous peoples and the cultural wisdom and knowledge that has been lost. Through the process of deconstructing colonial ideologies of superiority and the privileging of Eurocentric views and practices, decolonization challenges inequitable power dynamics and revitalizes Indigenous knowledge and practices.

As the chapters in this section demonstrate, decolonization is an ongoing, sometimes painful and sometimes joyous process requiring collective participation and responsibility. It is a process through which Indigenous peoples reclaim their traditional cultures and reclaim their distinct identities. It is through respectful listening to the voices of Indigenous peoples and attending to the artistic cultural representations they create that their identities and cultures can be reclaimed, remembered and valued.

Feminist aesthetic practices remind us of the power of visual representations to convey deep rich understandings of the world, and it is the visuality of the stories that bring their meaning back to life. Using intersectional decolonizing feminisms, we see that not only is the personal political in the ways it is represented and shared, but the personal is also collective (Weatherall, 2020). The representations in the three following chapters show the capacity of artistic representations through feminist lenses to highlight not only the injustices but ways in which the arts represent care and connection. The stories told through murals, installations, carvings and fashion remind us to listen and view with attention and caring – these stories guide our identity and inscribe our place in the world. As Clover (2019) reminds us, the feminist radical imagination allows 'that which can be seen, thought, known and produced once patriarchal relations of power are rendered visible' (p. xv).

Dorothea Harris ignites our imaginations with her chapter on cultural revitalization, drawing on her artistic family background to invigorate seven principles of Indigenous feminist aesthetic work. These principles of *Uy'skwuluwun* relate to reciprocal care and respect, physically, emotionally and spiritually connecting through arts-based work of beading, painting, cedar weaving, and knitting, locating us in place and time. Harris shows how Indigenous feminist aesthetic work is central to healing and wellness in Indigenous communities, particularly from the impacts of colonization. The intersectionality of matriarchal Indigenous arts-based storytelling speaks to the aesthetic work that women have engaged in over time, and tells the story, through women's voices and artefacts, that serve to bring us to a time before colonialization. Harris' chapter tells of the healing emotional work that is done through arts practices, challenging Eurocentric values and practices that have disconnected us from our lands, cultures and communities.

Carey Newman's *Witness Blanket*, a nationally acclaimed work of art created to address the atrocities of the Indian Residential School survivors in Canada, is explored in Chapter 11, *Decolonizing Aesthetics of the Witness Blanket* by Etmanski and Newman as a decolonizing aesthetics of remembering, and storying living history. The *Witness Blanket* both dismantles and recreates a colonial patriarchal time in Canada's history as demonstrated through the residential schools, bringing the voices of victims to life, telling their stories with beauty and reverence. Drawing on two of the 886 stories represented in the *Witness Blanket*, two braids of hair contributed by Ellen and Marion Newman, Carey's sisters, the authors interweave a feminist aesthetic with Indigenous understanding. They examine the intersecting stories, Kwakwaka'wakw epistemology, traditional ceremony and artistic treatment behind their inclusion. The *Witness Blanket* is a reminder to move beyond histories of pain and suffering to reimagine the possibility of living respectfully with the world and its inhabitants.

The final chapter in this section, *Murals as Storied Spaces: An Indigenous Feminist Practice of Hope and Healing,* tells the story of a participatory feminist arts-based project as it emerged from the imaginations of educators and youths working together to respond to the sweeping prevalence of murdered and missing women and girls (MMIWG) across Canada. Murphy and Ellsworth recount the mural project they created in response to this national epidemic that has only recently been recognized as the systemic racism and violence perpetrated against Indigenous women and girls. The final mural image, of an Indigenous woman surrounded by ancestral beings and the traditional medicinal plants of the W̲SÁNEĆ territories, powerfully illustrates how Indigenous women are nourished through deep-rooted connections to land and community teachings. They note that art is a powerful way of addressing issues that are difficult to talk about, particularly those who have been silenced. In this chapter, they highlight how Indigenous feminist proposals for activist art making offer generative possibilities to contest colonial patriarchal oppression.

Caring and the feminist imaginary

Care and caring have been central concerns in feminist literature for decades. As well as disrupting a notion of care and caring as essentially feminine characteristics and as naturally 'women's work', feminist scholars have underscored the importance of centring care and caring as core ethical concerns (Noddings, 2013; Tronto, 1994). At a time when carelessness and neglect prevail, not just in relation to how we humans care for each other but how we care for the environment and the planet, we need to query what if 'we were to begin instead to put care at the very centre of life?' (Chatzidakis et al., 2020, p. 5). It is this speculative 'what if' and the possibility enabled by reimagining the world that can be understood as the feminist imaginary. As Ahmed (2017) reminds us in *Living a Feminist Life*, self-care, particularly for people from marginalised groups, is a political act: 'In directing our care toward ourselves, we are redirecting care away from its proper objects; we are not caring for those we are supposed to care for; we are not caring for the bodies deemed worth caring about' (p. 239).

In *Matters of Care*, Puig de la Bellacasa (2017) centres caring (or what matters) in ways of knowing. For her (2017), knowing as a form of caring is about attending to 'neglected experiences' (p. 61) as well as 'being touched rather than observing from a distance' (p. 93). This is 'involved knowing, knowledge that cares' (p. 118) rather than a prevailing way of knowing in the academy which privileges *disinterest, being distant, neglecting*. Indeed, Collins (2000) centred an ethics of caring as a dimension of knowing decades ago when writing about feminist African-American women's ways of knowing. For Collins, connection and caring underpin African epistemologies rather than the Western philosophical emphasis on objectivity, distance and neutrality. And as she identified, these other ways of knowing are understood as dangerous as they challenge the Western philosophical tradition: 'Afrocentric feminist epistemology calls into question the content of what currently passes as truth and simultaneously challenges the process of arriving at the truth' (p. 271).

The centring of care ethics and caring is also not new to feminist adult educators. English and Irving (2015, p. 113) provide a reminder that Hart's idea of life-affirming work needs to be centred so that it becomes everyone's work and not just the work of women. O'Brien (2013) writes about the importance of practising transformation, care and 'becoming human' (p. 33) by integrating these elements into pedagogic programmes. Moreover, Etienne's concept of 'matriarchal learning hubs' centres 'older black Women's experiences of the concept of caring for the wider community' as integral to learning (2016, p. 26). The chapters in *Caring and the Feminist Imaginary* make an important contribution to feminist adult education literature through focusing on the possibility of aesthetic rupture and disrupting privileged ways of knowing. *What if* we were to centre *attending to, presence, paying attention, closeness, taking care* and *connection* rather than understanding these ways of knowing as aberrations and flaws when conducting research?

Kerry Harman commences this work in Chapter 13, *Creating Moments of Equality when Researching Sensory Ways of Knowing Homecare: Toward an Aesthetics of Care?*, by introducing a current research project she is developing with paid homecare workers in the UK and how 'taking care' is a central concern of the project. The political and pedagogical possibility of research, whereby it contributes to an aesthetic rupture of a prevailing 'subject/academic knower-object/research participant known' ordering reproduced in the academy is explored. The purpose is not to replace one research method with another 'better' approach but rather to expand thinking on how caring might be enacted when conducting academic research. The chapter directs attention to the performative aspects of research and the political possibility of research *as* intervention whereby research practices contribute to producing aesthetic rupture.

In Chapter 14, *Estrangement Pedagogy in Research-based Theatre about Madness,* Lauren Spring introduces a 'feminist mad aesthetic'. Mad studies scholars and feminist critics call attention to how psychiatry's deeply misogynist history continues to inform biomedical approaches to understanding human suffering and pathologizing individual behaviours, showing this model of care as problematic. Spring argues that a mad aesthetic, when applied to research-based theatre, is intrinsically linked to estrangement pedagogy. Estrangement pedagogy aims to upend gendered hegemonic framings of human distress and expectations through a theatre of storytelling. Spring includes excerpts from plays she has written in the chapter to illustrate the force of aesthetic rupture in making biomedical approaches to care and caring strange.

The theme of the possibility of aesthetic rupture is continued in Claudia Firth's chapter *Feminist Aesthetics and Mutual Learning in Turbulent Times: The Politics of Listening and Organization.* As a practitioner working with groups and organizations, Firth is interested in the possibilities offered by reconceiving listening as active (rather than passive) and political. To listen requires care and attention. However, in interrogating the ethical dimension of care and an implicit assumption that taking care when listening necessarily requires focusing on the other rather than focusing on self, Firth provides a more nuanced analysis of care work in listening. Drawing on a Bickford's work on the politics of listening (1996), Firth points to situations where caring might be understood as a constraint as well as a possibility. If caring in the context of listening requires failing to attend to oneself, then this can be problematic.

In the final chapter in this section, Amber Moore and Kaye Hare challenge patriarchal, heteronormative understandings of affection, care and support in the neoliberal university. Drawing upon Ahmed's figure of the feminist killjoy, they explore how love-letters can enrich feminist survival kits by providing a place to document and enact subversive care that challenges the logic of individual mobilities in the academy. Writing in feminist collaboration, they play with the romantic aesthetics of love letters by bending genre conventions to reimagine love letters as a place for feminist resistance, persistence and respite. Their letters illuminate how unabashed, brazen and experiential composition can thread together the past, present and future to surface an ethic of critical friendship in the academy. *On fostering feminist friendships for resistance and respite: Love letter making* is an apposite ending to this collection as it provides a useful guide for feminist adult educators as we live our feminist lives in and through caring and the feminist imaginary.

In summary, the chapters in *Feminism, Adult Education and Creative Possibility: Imaginative Responses* expand our understandings of the feminist imaginary by positioning aesthetic practices both within notions of art and creativity and more broadly, as a practice of caring, listening, digitally speaking and being. Chapters allow us to see how arts-based and making practices play a crucial part in reimagining 'who' and 'what' might exist, and equally a broader take on feminist aesthetic practices as those aimed to produce aesthetic rupture, and a reconfiguring of 'what' and 'who' can be sensed and made sense of. In illustrating both dimensions of the feminist imaginary the volume broadens the scope of 'who' and 'what' might be attended to in and through feminist adult education and research practices. The 'feminist imaginary' is introduced as a way of collecting and curating multiple threads and themes that are interwoven through the book to provide a rich narrative of creating, examining, imagining, practising and contesting existing relationships between adult education, power, gender justice, colonialism and social change at a time when hope and possibility can feel difficult to grasp and hold onto.

References

Ahmed, S. (2017). *Living a feminist life*. Duke University Press.

Akkent, M., & Kovar, S. (Eds.). (2019). *Feminist pedagogy: Museums, memory sites and practices of remembrance*. Istanbul Kadin Muzesi.

Andrews, M. (2014). *Narrative imagination and everyday life*. Oxford University Press.

Archibald, J. (2004). *Indigenous storywork*. UBC Press.

Atleo, M. (2016). All my relations: Networks of Firsts Nations/Metis/Inuit women sharing the learnings. In D. E. Clover, S. Butterwick, & L. Collins (Eds.), *Women, adult education and leadership in Canada* (pp. 33–44). Thompson Educational Publishing.

Baksh, R., & Harcourt, W. (Eds.). (2015). *The Oxford handbook of transnational feminist movements*. Oxford University Press.

Bickford, S. (1996). *The dissonance of democracy: Listening, conflict, and citizenship*. Cornell University Press.

Bishop, Etmanski, & Page (2019). Engaged scholarship and the arts. *Journal of Engaged Scholarship, 5*(2), i–ix.

Butterwick, S., & Roy, C. (Eds.). (2018). Finding voice and listening: The potential of community and arts-based education and research. *Special Edition, Canadian Journal for the Study of Adult Education, 30*(20).

Butterwick, S. (2016). Feminist adult education: Looking back, looking forward. In D. E. Clover, S. Butterwick, & L. Collins (Eds.), *Women, adult education and leadership in Canada* (pp. 3–14). Thompson Educational Publishing.

Butterwick, S., & Selman, J. (2003). Deep listening in a feminist popular theatre project: Upsetting the position of audience in participatory education. *Adult Education Quarterly, 54*(7), 7–22.

Clover, D. (2019). Introduction. In D. E. Clover, S. Dzulkifli, H. Gelderman, & K. Sanford (Eds.), *Feminist adult educators' guide to aesthetic, creative and disruptive strategies in museums and community* (pp. viii–xvi). University of Victoria.

Clover, D. E., & Sanford, K. (Eds.). (2013). *Lifelong learning, the arts, and creative cultural engagement in the contemporary university: International perspectives*. Manchester University Press.

Chanter, T. (2018). *Art, politics and Rancière: Broken perceptions*. Bloomsbury Academic.

Chatzidakis, A., Hakim, J., Littler, J., Rottenberg, C., & Segal, L. (2020). *The care manifesto: The politics of interdependence*. Verso.

Cocks, J. (1989). *The oppositional imagination: Feminism, critique and political theory*. Routledge.

Collins, P. H. (2000). *Black feminist thought: Knowledge, consciousness, and the politics of empowerment* (2nd ed.). Routledge.

Criado Perez, C. (2019). *Invisible women: Data bias in a world designed for men.* Abrams Press.

English, L. M., & Irving, C. J. (Eds.). (2015). *Feminism in community: Adult education for transformation.* Sense Publishing.

Etienne, J. (2016). *Learning in womanist ways: Narratives of first-generation African Caribbean women.* Trentham Books.

Freire, P. (2004). *Pedagogy of indignation.* Paradigm.

Fricker, M. (2007). *Epistemic injustice: Power and the ethics of knowing.* Oxford University Press.

Green, J. (Ed.). (2017). *Making space for Indigenous feminism* (2nd ed.). Fernwood Publishing.

Greene, M. (1995). *Releasing the imagination: Essays on education, the arts, and social change.* Jossey Bass.

Hall, S. (2013). The work of representation. In S. Hall, J. Evans, & S. Nixon (Eds.), *Representation* (2nd ed. Chapter One, pp. 1–59). Sage.

Harvey, M. (2017). Living well through story: Land and narrative imagination in Indigenous-State relations in British Columbia. Unpublished Doctoral Thesis. University of Victoria.

Helmore, E. (2021, March 28). *Writers grapple with rules of the imagination.* https://www.theguardian.com/books/2021/mar/28/writers-in-culture-war-over-rules-of-the-imagination

Hemmings, C. (2011). *Why stories matter: The political grammar of feminist theory.* Duke University Press.

Heng, L. (1996). Talking pain: Educational work with factory women in Malaysia. In S. Walters & L. Manicom (Eds.), *Gender and popular education* (pp. 202–28). London: Zed Books.

hooks, b. (2007). *Feminism Is for everybody: Passionate politics* (2nd ed.). Routledge.

hooks, b. (1984). *Feminist theory: From margin to center.* South End Press.

Kidd, J. (2015). *Representation.* Routledge.

Manicom, L., & Walters, S. (Eds.). (2012). *Feminist popular education: Creating pedagogies of possibility.* Palgrave.

McRobbie, A. (2009). *The aftermath of feminism: Gender, culture and social change.* Sage.

Mohanty, C. (2012). Foreword. In L. Manicom & S. Walters (Eds.), *Feminist popular education in transnational debates: Building pedagogies of possibility* (pp. vii–x). Palgrave Macmillan.

Moraga, C. L., & Anzaldua, G. (Eds.). (1981). *This bridge called my back: Writings by radical women of color.* Kitchen Press.

Nazneen, S., & Sultan, M. (Eds.). (2014). *Voicing demands: Feminist activism in transitional contexts.* Zed Books.

Noddings, N. (2013). *Caring: A relational approach to ethics and moral education* (2nd ed.). University of California Press.

O'Brien, M. (2013). Towards a pedagogy of care and well-being: Restoring the vocation of becoming human through dialogue and relationality. In A. O'Shea & M. O'Brien (Eds.), *Pedagogy, oppression and transformation in a 'post-critical' climate: The return of Freirean thinking* (pp. 14–35). Continuum.

Okri, B. (1997). *A way of being free.* Phoenix House.

Puig de la Bellacasa, M. (2017). *Matters of care: Speculative ethics in more than human worlds.* University of Minnesota Press.

Rowbotham, S., Segal, L., & Wainwright, H. (2013). *Beyond the fragments: Feminism and the making of socialism* (3rd ed.). Merlin Press.

Rose, G. (2001). *Visual methodologies*. London: Sage.

Scott-Dixon, K. (Ed.). (2006). *Trans/forming feminisms: Transfeminist voices speak out*. Sumach Press.

Shotwell, A. (2011). *Knowing otherwise: Race, gender, and implicit understanding*. Pennsylvania State University Press.

Solnit, R. (2014, April 24). Woolf's darkness: Embracing the inexplicable. *The New Yorker*. https://www.newyorker.com/books/page-turner/woolfs-darkness-embracing-the-inexplicable

Solnit, R. (2004). *Hope in the dark: Untold histories and wild possibilities*. Nation Books.

Speller, K. (2015, November 30). *A U.K. student is fighting to keep feminism in the classroom*. http://www.mtv.com/news/2616304/feminism-uk-a-levels-petition/

Tronto, J. (1994). *Moral boundaries: A political argument for an ethic of care*. Routledge.

Tuck, E., & Yang, K. W. (2012). Decolonization is not a metaphor. *Decolonization: Indigeneity, Education & Society, 1*(1), 1–40.

United Nations (2019). *UN75 2020 and beyond: Shaping our future*. United Nations. https://esaro.unfpa.org/en/news/un75-2020-and-beyond-shaping-our-future-together

Walters, S., & von Kotze, A. (2021). Making a case for ecofeminist popular education in times of Covid 19. *Andragoška spoznanja/Studies in the Adult Education and Learning, 27*(1), 47–62.

Weatherall, R. (2020). Even when those struggles are not our own: Storytelling and solidarity in a feminist social justice organization. *Gender Work Organ, 27*, 471–86.

Wenham, C., Smith, J., Davies, S., Feng, H., Grépin, K. Harman, S. Hertten-Crabbe, A., & Morgan, R. (2020, July 08). Women are most affected by pandemics – lessons from past outbreaks. *Nature*. https://www.nature.com/articles/d41586-020-02006-z

Wildermeesch, D. (2019). Adult education and aesthetic experience. *European Journal for Research on the Education and Learning of Adults, 10*(2), 1–6.

Yang, K., & Lawrence, R. (Eds.). (2017). *Participatory visual approaches to adult and continuing education: Practical insights*. Jossey-Bass.

Part I

VISUALIZING AND THE FEMINIST IMAGINARY

Chapter 1

Curating Visibility: The Disobedient Women Exhibition as a Representational Feminist Pedagogy of Possibility

Darlene E. Clover and Kathy Sanford

Women dominate their own experience by imaging it, giving it form ...
In their exact recording of their experience they establish women's claim as
individuals ... They define for themselves woman as she is and as she dreams.

Meyer Spacks, 1976, p. 414

Issues of vision, visibility, representation and imagination are central concerns
of feminist adult educators and cultural theorists. We speak collectively of the
historical invisibility of women, the need to give visibility to women's diverse
stories, perspectives and experiences, the visual power of self-representation and
the need to inspire an imagination of possibility (e.g., Butterwick & Roy, 2016;
Clover et al., 2017; Manicom & Walters, 2012).

The online *Oxford English Dictionary* defines vision as the ability to see or what
can be seen from a particular position or perspective. Visibility is how clearly or
easily one can see as well as the act of attracting attention. Invisibility is that which
cannot be seen straightforwardly or even at all. The imagination is the forming and
envisioning of new ideas, images or concepts whilst representation is the practice
of portraying these imaginings in order to call particular understandings to mind.
Despite the presumption of neutrality inherent in these definitions, they are in
fact riddled with relations of power and particularly, gendered relations of power.
Vision, visibility, imagination and representation are always political because
they are about what we are able, allowed or made to see and thus, to know and
to imagine about the world, ourselves and others (Vendramin, 2012). Feminists
Cramer and Witcomb (2018) refer to this pedagogically as people 'seeing what
they are being taught to see and to remain blind to what they are being taught
ignore' (p. 2). Over the decades, cultural feminists such as de Beauvoir (1949)
and Marshment (1993) have illustrated the historically problematic patriarchal
nature of our representations – our imagery, language and narratives – that have
been 'done by great men [with] singular obstinacy' (Pomata, 1989, p. 1). In her
2020 book entitled *Invisible Women: Data Bias in a World Designed by Men*,
Criado Perez shows that in fact little has changed. Both the chroniclers of the past

and the architects of the present and future have taken 'the lives of men ... to represent those of humans overall. When it comes to the lives of the other half of humanity, there is often nothing but silence' (p. xi). Criado Perez refers to this as a world 'disfigured by a female-shaped absent presence' (p. xi). Given this, what we are being taught to see is a world created and imagined for and about men and what we are being taught to remain blind to is the stories of women in all their diversity. Men, however, have not stopped at making their own lives and deeds central to almost every single story and aspect of the world. They have envisioned, imagined, storied and represented women through the 'male gaze', the practice of turning women into objects by robbing them of subjectivity. As a result, women 'participate unequally in the practices through which social meanings are generated and the world is made' (p. 2). We live in a world of female-faced poverty, sexualized violence and harassment, and movement control, and all too often, continuing low levels of self-esteem. Many women have a limited sense of future possibility, unhealthy obsessions with beauty and body image, a lack of historical memory and gender consciousness which causes them to blame themselves and other women rather than patriarchy, and to denigrate or dismiss feminism as a relic of the past (McRobbie, 2009; Scott-Dixon, 2006).

Our research over the past fifteen years has concentrated on museum exhibitions as important pedagogical spaces of vision, visibility, imagination and representation. Exhibitions are public representational structures, discursive imaginary formations through which people are able to see and thus come to know something about their topic. Benjamin (2014) calls them a 'play of forces ... ideal for influencing the public' (p. 29). For Bartlett (2016), exhibitions are important because they 'mark the significance of their subject', lending it authority, legitimacy and socio-cultural value (p. 307). Museum and gallery exhibitions are also visited yearly by millions of people who come to be entertained but more importantly, to learn, and visitors tend to trust what they are learning through the exhibitions as 'truth' (e.g., Hannay, 2018). This is problematic because our studies over the past twelve years have uncovered what we call in feminist adult education a hidden curriculum nestled in the folds of displays and exhibitions worldwide that contributes actively to the female 'absent presence' and our current state of gender blindness. Through means both visible yet invisible, representational yet misrepresentational, imagined yet misconceived, men are persistently visualized and storied in exhibitions and displays as 'knowers' who perform actively, deeply and intentionally upon the world. When it comes to women, however, it is as though there is 'nothing to see here so kindly move along'. Until women are able to represent themselves visually and to tell their own stories publicly, they will remain subject to the disempowering voyeurism of the 'male gaze' (e.g., Marshment, 1993; Clover et al., 2017; Sanford, et al., 2020).

Although imagining and storying women's lives as material for exhibitions is a relatively recent phenomenon, women worldwide are in fact curating feminist exhibitions as sites of resilience and resistance. The very act of their staging makes a statement about women's substantive contributions to the evolution of humanity and the 'radical feminist ideologies and collective activities' (Crane, 2000, p. 2) that exist in the interest of gender justice and change. By showcasing women in all their diversity, feminist exhibitions not only lend them authority, value and legitimacy, they also pedagogically incorporate their content 'into the extra-institutional memory of the museum visitors' (p. 2).

In this chapter, we focus on our own exhibition as a site of resistance and feminist interventionist strategy. In 2017–18 we curated a multi-media research exhibition entitled *Disobedient Women: Defiance, Resilience and Creativity Past and Present* in two separate galleries in Victoria, British Columbia. Drawing on feminist exhibition praxis and adult education we tell the story of how this exhibition came into being and its pedagogical intentionality. We focus on both design and content because the power of this feminist exhibition – and one could argue all exhibitions – is that it performed as both the messenger – the educator and carrier of a tale – and the message, a feminist imaginary of paintings and posters, poetry and puppets, videos and newspaper clippings, textiles and installations that told a tale of historical and contemporary defiance, resistance and resilience, and it offered another way of seeing and knowing the diversity of feminist power and activism.

Impetus and title

Disobedient Women was designed around a number of key features that scholars argue are inherent to feminist exhibitions (e.g., Best, 2016; Robinson, 2013). The first is that on one hand, feminist exhibitions can materialize as a result of work over time, a long, slow development, yet at other times, they are curated more hastily in response to a critical moment. *Disobedient Women* in fact combined these two elements. The idea for this type of exhibition had percolated in our more than two decades of studying feminist activisms and arts-based and creative practices as well as our need to 'represent' our findings in more creative and accessible ways. The actual act of curating *Disobedient Women* was, however, a more immediate response to a very immediate problematic moment in time. The Canadian government was in the midst of planning a 'celebration' of the Sesquicentenary of Confederation, the coming together of separate provinces into one nation called Canada. The narrative surrounding this event, however, was deeply patriarchal, showcasing stories of 'white' male colonial discovery, muscularity and war. Not only did this narrative exclude women but it ignored a century of challenges to its neat patriarchal ordering of things. Based on this, as well as a visit Darlene had made to a wonderful exhibition entitled *Disobedient Objects* at the Victoria and Albert Museum, London, we decided to adopt the term 'disobedience' for the title of the exhibition. Disobedience means a 'refusal to obey rules or someone in authority' (*Oxford Dictionary Online*, n.p.). For Bachelard, 'to disobey in order to take action is the byword of all creative spirits and … the spark behind all knowledge' (cited in Flood & Grindon, 2015, p. 7).

A second feature of feminist exhibitions identified by Robinson (2013) is that they are surveys rather than themed shows, illuminating specific or diverse

Figure 1.1 *The exhibition*. Photo by Darlene Clover.

elements of women's movements. Based on both our research and the moment in time noted above, we decided to centre the exhibition at the intersections of women's activism and political-activist artworks. The 'survey' quality of *Disobedient Women* is captured best in the *Call for Objects, Belongings, Images and Stories* we created and disseminated widely through a variety of social media platforms as well as to women's organizations, transition houses, artist collectives, art galleries and museums and by word of mouth. The Call adopted Bachelard's view that 'the history of human progress amounts to a series of Promethean acts' (cited in Flood & Grindon, 2014, p. 7). On one hand, they are public acts that aim to break the bonds of oppression. Women enter the public sphere with extraordinary courage, raising their heads above the parapet and taking to the streets to speak truth to power and challenge injustice. We invited women across the province to submit representations of the past and the present that illustrated highly visible and political acts of resistance and defiance in the public sphere. We received a variety of protest placards, puppets, protest buttons, quilts, pamphlets, record albums, puppets, banners, t-shirts, videos, newspaper clippings of women being arrested and more. On the other side, however, Bachelard speaks to disobediences that are 'patiently pursued, so subtle at times as to avoid punishment entirely' (p. 7) but they are nevertheless critical processes of refusal and defiance. To showcase these acts, we invited representations and stories by and about women who had made more understated yet equally important 'activist' contributions. These women sent us altered books, quilts, poetry and much more (Figure 1.1).

Curatorial activism: Inclusion, participation and agency

When you asked me to write my own label, I was shocked because I had no
idea what to say and I expected you to do it. That's been my past experience
with galleries … I just want to say thank you for giving me this chance.

                                   Email excerpt from a commissioned artist

Another key design element of *Disobedient Women* was curatorial activism.
According to Message (2013), curatorial activism is 'attempts by individuals
to engage with, represent and often contribute to social and political protest
and reform movements' (p. 1). Our intent was to not only represent women's
movements of activism and creativity in the province of British Columbia
(BC), but also to join with and add to the numerous protests emerging around
the explicit colonial history shrouded in the celebratory narrative of the
Sesquicentenary. As feminists, however, we also took curatorial activism in a
different and participatory direction which was an antithesis to the normative
practices of curation where exhibitions are designed, conceptualized and narrated
by the curator. Having said this, we did have a role to play in the curation, but in
the interests of contributing to social movements we let go of as much power as
was possible. The first participatory strategy we used was the *Call* noted above,
which we disseminated far and wide to get the most diversity of representation
and items as possible. The second strategy was to establish an advisory group
of women who could guide the thinking, framing, design and curation of
Disobedient Women. We pulled together a very diverse group, consisting of
Indigenous and non-Indigenous artists, an art education professor, two PhD
students with experience in museums, curators from a local heritage site and
the Legacy Maltwood Gallery, adult educators from the provincial museum and
an art gallery respectively. We also included four very interested UVic graduate
students, one of whom centred her project around the exhibition. We met
individually with members over the months and five of these women contributed
artworks to the exhibition. What was most important about this group of artists
and curators, however, is that they asked us critical questions about curatorial
responsibility, the look and the feel of the exhibition, and the argument, narrative
or allegory that would hold it together to withstand interrogation but equally
provoke dialogue and challenge.

   Our third curatorial activist strategy was to commission seven artists to create
pieces for the exhibition around the theme of 'disobedience'. We identified these
women through our own networks, and they also supplied names of feminist
activist artists. We met individually with each artist to outline the exhibition focus
and their particular artistic genres and ideas. Artists' backgrounds were diverse
in culture, gender and age. The works they submitted included paintings, videos,
installations, two sets of puppets, protest buttons and posters. All the artists were
asked to compose their own label descriptors because, borrowing from Cixous's
(1976) comment above, we wanted the women to literally write themselves into
the language and texts of the exhibition.

Our third participatory strategy was to interview two older women for their stories of resistance, resilience and solidarity. One interviewee was a local woman physician, Mary Wynne Ashford, who had for decades been a highly visible anti-nuclear activist. As an artist, Mary Wynne also produced a set of puppets for the exhibition (see Figure 1.2). Another interview was with Indigenous Elder May Sam. Feminist Indigenous adult educators remind us of the importance of rendering visible the diverse leadership roles Indigenous women have played as well as their use of arts-based practices to resist the sexist foundations of Canada's colonial relations (e.g. Harris, in press). May Sam's work often goes unnoticed because it is representative of the quieter side of activism, specifically, keeping her culture alive by knitting traditional sweaters and teaching the traditional practices to youth. But she is a powerful force in both her own community and as a (university) elder in residence. As a fourth strategy, we reached out to archivists at the University of Victoria and the Royal BC Museum to identify items in their collections. We will discuss some elements of this shortly.

A fifth feminist curatorial strategy was to curate the exhibition in two different locations. One was a free municipal art gallery in the city centre. This location gave access to a wide audience that ranged from locals to homeless and street-involved people to tourists. The second space was the University of Victoria Maltwood Legacy Gallery, housed on the lower ground floor of the main library. Curating

Figure 1.2 *The clothesline.* Photo by Darlene Clover.

the exhibition in this space gave on-campus students easy access to the exhibition as well as faculty members, administrators, alumnae and library staff.

A final participatory element of *Disobedient Women* responded to Perry's (2012, p. 27) call for activist curatorial 'strategies that facilitate active visitor participation' and Weiser's (2017) belief that exhibition stories become more meaningful to visitors when their ideas are used to expand the story. We designed six different comments cards for each site. The cards had a different image from the exhibition and a question to which visitors could respond. To weave these comments into the existing story told in the museum, we designed a vertical clothesline installation (see Figure 1.3). Over 320 visitors pinned completed comment cards to the line. Most visitors answered the questions although many others used the back of the cards to tell us stories of their own acts of disobedience and connections to the exhibitions.

Epistemic justice through the messenger and the message

I was struck by the inclusion of Indigenous women's voices and how constant they have been in the struggle to assert rights and defend the Earth.

Comment Card

Fricker (2007) reminds us that we live in a world of 'epistemic injustice', which for her is an intentional discounting or belittling of the credibility of an individual or an entire group, such as those who identify as women, by misrepresenting, invalidating or silencing their experiences, knowledge and perspectives. Epistemic injustice hinders women's abilities to put themselves, as Cixous (1976) argues, into the text of world, into the history of the world 'by their own movement' (p. 872). Equally, it stifles their abilities to make sense of experiences they have, being underpaid, excluded or controlled, 'which it is strongly in their interests to render intelligible' (Fricker, 2007, p. 7). The antithesis to epistemic injustice is, of course, epistemic justice and resistance, both of which lay at the heart of *Disobedient Women*. Feminist epistemology, as represented in and through *Disobedient Women,* aimed to destabilize and decentre accepted descriptions or depictions 'of the world and how the world should be perceived' during the Sesquicentenary (Vendramin, 2012, p. 82). To borrow from hooks, what *Disobedient Women* offered was an 'oppositional look', 'a process through which the gaze', and in this case the feminist gaze, 'functioned as site of resistance' (Bloom, 1999, p. 3). Feminist epistemology is also, however, a struggle for a new and broader knowledge of the world and a means to construct of new or common meanings (Vendramin, 2012). In this framing, *Disobedient* was constructed as a way to see a very particular part of the world through 'other eyes', that is, feminist activism. We wanted to destabilize common assumptions and stereotypes of feminist activism as white, old-fashioned, stodgy, misguided and aggressive by placing a very different story in the minds' eyes of visitors: combining historical and present views of diversity in action, of humour and power, of playful tricksters and rebels.

Knowable pasts, imaginable futures

[I learnt] that we have come a long way but not far enough.

Comment card response

How we can come to know history in ways that help us to understand and shape the future was a central pedagogical feature of *Disobedient Women*. Giroux (2004) reminds us that 'history is not an artifact [*sic*] to be merely transmitted, but an ongoing dialogue and struggle over the relationship between representation and agency' (p. 68). He calls on educators to blast open history, to rupture its silences with an 'open and honest' concern for the legacy of the unrepresented or misrepresented.

To design *Disobedient Women* as a site of historical interruption and a pedagogy 'in the service of remembering' (Bartlett, 2016, p. 310), we worked with the archivists as noted above. Within weeks of our first meeting, these women had mustered an assortment of images and objects that illustrated the diversity of women's historical activist pasts across the province. For example, we received various photos of groups of women who belonged to Women's Institutes and to Ladies Auxiliaries. The work of these institutions and auxiliaries often includes things such as holding dances and organizing teas or craft sales to raise funds for worthy causes. As such, they are seen as too tame to be part of the women's movement (Moseley, 2017). However, behind the scenes, using what Moseley calls 'leadership that [does] not show', these women's groups have done far more than this. Many worked to facilitate women's entry into the workforce, which was both into more 'feminine' work but also into more masculine spaces such as the fire brigades. A most interesting image was titled the *First Chinese and Japanese Ladies Auxiliary, circa 1900*. While little is known about this group, not surprisingly there were hints that they had helped with the preservation of Chinatown. What is also fascinating is that China and Japan were in many ways adversaries yet in the 'new' country, this group of women was reaching out across enemy lines to create a different way forward.

We also pieced together from the archives a story of Rosemary Brown, the first Black woman to be elected to the BC legislature. Despite this incredible feat, there is only a brief mention of her in the large, provincial museum and she is relatively unknown. Additionally, archivists at UVic supplied us with the entire collection of *Zenith Digest*, a newsletter edited by trans-woman Stephanie Castle. There were two important things about these newsletters. The first is that they challenge Scott-Dixon's (2006) assertion that although much has been written about trans people, 'much less has been written by trans people about themselves, in their own voices' (p. 21). The *Digest* showed that trans-women were in fact writing about themselves and their issues, but what was lacking was the visibility. Secondly, Castle self-identified as a feminist, and therefore for her, trans issues were neither outside nor irrelevant to feminism as is a common assumption. This was noted by a visitor who left this comment: '[I learnt that] feminists had been focusing on trans issues for a long time and that trans-women can be feminists.'

We also designed an installation from the many items that were donated to the exhibition by a feminist lawyer (see Figure 1.4). She arrived at one of our group meetings with four bins filled with the memorabilia from a feminist life, including feminist phonographic records, protest T-shirts, magazines, books and posters. This is the label she wrote to tell her story:

> Our formative years have a great influence on the music we listen to, the art we are drawn to, and how we choose to dress. For me it was those years when I became a feminist, acutely aware of the injustices in the world around me. My bedroom became an extension of myself, and the ideas I was beginning to form as a young woman. I spent many hours reading, listening to music and adorning my walls with posters, photos and art. I read.

For feminist Hemmings (2011, p. 16), what enables us to imagine the future differently is when we 'shuttle back and forth between the past and present'. We created a number of visual shuttles in *Disobedient Women*. In one instance, we placed a blanket covered with protest buttons created by a woman's organization that had been active from the 1960s to the 1990s that had been in archives alongside a series of contemporary protest buttons made by a young, commissioned artist, who had not in fact seen this blanket. What this juxtaposition showed was while some issues such as childcare and the gender pay gap were more prevalent in the more historical buttons, the issues reflected in both sets of buttons were problematically similar. Numerous visitors left messages that showed their great surprise that challenges of the past remained so ubiquitous in the present, and this

Figure 1.3 *Feminist bedroom installation.* Photo by Darlene Clover.

best captured in this comment: 'I never would have believed it. I thought equality was pretty much fixed. Geez.'

A second shuttle was around protest images. We had received a number of newspaper images of women being arrested for civil disobedience. One in particular was a white woman being 'man-handled' by two male police officers into an awaiting paddy waggon. In her story, she self-identified as a committed activist from an early age, and that while this was her most public arrest, it was one of many. We placed this alongside an image of Qwetminak, a grassroots Lil'wat nation Elder, who was handcuffed, on her knees and flanked by two male RCMP officers. Her accompanying story tells us that she had never in her life protested publicly and had never identified as an 'activist' but had been compelled to take a stand because her lands were threatened.

Courage and humour: Rebels and tricksters

[I learnt] that feminism is fun. That is not what I had heard.

Comment Card

As noted above, feminism is often cast as what McRobbie (2009) calls 'implicitly unattractive and embittered' (p. 157). Yet Ahmed (2017) reminds us that feminism

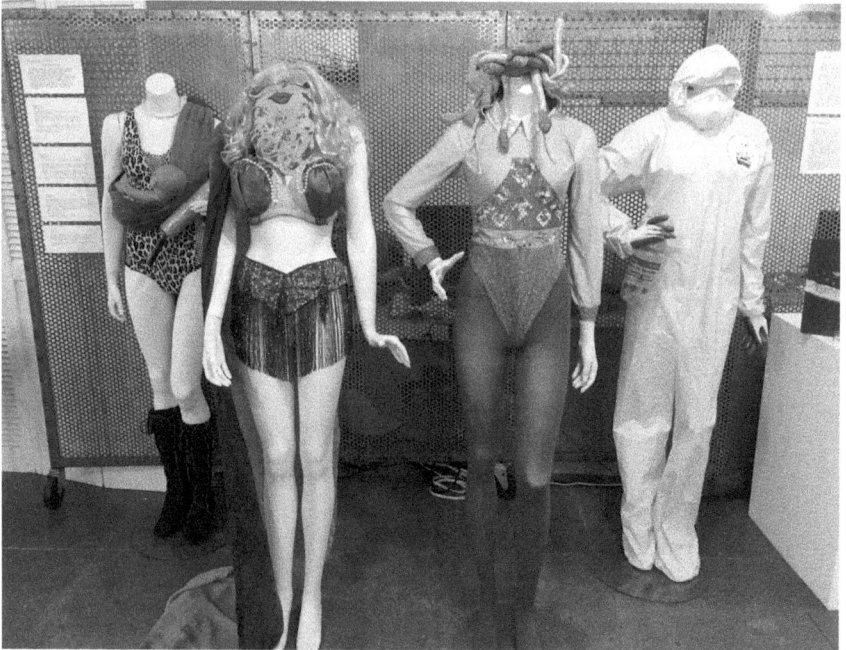

Figure 1.4 *Costumes of the West Coast League of Lady Wrestlers.* Photo by Darlene Clover.

Figure 1.5 *Feminist ravens.* Photo by Darlene Clover.

is a practice of hope, courage, humour and creative energy. While not fully by design, these were the elements that were rendered visible through the assembly of *Disobedient Women*. One major installation was composed of mannequins and items from the West Coast League of Lady Wrestlers, a group of young, very diverse women artists who explore the intersections between performance and the male gaze (see Figure 1.4). Using humour and satire they wrestle with issues that range from the environment to identity or dress, for example, like a Black Widow, a shapeshifting spider who emerges in her true form to untie and reweave the histories of spinsterhood. Her signature move is 'The Female Gaze'.

A second installation showcased the rebellious and feisty Raging Grannies, a courageous group of elderly women who raise awareness about diverse social, ecological and gender justices through humorous and satirical acts of protest, direct action and performances. Among other things, the display included a life size cut-out of a granny complete with feather boa (from the archives), books and song sheets they had written and a photograph of two grannies wading naked into a freezing lake to protest water pollution.

A third donation included a series of paintings entitled *Feminist Ravens* (see Figure 1.5) created by Indigenous artist and law professor, Val Napoleon. In her label she defined the ravens as 'tricksters', who

teach us by being a troublemaker and by upsetting the log jams of unquestioned assumptions. She can also teach us with love, patience, and a wicked sense of humour. She can create spaces for conversations and questions – that is her job as a trickster and as a feminist so that nothing is taken for granted and all interpretations are laid bare.

(from the label)

Ticksters, according to Priyadharshini (2012), are important feminist tools because they combine 'humour and education' in ways that satirize and provoke us question our assumptions and also provide a provocative form of inspiration for action (p. 548).

A final display in the exhibition we will highlight in this chapter was a photographic series by a group of Sikh feminists from Vancouver entitled *(Mis) Interpretation: Sikh Feminisms in Representation*. The aim was to decentre the notion of a normatively androcentric faith by visually introducing Sikh feminist thought and ways of being through self-imagery/definition. The perspective and sense of identity presented is rarely addressed within Sikh culture, and all but unknown beyond. It offers a new presence through its oppositional gaze – of how Sikh feminists see themselves as vital meaning makers of the faith, by offering new interpretations of the religion and its inherent impact on their and others' lives.

Final thoughts

Disobedient Women was a result of our urge to intervene into a problematic historical narrative, to exhibit radical and less radical feminist visions and actions, to capture a world of imagination and creativity, to showcase a history of diversity, and to use a more participatory curatorial process. Although we noted only a very few of the comments shared by visitors, this proved to be an inviting pedagogical space where those who came acknowledged that they had been challenged to see and to think differently, to make connections where none existed before, and most importantly, to laugh and feel a sense of hope and optimism for the future. As Greene (1995) once noted, it is against the backdrop of things remembered and 'the meanings to which they give rise that we grasp and understand what is now going on around us' (p. 20). Moreover, 'consciousness always has an imaginative phase, and imagination, more than any other capacity, breaks the inertia of habit' (p. 21). On this note, we give the last word to a visitor who wrote, 'I am leaving here just so inspired … I will never forget what you have done for me.'

References

Ahmed, S. (2017). *Living a feminist life*. Duke University Press.
Bartlett, A. (2016). Sites of feminist activism. Remembering pine gap. *Continuum: Journal of Media and Cultural Studies, 30*(3), 307–15.
Benjamin, W. (2014). The work of art in the age of its technological reproducibility. In L. Steeds (Ed.), *Exhibition* (pp. 26–34). Whitechapel Gallery.

Best, B. (2016). What is a feminist exhibition? considering contemporary Australia: Women. *Journal of Australian Studies, 40*(2), 190–202.

Bloom, L. (Ed.). (1999). *With other eyes: Looking at race and gender in visual culture.* University of Minnesota.

Butterwick, S., & Roy, C. (Eds.). (2016). *Working the margins of community-based adult learning: The power of arts-making in finding voice and creating conditions for seeing/ listening.* Sense Publishers.

Cixous, H. (1976). The laugh of the Medusa. *Signs, 1*(4), 875–93.

Clover, D. E., Murphy, T., & Delaronde, L. (2017). In defiance: A case study of exhibitory praxis as feminist adult education. In *Proceedings of the 36th Annual Conference of the Canadian Association for the Study of Adult Education* (pp. 83–7). Ryerson University, Toronto.

Criado Perez, C. (2019). *Invisible women: Data bias in a world designed by men.* Abrams Press.

Cramer, L., & Witcomb, A. (2018). Hidden from view? An analysis of the integration of women's history and women's voices in Australia's social history exhibitions. *International Journal of Heritage Studies, 25*(2). Online: Doi.org/10.1080/13527258.2018.1475490

Crane, S. (Ed.). (2000). *Museums and memory.* Stanford University Press.

de Beauvoir, S. (1949/2011). *The second sex.* Vintage.

Flood, C., & Grindon, G. (2014). *Disobedient objects.* V&A Publishing.

Fricker, M. (2007). *Epistemic injustice: Power and the ethics of knowing.* Oxford University Press.

Giroux, H. (2004). Cultural studies, public pedagogy, and the responsibility of intellectuals. *Communication and Critical/Cultural Studies, 1*(1), 59–79.

Greene, M. (1995). *Releasing the imagination: Essays on education, the arts and social change.* Jossey-Bass.

Hannay, C. (2018, September 15). Canadians visiting museums, galleries more than ever, survey shows. *Globe and Mail.* Retrieved March 20, 2019, from https://www. theglobeandmail.com/canada/articlecanadians-visiting-museums-galleries-more-than-ever-survey-shows/

Harris, D. (in press). Indigenous feminist aesthetic work as cultural revitalisation: Facilitating Uy'skwuluwun. In D. E. Clover, K. Sanford, & K. Harman (Eds.), *Feminism, adult education and creative possibility: Imaginative responses.* Bloomsbury Publishing.

Hemmings, C. (2011). *Why stories matter: The political grammar of feminist theory.* Duke University Press.

Manicom, L., & Walters, S. (Eds.). (2012). *Feminist popular education in transnational debates: Building pedagogies of possibility.* Palgrave Macmillan.

Marshment, M. (1993). The picture is political: Representation of women in contemporary popular culture. In D. Richardson & V. Robinson (Eds.), *Thinking feminist* (pp. 123–50). The Guildford.

McRobbie, A. (2009). *The aftermath of feminism: Gender, culture and social change.* Sage.

Message, K. (2013). *Museums and social activism: Engaged protest.* Routledge.

Meyer Spacks, P. (1976). *The female imagination.* Avon Books.

Moseley, S. (2017). A strong leadership that does not show: Ladies Auxiliaries as women's first entrance points into the fire department. *Rhetoric Review, 36*(4), 348–62.

Perry, D. (2012). *What makes learning fun? Principles for the design of Intrinsically motivating museum exhibit*s. AltaMira Press.

Pomata, G. (1989). Versions of narrative: Overt and covert narrators in nineteenth century historiography. *History Workshop, a Journal of Socialist and Feminist Historians, 27,* 1–17.

Priyadharshini, E. (2012). Thinking with trickster: Sporadic illuminations for educational research. *Cambridge Journal of Education, 42*(4), 547–61.

Robinson, H. (2013). Feminism meets the gig exhibition: Museum survey shows since 2005. *Anglo Saxonica, 3*(6), 129–52.

Sanford, K., Clover, D.E., Taber, N., & Williamson, S. (2020). *Feminist critique and the museum: Educating for a critical consciousness.* Brill/Sense.

Scott-Dixon, K. (Ed.). (2006). *Trans/forming feminisms: Transfeminist voices speak out.* Sumach Press.

Vendramin, V. (2012). Why feminist epistemology matters in education and educational research. *Solsko Polje, 23*(1/2), 87–96.

Weiser, E. (2017). *Museum rhetoric: Building civic identity in national spaces.* The Pennsylvania State University Press.

Chapter 2

Migrant Women Drawing Themselves into Their Homes and Communities

Sondra Cuban

This chapter is a story about a feminist visual mapping project focused on with a group of migrant women and their gendered im/mobilities. In my exploration of migrant women's lives in Chile, I used an im/mobilities lens to make sense of the maps that they drew of their daily movements and worlds and its relation to gender. 'The back slash separates the concept of immobility from mobility, to underscore the mutually constitutive relationship between particular forms of movement and the regulations and disciplinary pressures that delimit that movement' (Belanger & Silvey, 2019, p. 2). I started with the idea that mapping as a data visualization method would be a critical and creative feminist approach to understanding the full spectrum of migrant women's movements and which could lend them agency and visibility because they were drawing their lives. Feminists recognize that visual maps are both cartographic spatial data and expressive arts and legitimate ways of knowing about women's lives (e.g., Pirani, Ricker & Kraak, 2020; Brickell, 2012; Garda-Rozenberga, 2019; Lee, 2017). My feminist visual approach to mapping highlights the complex, mundane, subjugated knowledges and identity constructions of migrant women's realities that lay hidden and unarticulated (Buch & Staller, 2007; Jung, 2014; Rose, 2014).

Feminist visual mapping lends visibility to an invisible group like the migrant women in Chile whose stories have not been told or captured in political or Google maps. In focusing on the handmade maps these migrant women drew of their lives, their moves and routes around the city, and their inner landscapes, I got a wider and deeper perspective on their views of home and belonging. In this chapter, I highlight this marginalized group of women and their 'emotional geographies' (Sheller, 2004, p. 223); ones that go deeper than the 'surface geographies' of most studies of urban migrants (Tolia-Kelly, 2011, p. 153). In drawing their own maps, these invisible women inscribe themselves on a new place of settlement – Chile – and in doing so they turn themselves into visible actors whose perspectives matter.

The stories are drawn from a 2017 Fulbright Commission study that used feminist research methods.[1] Fifty-five migrant women from various Latin American and Caribbean (LAC) countries told me stories and drew maps of their im/mobilities within their homes and communities. They represented Chile's newest and largest migrant nationalities, who are predominantly women, and often hidden in the statistics. They were Venezuelans (13), Colombians (9) and Haitians (13) who arrived in Chile recently because of the economic, political and environmental crises occurring in their countries. There were also migrant women from Southern Cone countries in South America, Uruguay, Argentina and Brazil (4), as well as nearby countries like Peru and Ecuador (6). Additionally, there were international (exchange) students from Mexico, as well as Cubans (8). Mostly in their thirties about half of them were partnered and had children.

Many of these migrant women were newcomers and were just trying to survive and adapt to their new homes. I asked them to draw maps about their everyday worlds and encouraged them to draw whatever they liked in these maps. They drew two kinds of maps. The first type of map illustrated contemporary everyday life in Chile including what the city looked like on the ground level from their perspectives, the places they went as they walked, cycled or drove around and the people they met while on the move. These maps emphasized the migrant women's geographical knowledge and contained carefully detailed city landscapes, with stick figures moving around buildings, streets, green spaces and vehicles. Arrows and other directional symbols were often used to show time sequences of daily rituals and what they saw, did and experienced while on the move. The other kind of map focused on the inner worlds of the women and was abstract mental maps. The forms they drew reflected their cultural, religious and personal beliefs, about familyhood, traditions, love for their countries, or they were symbolic of feelings like happiness or sadness. These maps contained iconic forms, poetry and key words, as well as universal symbols like hearts and crosses, that were floating in space with little background context, some bigger than others. These maps showed little of the migrant women's external worlds in Chile and instead signified concepts like loss, hope and change.

I begin this chapter with a discussion of mobilities and immobilities, and then move to hand-drawn maps as feminist visual practice. I conclude with an in-depth look at two particular maps in order to illustrate differences in immigrant women's practices of mobility. Nelly's map shows how she inhabits the external world by walking the streets of her city. She didn't have a safe place to live where she could wait and strategize, so she walked and mapped the city landscape as part of her active movements. Nelly lives a far more external, albeit solitary life. The other map by Mariam is much more of an internalized representation of waiting at home. She spends much of her time in the domestic sphere with compatriots, waiting and strategizing her next moves. Central to her map was of a flower that symbolized her rich interior life and illustrated her inactive movements.

An im/mobilities lens for understanding home and belonging

The maps the women made illustrated their active movements, or active mobilities around their homes, neighbourhoods and the city where they lived in Chile including walking, driving or being passengers. They also delineated inactive movements, or passive mobilities, such as waiting, hanging out and pausing before or after moving. Stillness could mean potentially moving and determining routes to be taken or immersing oneself in surroundings and/or reflecting in a quiet moment. It could also mean being paralysed by a thought or an incident and unable to move. Women's movements, after all, are often blocked, constrained or prevented. The maps, then, represented systemic forces both propelling and limiting migrant women's movements. Yet the maps also represented their persistence, particularly in establishing a new home and a sense of belonging.

I use a feminist analysis of migrant women's im/mobilities; one that is nuanced and complex, to show the spectrum of movements practised by diverse migrant women as part of their everyday adaptations. Most active movement however has been characterized in terms of 'masculine subjectivities and privileged access to freedom of movement … ignor[ing] the gendered, sexualized, and racialized production of space' (Sheller, 2014, p. 795). These types of mobilities represent foreign settings, peaks and climaxes, and individual acts of heroism. Action is celebrated while inaction is seen as weak. Most of the women's movements defied this didactic notion of mobilities. Instead, their maps represented their 'everyday mobile lives', ones defined more by plateaus, routes, short distance moves, rituals, and blockages, a combination of both active and passive mobilities (Elliot & Urry, 2010, p. 23). Their maps captured their localities, with rhythms associated with moving around neighbourhoods and communities on a day-to-day basis. The maps illustrate migrant women's movements with gender and power in urban spaces, each map emphasizing active or passive mobilities.

Mapping active and passive (im)mobilities

Active mobilities are physical movements which are energetic, embodied and aesthetical in space and time (Urry, 2007). The women's maps that represented active mobilities illustrated short-distance urban walking or driving interspersed with the sensory experience of moving in unfamiliar urban environments. Many migrant women engaged in active mobilities like walking to search for jobs. But they also moved for therapeutic reasons, for example, walking through a park and sitting on a bench to experience quietness and escape from the noisiness of urban street life. Additionally, they ran errands, for example, shopping, and securing items for survival and hurried to get home to take care of their families. Moving around in public on sidewalks and streets also meant migrant women bore the risks associated with interacting with strangers. There were many stories of being harassed while on the streets. One Mexican student recalled Chilean men yelling, derogatory terms such as 'Tacos' and 'Cabrón' after they heard her accent. An Indigenous Otavaleña street vendor was solicited for sex while an Afro-Colombian woman had her hair touched by passers-by. Likewise, unwanted public encounters occurred on public transport. A Haitian woman said her bus driver refused to touch her hand when he gave her back money for the fare. Another Haitian passenger felt 'different' on the bus and said few other passengers would sit next to her. These examples show ways that women's active mobilities are constrained within a patriarchal and racist society.

Active movements were more controlled by migrant women who drove cars around the city. While they had less direct contact with strangers they too could be controlled in their 'mobility management' role, as mothers carting their children around (Murray, 2008, p. 56). One Peruvian woman described her entire day framed by her children's activities according to a timeline that dominated her every activity in her car and in her home. Other migrant women with cars like her drew maps with circular routes they travelled on every day to and from buildings as if on a track course with arrows representing sequences of school schedules and after-school activities. They were in a sense, 'mooring' for their children, tethered to their cars and phones (Merriman, 2014).

On this end of the mobilities spectrum were also migrant women's passive mobilities such as hanging out, staying put and 'being' in the moment. Passive states might be voluntary or involuntary, but they are always imbued with social and cultural power. Some migrant women felt stuck or weary of their lives and discussed their potential movement and aspirations to move while resting, thinking or sitting and they depicted these states in their maps. One woman's map was of her desk and a window she stared out of every day. These potential movements were 'moments in which further movement is renegotiated, resisted, or restrained' (Schewel, 2019, p. 3).

Then there were longer periods of sedentariness, what can be called immobilities (Hannam et al., 2006). Immobilities are 'distinguished by continuity in one's centre of gravity, or place of residence, relative to spatial and temporal frames' (Schewel, 2019, p. 329). Migrant women may work in closed spaces that immobilize them, or they may be dispossessed and stuck in refugee camps. They may experience occupational immobility which suggests highly skilled women migrants becoming deskilled in jobs that are under their qualifications, particularly in care work (e.g., Elliot & Urry, 2010). Immobilities could bring on despair such as anxiously waiting for a visa or paperwork, like several of the Haitians who applied for residency were denied and appealing their verdicts. Or migrant women may be immobilized through illness, disability, deportation of friends or the death of a loved one. In one case, a woman's boyfriend who had planned to follow her to Chile died in a motorcycle accident in Haiti right after she emigrated. She spent so much time crying about him that her uncle in Chile tore up all of his photographs to motivate her to get out of bed and literally move on with her life. Her map was of a small flower in a pot that symbolized her state of being. She said, 'I don't move a lot.' On the other hand, immobilities may have a positive connotation such as relaxing and appreciating nature, like one Mexican woman's map which was of her in a park, talking to her boyfriend in Mexico, and people-watching.

The women's maps illustrating their active and passive mobilities importantly represented what Boccagni (2017, p. 8) calls 'homing pathways' as some circled their communities to get to know the spatial geography of their new dwellings and moved quickly over much territory, like Nelly, while others waited, only moving when necessary, because staying put inside their homes was a way to be safe from harassment on the streets. Nelly exhibited a type of what Brah calls 'homing desire' that drove her to the far corners of her community, while Mariam exhibited imagined and mythic states of belonging by 'desiring home' (cited in Blunt & Dowling, 2006, p. 199). Mariam spent more time homemaking and creating diasporic communities in order to 'feel' at home. While Nelly figured out new routes outside, Mariam developed cultural roots, inside.

Hand-drawn mapping as a creative feminist practice for understanding im/mobilities

The maps were open and dynamic enough to capture migrant women's active and passive mobilities as 'multiple socio-mobile constructions of everyday life' (Jungnickel & Hjorth, 2014, p. 137). Their graphic elicitations focused on the 'position of the inbetween' of both interior consciousness and exterior landscapes (Garda-Rozenberga, 2019, p. 147). The women possessed complex and diverse views of home and community as well as perspectives filled with tensions, born of their gender, nationalities, cultures and races. Whether the maps were of migrant women's inner or outer worlds, they represented the cartographies of emotion and observation.

I respected the content the migrant women chose to draw, the ways they drew and what they said about it as part of the ethics of feminist visual ethnography (Barrantes-Elizondo, 2019; Rose, 2014). Some of these maps particularly the more abstract maps yielded memories and metaphors of sensitive topics. A number of the women used words in these types of maps that enhanced the imagery and symbolized change and added intertextual dimensions. One woman said, that in, 'drawing my map, I reflected on everything I am undergoing'. Her sense of home and belonging had been shaken to the core through intimate partner violence and her map symbolized a re-establishment of a new identity in a new home.

The women seemed to enjoy the accessibility of drawing their worlds. It was an accessible tool to 'bypass the difficulties of language' especially for sensitive content (Lee, 2017, p. 2). These hand-drawn maps are another way of communicating expressively 'to secure an empathic participation in the lives of others' (Barone & Eisner, 2012, p. 12). Drawing with coloured pencils or markers served as a memory mechanism that brought up embodied experiences and reflections as women being inside and outside their new homes.

I undertook a feminist analysis of all of the hand-drawn maps. Though the drawings were fixed creations, I interpreted and analysed them from different angles to see patterns and develop themes of (im)mobilities so that they came alive. The subjective content, colour, numbers, words and loose styles of these expressionist maps were lenses onto how migrant women identified and engaged with their local worlds. Discourses of power in their maps were read by me as part of an embodied feminist aesthetic of im/mobilities; in using their intuition and sensory experiences these migrant women effectively created DIY maps that profiled their chains of activities, bodies in motion or sense of paralysis (such as when they were not moving). A spatial feminist language of adaptation emerged to frame the ways migrant women's lives were entrapped and constrained by misogynistic and racist barriers and thus served as a 'representational crisis of vulnerable subjects' (Jung, 2014, p. 986). At the same time their maps revealed the strategies they used to cope with such barriers. The migrant women's hand-drawn maps became cartographic persuasive 'mashups' of their everyday lives, containing both barriers and supports, in a new place of settlement (Muehlenhaus, 2014; Pink, 2011).

Nelly's map shows a familiar street route she took in her search for jobs as part of her active mobilities and she depicted herself on the move, walking and talking to strangers, at all times of the day. She waited too, but she did so on the streets because she had no home in which to stay put. Mariam, on the other hand, who was doing the exact same thing as Nelly – walking and searching for jobs, chose to symbolize her world as part of passive mobilities, waiting and strategizing inside. Both adapted in different ways, as part of homing and belonging.

Nelly's map of walking

This map is by Nelly (Figure 2.1). In her forties and a former nurse from Caracas, Venezuela, she recently migrated to Chile on the tip of a friend. She had previous working vacations in Mexico and the United States but moved to Chile this time to send money back to her ill parents to pay for medicine which they couldn't afford with the current economic and political crisis there. She depicts herself walking the streets of this Chilean city job-seeking and crying, turning her map into a mobile geography of her emotions. She pauses to eat the cheapest food available,

Figure 2.1 *Nelly's map.* Photo by Cuban.

sopaipillas, from street vendors and keeps walking 'all day and come[s] back at 8', wondering how long she can couch surf at her friend's, who demanded that she leave the apartment during the daytime. She explained that every day she will 'walk and walk and walk to find a job. ….I go walking and come back and go straight to sleep'. Walking along the main avenue with her resume, close to a Casino, the orange colour, feelings, curves, twists and words on her map illustrate dreams turned to despair, her map a deep mining of her in this city landscape. Her walking covers a large swathe of the central area of the city as she makes this terrain hers. In calling attention to her embodied emotions of moving through the streets homeless and jobless and alone with her signature footprints, like so many other recent migrants, she makes herself visible and traceable. Her belonging and homing are evident in the fact that she still identifies her walking forward from an uncertain home base, which she labels, 'apartamento'.

She is the key figure in her map, with the streets as a backdrop. Nelly is a highly skilled migrant who uses the streets as a homing device to feel like she belongs to this new place of settlement, her map becoming an artefact of the tracks left by her as she moves through her new community. Nelly had neither a home nor many artefacts to show. She did however have a large nursing degree document, one which is evident on the map. The degree, however, was useless in Chile because it needed to be validated first in her country which she didn't have time to do before she left. Nelly's plan was to become 'stable and move on, to keep going'. The newcomer migrants like Venezuelans, Haitians and indigenous Ecuadorians who arrived under desperate terms used walking and public transportation and which contrasted to those settled migrants who married Chileans and could afford private transportation, especially cars. Nelly said, 'what I've been doing, is I leave as early as possible and come back as late as possible. I walk a lot, so I don't have to pay for buses'. She often met strangers on these walks some who helped her. Nelly's trajectory could be described as physically hypermobile yet occupationally and socially immobile.

The Ecuadorian street vendors in the study drew similar maps as Nelly, from the ground level walking because they spent their lives working on the streets. The streets were important to know when they were running from the police who chased them because their work was criminalized. Often, they lived in temporary homes and never knew whether or not they would return to them at night after a long day of work. Their maps more frequently illustrated their central city routes and had important landmarks and shops where they sold artisanal crafts. Likewise, those migrant women who had access to cars often illustrated roadways and their perspective as drivers, cruising through the city on their way to work, running errands and taking children from one activity to another.

Mariam's map of waiting

Mariam is a Haitian also in her forties (Figure 2.2). Like Nelly, she walked around the city looking for work: 'I go out the house and walk anywhere and try to find any job to get a contract and I am expecting the season of blueberries and work.' Unlike Nelly,

Figure 2.2 *Mariam's map.* Photo by Cuban.

however, she was not talking to strangers on the streets due to her very low Spanish language fluency, and she spent most of her time indoors in her home, talking to her Haitian roommates in Haitian-Creole, one of whom was her sister. She was often online too with Haitians in Chile and with her family in Haiti. Mariam said she migrated to Chile with her sister 'to find a better life. I thought Chile was better. It was to help my family. I heard that in Chile more jobs were available, and I thought I'd come here to improve my daughter's life'. When she first arrived in Santiago, she found herself in a tight spot after receiving a fraudulent contract followed by her visa expiring. She then had no 'legal papers and I can't work'. She wrote a letter to the government so they could 'reconsider my situation' but received a rejection and was currently undocumented. Her situation was doubly difficult because in Haiti she had a farm and animals that she sold in order to pay for her trip to Chile. She despaired that 'I lost all of that plus I have no job. I can't repair what I lost, and I have no money to send to my daughter'.

Her stated goal, however, was 'to go really far'. Rejected by the Chilean government and unwilling to return to Haiti, she contemplated her difficult situation and waited. She spent most of her time staying put, thinking about her family especially her teenage daughter, and strategizing her goals. She nurtured her dream and this materialized on her map as a large pink detailed flower that was the Haitian national flower, the hibiscus. She explained that it symbolized herself as a migrant in Chile: 'the flower is my life. I am like a flower. Flowers go through blooming. And they also fall. I fell and I want to bloom again.'

Nearly all of the maps of the Haitian women represented Haiti, not their contemporary daily life in Chile, which was so difficult due to the intense discrimination against them and their exclusion. Most of their maps were of pretty flowers, often the hibiscus. It was a symbol of pride, beauty and resilience as well as community. The flower centred Haitians' presence in a way that enabled them to go out of their homes and face Chilean society. Haitians like Mariam often stay inside because they are racially targeted (e.g., Lube-Guizardi & González Torralbo, 2019; Walsh, 2019). One Haitian noted posts on Facebook by Chileans who claimed that Haitians were disease carriers while mainstream media reports speak derogatorily to their influx as invasions. The Afro-Colombian and Afro-Brazilian women too found the public arena and civil society to be unsafe for them because of the amount of racial discrimination they experienced. Many of these migrant women began to share information online and were more strategic in terms of the neighbourhoods and areas where went and their activities.

These more symbolic mental maps were also drawn by others. For example, a Colombian non-profit coordinator drew an image of prayer hands and a cross that symbolized her strength to care for her son, husband and clients at work. A Venezuelan, who was a Buddhist, wrote a mantra and drew a Buddha, a heart and prayer book to represent the importance of inspiration and grace in her life in Chile. Faith was an important aspect of many of the women's lives. Still other women drew images such as suns, representative of the light and hope and they wanted so much in their lives. Another Haitian created a flag of her country, in her hope to return there someday and as a member of the Haitian diaspora in Chile. Still another Colombian who was recently divorced drew one large house that symbolized her new life after a divorce. It was bright red and centralized on her map. It represented her love of the arts, her freedom and her new foundation.

Final thoughts

Many of the maps, and particularly those of Nelly and Mariam, show a sense of hope and agency that defies the immigration and geography literature describing migrant women as embedded only within the domestic sphere and as passive followers of migrant men. These migrant women, on the other hand, were feminist pioneers, and they engaged fully in public life with their highly emotional and (im)mobile geographies. It is important to note that they were caring for their families abroad by moving countries and sending remittances, Nelly for her parents and Mariam for her daughter. Women's stories about caring for family at-a-distance 'does not initiate a complete shift in gender practices but instead results in a confluence of gender retentions and contestations in transnational family life' (Parreñas, 2008, p. 81). In her active mobile state, Nelly became visible in the public and she circulated around to let people know who she was as a high-skilled Venezuelan. She engaged in a feminist project of inscribing her privatized troubles onto the public arena in the embodied map that she drew of her new home as a streetscape, with her nursing degree, her tears and her footprints. Mariam too disrupts the mainstream media view of Haitians as helpless and instead shows Afro-Caribbean women as agentic in their new homes, forming diasporas, calculating their next moves, and using as much information as possible to build new lives in a place where they are not wanted. With her passive mobilities she developed hope and strength through a process of connecting to her inner self, as depicted by the Haitian national flower, which inspired her to move forward and progress her life.

From these migrant women's maps we see and experience the different worlds they inhabit from their marginalized and (im)mobile positions; ones which change, are open-ended and resilient. Their maps offer a deep visual pedagogy to rethink decolonizing and gendered lines of power in society for migrant women (D'Arcangelis & Huntley, 2012).

Note

1   Parts of this chapter have been adapted from my book, Cuban (2021, in press).

References

Barone, T., & Eisner, E. (2012). *Arts-based research*. Sage Publications.

Barrantes-Elizondo, L. (2019). Creando espacio para la etnografía visual en la investigación educativa. *Revista Electrónica Educare, 23*(2), 1–15.

Bélanger, D., & Silvey, R. (2019). An im/mobility turn: Power geometries of care and migration. *Journal of Ethnic and Migration Studies, 46*(16), 3423–40.

Blunt, A. and Dowling, R. (2006). Home. Routledge.

Boccagni, P. (2017) *Migration and the Search for Home Mapping Domestic Space in Migrants' Everyday Lives*. Springer.

Brickell, K. (2012) 'Mapping' and 'doing' critical geographies of home. *Progress in Human Geography, 36*(2), 225–44.

Buch, E. D., & Staller, K. M. (2007). The feminist practice of ethnography. In S. N. Hesse-Biber & P. L. Leavy (Eds.), *Feminist research practice: A primer* (pp. 187–221). SAGE Publications.

Cuban, S. (2021, in press). *Mapping southern migration routes of women*. Palgrave Macmillan.

D'Arcangelis, C. L., & Huntley, A. (2012). No more silence: Towards a pedagogy of feminist decolonizing solidarity. In S. Walters & L. Manicom (Eds.), *Feminist popular education in transnational debates: Building pedagogies of possibility* (pp. 41–58). Palgrave Macmillan.

Elliot, A., & Urry, J. (2010). *Mobile lives*. Routledge.

Garda-Rozenberga, I. (2019). Mapping life stories of exiled Latvians. *Trames, 23*(2), 145–57.

Hannam, K., Sheller, M., & Urry, J. (2006). Editorial: mobilities, immobilities, and moorings. *Mobilities, 1*, 1–22.

Jung, H. (2014). Let their voices be seen: Exploring mental mapping as a feminist visual methodology for the study of migrant women. *International Journal of Urban and Regional Research, 38*(3), 985–1002.

Jungnickel, K., & Hjorth, L. (2014). Methodological entanglements in the field: Methods, transitions and transmissions. *Visual Studies, 29*(2), 136–45.

Lee, J. (2017). Drawing life maps of New Malden: Ethnographical enquiry into the joseonjok people in New Malden by means of drawing practice. *Waypoints, 2*, 1–15.

Lube-Guizardi, M., & González Torralbo, H. (2019). Women in (dis)placement: The field of studies on migrations, social remittances, care and gender in Chile. *Revista de Estudios Sociales, 70*, 100–14.

Merriman, P. (2014). Mobilities I: Departures. *Progress in Human Geography, 39*(1), 87–95.

Muehlenhaus, I. (2014). Going viral: The look of online persuasive maps. *Cartographica, 49*(1), 18–34.

Murray, L. (2008). Motherhood, risk and everyday mobilities. In T. P. Uteng & T. Cresswell (Eds.), *Gendered mobilities* (pp. 47–63). Routledge.

Parreñas, R. S. (2008). The *forces of domesticity: Filipina migrants and globalization.* University Press.

Pink, S. (2011). From embodiment to emplacement: Re-thinking competing bodies, senses and spatialities. *Sport, Education and Society, 16*(3), 343–55.

Pirani, N., Ricker, B. A., & Kraak, M. J. (2020). Feminist cartography and the United Nations Sustainable Development Goal on gender equality: Emotional responses to three thematic maps. *The Canadian Geographer/Le Géographe Canadien, 64*(2), 184–98.

Rose, G. (2014). On the relation between 'visual research methods' and contemporary visual culture. *The Sociological Review, 62*, 24–46.

Schewel, K. (2019). Understanding immobility: Moving beyond the mobility bias in migration studies. *International Migration Review, 53*(1) 1–28.

Sheller, M. (2004). Automotive emotions: Feeling the car. *Theory, Culture & Society, 21*(4/5), 221–42.

Sheller, M. (2014). The new mobilities paradigm for a live sociology. *Current Sociology, 62*(6), 789–811.

Tolia-Kelly, D. P. (2011). The geographies of cultural geography III: Material geographies, vibrant matters and risking surface geographies. *Progress in Human Geography, 37*(1), 153–60.

Urry, J. (2007). *Mobilities.* Polity Press.

Walsh, S. (2019). The Chilean exception: Racial homogeneity, mestizaje and eugenic nationalism. *Journal of Iberian and Latin American Studies, 25*(1), 105–25.

Chapter 3

Conversations from Creative Toolboxes: Journeys as Artists, Educators and Curators

Beverley Hayward

Tales from the Creative Toolbox: Turning the Tide

Diverse are the texts of knowledge creation.
We are exhibiting, crafting our curation.
Finally displayed on those whitewashed walls,
On par with the work hung in those hallowed halls.

Our art and craft in all its Majesty, stands tall.
No longer relegated to those dusty backroom stalls.
In place of all those old, white masters of the arts,
We are here, this is just the start.

Oh, what joy, oh what pride,
Our art-craft is crammed high and wide.
We have found our own Truths; we have the keys.
Our oeuvre is a cornucopia of beauty and fecundity,

See us here: we WILL NOT hide,
In a Feminist Aesthetic, we have turned the tide!

(Hayward, 2021)

Introduction

For many years, I worked alongside a group of other women artists-educator Learning Support Assistants (LSA) at a university in London, England. An LSA is a support worker in an educational institution who assists students who are neurodiverse or seen to have a disability. Whilst working together as a collective community of women, we had many conversations in many different spaces in the academy. For example, our conversations took place in the staff room, my office, the corridors and over a coffee in the refectory. It was whilst having these conversations that we realized the extent of our marginalization in the academy. We were marginalized as artists, women, support workers and, as what Clover (2010) calls, 'artists as educators' (p. 243). My chapter draws on our conversations to illustrate some of the struggles we faced as marginalized educators – the paradox of our actually seeing ourselves as powerful artists-educators, whilst most academics saw us as mere helpers and carers. The struggles were distressing as we attempted to overcome the dominance of 'the masters' in both the academic and the art world who, for the most part, upheld patriarchal class structures in ways that tended to silence us. We were in essence what Parker and Pollock (1981) called the 'mistresses' in *Old Mistresses,* which carries a very different power connotation to 'The Masters'. In addition, it was difficult for working-class women like us to break into the exalted practices of curating and exhibiting. Yet we challenged and surpassed these in our own way and this chapter shares our journeys from entrance into the academy as LSAs to our exits as artists-educators and curators. While there were many different types of conversations, I focus in this chapter on the conversations I had with Luna. For me, these conversations were the richest in language, poetry and imagery and best represent feminist art and pedagogic praxis. It was also Luna who educated and advised me on the practices of curating and exhibiting, as she had actually exhibited at The Halpern Gallery, and provided me with the contact Genevieve Tullberg, the gallery manager. Through this connection we will be able to exhibit collectively our textiles, painting, ceramics, photographs and craft pieces when the gallery re-opens following Covid-19.

For me, as I describe in the poem which opens this chapter, to exhibit my work publicly is a liberating force against 'all those old, white masters of the arts' and what Pollock (2003) calls 'the idealised masculine self, the artist-hero' (p. xxvii). However, I am always mindful of Pollocks assertion that to challenge the norms of the male, European artist 'with the ordinariness of class, culture and other difference, or sexuality [is seen] by the curators of art's purity as a kind of contamination, soiling its transcendent beauty with the messy business of life' (p. xxviii). It is precisely our foray into this messy business of life that makes our story, mine and Luna's, so significant and so feminist. Further, it is the importance of the everyday and the conversations and experiences we had which gave our practice as artists-educators meaning. As I state in my poem, in the act of 'exhibiting, crafting our curation' we resisted the masters and their arts, and the professors/academics positioned so safely in what is often called their ivory towers (e.g., Jackson, 2004). In this chapter I share our conversations about the injustices of our situation and our acts of resistance to the class and gender-assigned positions. In the telling of our stories, however, there was a shadow, an urgency because our redundancy from university was imminent and in fact our positions came to an end in 2019. What I outline in this chapter is how, as we talked and created our artworks, pulling ideas and images from our feminist artistic and pedagogic toolboxes, we actually showcased our imaginations, and the breath and spirit of our creativity that is not redundant and will never disappear.

A collective participation of resistance

In the knowledge that we would soon be unable to have spontaneous and significant conversations as LSAs, I brought together a group to tell our stories.[1] The stories are a celebration of our subjectivities as artist-educators, and acts of political act of writing. The opportunity to exhibit our work as a collective community of artists, through poetry, imagery and text, was in itself an act of power. Public feminist exhibitions are important as they rupture the legacy of the elitist mastery canons of art, noted above and give women like us a platform from which we can be seen in all our creativity (Parker & Pollock, 1981). The need to hold this exhibition has its genealogy in the marginalization we felt. From our shared experiences, we learnt a lot from each other and it was imperative to gather these new knowledges of feminist artistic and pedagogic practices before the stories were lost. This loss was due to neoliberalism's collision with austerity, often the landscape in which education is situated. The UK government decided that the work of LSAs was no longer required in higher education. Therefore, this chapter makes a contribution to the limited knowledge produced about LSAs and goes some way towards understanding the work of the LSA in this particular space and time. We are positioned in a legacy of care and the 'good woman' discourses, which are presented in the limited literature written about, but not written by, support workers, for example, the discursive positionings of the poor student, good woman-support worker, carer and othering narratives (e.g., Watson, Bayliss & Pratchett, 2013; Veck, 2009; Barkham, 2008). Yet this is a story about resistance, resilience and a celebration of ourselves as feminist artist-educators. We did fail in the compulsory schooling system but returned to university as mature students and then as educators. Now we are educators and our pedagogic-artistic tales are overflowing from our feminist creative toolboxes, for packed in these boxes we have found a wealth of knowledge and imagination.

In many ways we have processed and problematized what Hoult (2012) called the discourse of the 'poor student' which is so frequently read as a negative identity and taken on the subject position of the resilient learner. We returned to education as mature students to study the creative arts, benefiting from the university's widening participation programme which reached out to people like us and enabled us to complete either access courses or full degrees. The LSAs with whom I worked and who part of my doctoral study had an interest in art and craft, in fact many of us were practising artists, with a desire to become a more recognized artist or to work in the creative industries. It is also important to note that many of us also 'protected' under two categories as we entered the university. The first was as dyslexic which is protected under the *Equality Act*, 2010, and the second, as disabled. However, although entry was permitted and we were sheltered behind an act that disallowed discrimination, there were unspoken conditions attached. One was that we would not be considered artists despite our training in that area. It is the coming to see ourselves artists that has enabled a different story to be told.

Curating our stories

Our story is different to the poor student, carer, helper narratives presented in the literature discussed above and perpetuated by the academics/masters in the academy. Just before the dissolution of the department I, in collaboration with other LSAs, decided to curate an exhibition of the artistic representations of our lives and selves we had created over the many years working collectively as a community. To begin, we used the staffroom walls to display an art history timeline. LSAs frequently attended many major art exhibitions as part of their role was to accompany their students on these trips. Frequently, we noticed that lesser-known artists seldom featured in these exhibitions. From our visits to these exhibitions, we collected a variety of posters which we pasted on the staffroom walls. We also used a pinboard to post newspaper articles of significance, for example, about the then Education Secretary Michael Gove, who was advocating a fervent promotion of white European male artists in the revised curriculum. Mansell (2013), writing about this for the *Guardian News*, stated that:

> In art and design, the draft [curriculum] is criticised for having 'substantially weakened content' and for lacking 'breadth, depth or cohesion'. It has a 'regrettably narrow' view of the subject, with a focus only on the history of western art produced by 'white European men', 'thereby ignoring the realities of the contemporary world'.

Fortunately, the proposed policy was not put into practise and the ideologies that sustain these colonial and gendered discourses were a concern that ignited the first earnest conversation about organizing our own exhibition. We were incensed by the perpetuation, preservation and reproduction of what Cixous terms the 'Empire of the Selfsame' (1975, p. 79). These selfsame mastery/masculine, class and race discourses attempt to sustain an elitist canon of what art is, the spaces in which art can be taught and those who is considered to be an artist. We spoke about this and how we could resist this entrenchment. One such way was to hold our own exhibition that was not dependent upon a universalising theme and was open to all support workers. The importance of the exhibition was to act as a pedagogical force to visualize a change to the monolithic norms upheld by those white men in power/government. By exhibiting the LSAs' artwork in an exhibition of a feminist creative praxis, new knowledges are visualized.

Therefore, I encouraged the whole department to prepare for an exhibition in the university's designated gallery space. During our years working at the university, we had many conversations about our artwork and I was eager to showcase this in the gallery space that was reserved for exhibitions. I curated the entire exhibition only to be told one week before the hanging that the gallery was no longer available as students were to have priority over the space. Deeply disappointed, I asked to reschedule the event and was told it was reserved for students for the remainder of the year. Although dismayed by this outcome, I accepted that the students should have priority. However, upon my next visit to the gallery I found the work exhibited had actually been produced by tutors at the university. I was angry and frustrated by what I saw as the continuation of both aesthetic and knowledge hierarchies exercised in the academy that clearly excluded the 'lowly' LSAs. I immediately informed all the LSAs of what was going on because I felt a certain responsibility for the injustice of the situation as I instigated expectations that the university would acknowledge and curate our work as 'equal' artists in the institution. I felt guilty that I had built up their hopes, only for them to be dashed by those who saw little if any value in us as artist-educators.

Figure 3.1 *Self-portrait*, 2014. Photo by Luna.

Figure 3.2 *Mocking the master' narrative: The masquerade*, 2015/2019. Photo by Hayward.

By exhibiting in this space, we would have been on par with those exercising the class and gendered discourses that situate the masters as the privileged subject. We were deeply hurt and frustrated, as I state in my poem, for once more we were 'relegated to those dusty backroom stalls', not able to showcase our work (Hayward, 2021). However, we were not deterred. Fortunately, at the time I had a very large office and made the space a small gallery where we all had the opportunity to exhibit. We displayed an abundance of art which instigated many conversations about our feminist art practices, stories about our lives and pedagogic experiences.

Our curation was an example of a disruption, a challenge to the gallery spaces of the university, where an alternative space of resistance was constructed. In this way, a small space of belonging to a community of artists is revealed and a different reality to mastery discourses is opened up to show that we too are artists. Many students and staff saw our work in this alternative gallery space and, as Clover et al. (2016) consider, we were using the space of the gallery to educate. It was here that we discussed our work together and Luna created a drawing (Figure 3.1). She said it was a representation of how she sees her role as an LSA and her work as an artist. In conversation with her and her self-portrait, I responded (see Figure 3.2). Some of the stories and conversations embodied in these images are told in the next section.

Painting resilience

'Learn to know yourself well', 'trust your own talents to correct, design and remake', 'mould yourself into being', 'become the artist, change the world'. These were the words that Luna wrote to accompany her *Self-portrait*. She summed up our position perfectly; as artists as educators, we supported the students, each other and ourselves. Over many years we discussed the power of art and exhibiting in our conversations about our oeuvres. We chatted about our art practices within a feminist pedagogic praxis, about different knowledges and alternative lifestyles. In the past, Luna's had lived in a counter-culture where she practised paganism, naturalism, tokenism, mysticism and meditation. She often spoke about her time living in a tepee, where she gave birth to one of her daughters, and the spirit guides who are an extension of her life. In her *Self-Portrait* the crow her spirit guide, although positioned to point to the future, is very much in the present. She said she took the crow as her totem which embodies knowledges that are no longer valued in our society, such as prophecy, foresight and intuition. This we discussed in a conversation we had during an exhibition we went to on Georgiana Houghton. I knew about Luna's past life experiences and I suggested that we went to this exhibition at the Courtauld Gallery in London. I felt it would be a nice day out in the summer holidays. I and a few of the LSAs, including Luna, attended this exhibition on this long-forgotten artist, a Spiritualist medium. Houghton created a series of abstract watercolours in the 1860s and 1870s and wrote on the back of each work the spirits that guided her hand. These included family members and high Renaissance artists. Like many female artists, her work was ignored by the masters, only to be recently re-discovered.

During the visit Luna told me about her experiences as an artist and how *Self-portrait* incorporates the fixed and familiar with an organic fluid potential for change. The crow symbolizes that part of the self that is constant, the unchanging element; she said 'it comes to visit me in my garden, everyday'. Looking to the future it is a symbol of hope, whereas the gold-finch, also included in her drawing, is a sign of endurance and is depicted just in the process of taking flight. She drew upon the imagery of birds as a metaphor for artists to fly to new spaces, to fly above that glass ceiling put in place by the masters of the canons of art history. I told her that the ambiguity and vulnerability, interlaced with the passion and power of the direct and forthright gaze, rivets me as the viewer. She said that it is a representation that subverts normative gendered identities and a canon that is cemented in linear time and established spaces.

My own tapestry, *Mocking the Master Narrative: The Masquerade* (Figure 3.2) further complicates and problematicizes normative gendered presentations and responds to Luna's representation. Here the socially constructed gendered identities that code the feminine norms are subverted as I play with these social codings. My artwork was created as part of my own self-study. To create it, I turned away from a history that reproduces the universal narratives of that which Cixous (1975, p. 79) critiques as 'mastery discourses' towards a feminist aesthetic, a tapestry that is an embodiment of the many selves' women like me perform in a daily masquerade. We mask certain parts of ourselves, only to reveal others when required by discourses of mastery/patriarchy that surround and shape us. This is necessary in order to operate in the prescriptive, overbearing institutional structures and discourses of higher education and the artworld. In our roles as support workers, we are seen as carers employed from what Steven's (2013) terms the Mum's Army. So masked were we in our 'poor student' as well as 'good caring woman' discourses that the artist as educator identity was almost completely hidden. As 'artists as educators' and educators who are artists, we resided outside the establishment and our collective community of practice was unknown to most in the university. Thus, my conversation with Luna explored the possibilities of who could be seen as an artist and what art could be. As we came together in conversation, we talked and represented ourselves as artists, educators and even, curators, moving differently in the spaces that tried to contain us. The freedom and agency to represent ourselves as we see ourselves and to move freely is in both images and also in the fact that neither picture has a frame. There are no boundaries to contain the formation of the subject.

In my image the possibilities for transformation are metaphorically symbolized in the spaces that are left open on the border at the bottom of the image. It is an embodiment of the ways in which women can disrupt the essentialist gendered positions; they can break the frame of their being, where the creative subject breaks the confines of colonialism, class and the reproduction masculine discourses (Cixous, 1975). I challenge the conventions of the canon, Greek mythology's use of the transformation of women, such as Myrrha and Daphne, into trees. Further historicization of the canon recalls Botticelli's *Primavera* (1482), the likes of which was created to stimulate the gaze of the male viewer and reinforce the traditions of the grand narrative that idealizes and genders the subjectivity of women. Conversely in our stories, both Luna and I celebrate Nature and the feminine. We are at one with Nature, opposing individualism, Western capitalism and the norms of the canon. In drawing upon the oeuvre of Frieda Kahlo, who stated that 'I paint my reality', evident too in the images presented is a compelling, influential and inspiring visual reality, our reality (see Burrus, 2008).

Therefore, I confront the masculine, colonial narrative that makes up the canon of what art is. I mock the masters of the arts by making this a deliberate feature in my tapestry where threads hang down and found – bricolage, laurel leaves, have been stitched and embellished. They are loosely attached in a space that should be the frame. The piece is a truth to the materials and techniques, as there is an authenticity in the obvious presentation of the materials. However, there is more to it than a Modernist's need to show the nature of those materials. The practise of my art is clearly illustrated in the techniques and mediums used. I enjoy sewing; it is a form of relaxation. My mind is able to empty in the concentration of the repetitive task. I do it most days; it is a daily routine that in this piece connects me to the memories of my mother, who was a seamstress. The process reminds me of Louise Bourgeois, where she says that sewing was a familiar activity and a form of emotional repair, as 'the needle is used to repair damage' (cited in Parker, 2010, p. xix). I was physically repairing the trauma of the sudden and disturbing nature of my mother's death. When thinking about the conceptualization of the piece, the death of my mother was very much in my thoughts. It brings to mind Cixous's (1977) writings on the death of her father and how this space of emptiness was required in order to be filled with the creativity needed to be able to write and create.

Whilst my work shares this emotional space with Cixous, in my consideration of death and bereavement, it is a position that is not shared by Luna. Our artworks

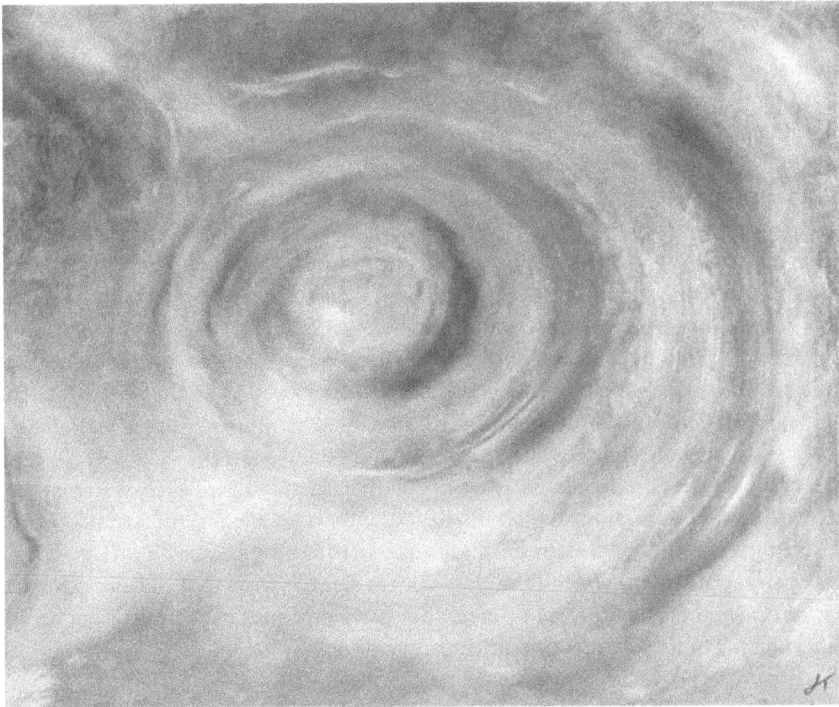

Figure 3.3 *Plato's Atlantis*, 2016. Photo by Luna.

embody experiences that are of the moment, but it also paints a wider context. In this wider context Luna and I both disrupt and mock the mastery narratives of patriarchal norms. O'Farrell (2005) makes this point when she says that 'it is not a matter of analysing the motivations, creativity and discoveries of an individual who is the originator of that work, but in looking at what structures and patterns that work shares, and also does not share, with others' (p. 111). For example, *Self-portrait* presents alternative possibilities and avenues of being. Luna spoke about the artist being able to move through portals not being fixed in space and time, suggesting that she is outside the norms of realities. This was a recurring theme that she discussed with me and one that was not present in my own work. Luna conceptualizes the creative process as being immersed in spaces of possibility, imagination, nature and the mythical when she created (see Figure 3.3). She said,

> So, I think that's in my artwork; it's the job of the artist, ... to stand on the edge of two worlds and communicate what he (sic) sees. I think that, that is just a fantastic way, cause when I paint, I go into a zone and the zone always takes me back to nature, it takes me back to the space to be in a different world.

In conversation, Luna explains that the painting process is often long, complex and challenging, developed through much immersement in the medium and application of the paint that may be intuitive and at the same time deliberate. But, like me, she also explored an understanding of power and knowledges and the ways in which society is constructed through sustained dominant discourses. In the painting Luna said she avoided demarcations by merging the boundaries. I viewed the image in situ, and in conversation with her, she says that there are no delineations of hierarchical powers. And to me it did appear three dimensional, multidimensional, other-worldly, a vortex into another space of myth. The paint shimmers, dazzles, transports the viewer to different spaces, to different land-seascapes. Luna says it is a portal, a space, where time has no meaning. Transitions, new beginnings and possibilities are envisioned, for in Luna's depiction of power, it is not centralized and possessed, but local, mobile, changeable and thereby exercised by those individuals that take up alternative subject positions. This she understood from the post-modern and post-structuralist unit she studied as a mature student. Luna articulates and visualizes how she sees the social structures and patterns of power. In her work, she focuses on problematizing normative class and gendered systems, the injustices and oppression she felt. Plato's Atlantis is an allegory of social control where the elite must maintain the status quo in order for society to thrive. There is a central point of power and the class system extends from that circular point of significance; this is the form of power that Luna critiques in her representation. She explains in the process of painting:

> Plato was talking about this Atlantis, it is almost like this mythical place, it could have been so beautiful, but it was built on power, but the power was at the centre

and went out. … but that's a misuse of the power and it was overridden; the law of nature took it out, so that's like his message to society.

Within the discourse of Eurocentric and mastery power and knowledge hierarchies, her art is a pedagogic visualization of feminist democratic positioning that looks to equalize social and cultural relationships. Our stories told and how we visually represented them challenge the elitist and normative canon of art. Art is a decayed tapestry using found objects and frayed thread. The spaces in which art can be taught are for us the spaces of everyday conversations. Those who can be seen as artists are now working-class women. The stories and artworks celebrate and remember the genealogy of all those hidden women, artists as educators, craftswomen and knowledge producers. The stories unmask the lost tales from our creative toolbox and the artwork will be seen in the up-and-coming exhibition that seeks to educate those to what West (2016) suggests are 'new ways of seeing' (p. 38). But as artists we wanted to inform others that women can be artists in gallery spaces in the public arena. It was important to have a public space to be seen and heard, to paint stories from a woman's perspective and create a conversation with the viewers, staff, students and the general public. The exhibition(s) showcase feminist creativity in the narratives of our artwork; we deliberately chose an exhibition to claim these spaces.

Reflections: Imaginative possibilities realized

In this chapter, we told our truths as artists, as educators, as artist-educators. We felt compelled to write our story and to organize an exhibition to challenge the institutional norms in which we worked that dismissed both who we are and what we know and do. As a result of the exhibition of our work and through our conversations, the silence of our knowledge and aesthetic production is not as loud in our consciousness as it was previously. Our weaving of our tales and visualizing our worlds through a feminist consciousness brought into the light our vast aesthetic experiences, our importance as artists. As I state in my poem: 'We have found our own Truths; we have the keys. Our oeuvre is a cornucopia of beauty and fecundity, See us here: we WILL NOT hide.' We pulled our imaginations from the creative toolbox, sought a new political subjectification through exhibition, a new sense of agency and need to interrupt the normalizing masculine and hierarchical codifications of the academy and the gallery. Although relegated to normative gendered roles in the academy and excluded from the normative gallery space, we created an artistic pathway, took a journey to develop our own subjectivities of artist as educator anyway. By telling out stories in the public spaces of our own choosing, we are able to educate, to show our differences, our power and knowledges. Importantly, Luna was actually commissioned by Medway Council to create a twenty-foot mural for the Corn Exchange in Rochester, Kent, England. Her response was *The Rose Garden* (see Figure 3.4 entitled *Detail*), inspired by both an ancient Persian poem *The Conference of the Birds* and her own artistic journey

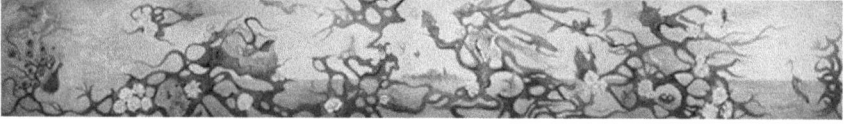

Figure 3.4a *The Rose Garden*, mural. Photo by Luna.

Figure 3.4b *Detail.*

(Zsigo, 2020). As my poem reminds us, in the public act of displaying our work 'we have turned the tide!' for we are no longer accepting of the old elitist normative structures. Imagination and creativity are the power tools from our toolbox that enabled us to risk-take and to claim our place in public curation (Cixous, 1976). Now the storytellers, we swim against the mastery tides towards and in an ocean of imaginative and creative feminist praxis.

Note

1   Some of the conversations we had formed part of my PhD research (Hayward, 2019). We and us refers to the support workers that took part in my study including myself, as there was an autobiographic element to my project.

References

Barkham, J. (2008). Suitable work for women? Roles, relationships and changing identities of 'other adults' in the early years' classroom. *British Educational Research Journal, 34*(6), 839–53.

Clover, D. E. (2010). A contemporary review of feminist aesthetic practices in selective adult education journals and conference proceedings. *Adult Education Quarterly, 60*(3), 233–48.

Clover, D. E., Sanford, K. Bell, & Johnson, K. (Eds.). (2016). *Adult education, museums and art galleries animating social, cultural and institutional change.* Sense Publishers.

Cixous, H. (1976). The laugh of the Medusa. *Signs, 1*(4), 875–93.

Cixous, H. (1975/1986). Sorties: Out and out: Attacks/ways out/forays. In H. Cixous & C. Clément (Eds.), *The newly born woman* (pp. 63–132). Tauris.

Cixous, H. (1977/1991). Coming to writing. In D. Jenson (Ed.), *Coming to writing and other Essays* (pp. 1–58). Harvard University Press.

Equality Act (2010). HMSO. https://www.legislation.gov.uk/ukpga/2010/15/part/7/crossheading/special-provision-for-political-parties

Hayward, B. (2019). Positionings, policies and practices in the UK's current higher education sector in the context of neo-liberalism: An exploration of the subject positions of the female learning support assistant, as they practise their art and craft in the everyday. Unpublished Thesis. Birkbeck College, University of London.

Hayward, B. (2021). Tales from the creative toolbox: Turing the tide. Unpublished Poem.

Hoult, E. (2012). *Adult learning and la recherche féminine: Reading resilience and Hélène Cixous.* Palgrave Macmillan.

Jackson, S. (2004). Language and discourse in the academy. In *Differently academic.* London: Kluwer Academic Publishers.

Kahlo, F. in Burrus, C. (2008). *I paint my reality.* New Horizons.

Mansell, W. (2013). National curriculum experts criticise Government. Accessed November 8, 2017, from https://www.theguardian.com/education/2013/jun/24/national-curriculum-experts-criticise-government

O'Farrell, C. (2005). *Michel Foucault.* Sage Publishing Ltd.

Parker, R. (2010). *The subversive stitch: Embroidery and the making if the feminine.* I.B. Tauris.

Parker, R., & Pollock, G. (1981). *Old mistresses: Women, art and ideology.* Pandora Press.

Pollock, G. (2003). *Vision and difference.* Routledge Classics.

Stevens, J. (2013, June 2). Army of teaching assistants faces the axe as Education department attempts to save some of the £4billion they cost each year. *Daily Mail.* http://www.dailymail.co.uk/news/article-2334853/

Veck, W. (2009) From an exclusionary to an inclusive understanding of educational difficulties and educational space: Implications for the learning support assistant's role. *Oxford Review Education, 35*(1), 41–56.

Watson, D. L., Bayliss, P. D., & Pratchett, G. (2013). Pond life that 'know their place': Exploring teaching and learning support assistants' experiences through positioning theory. *International Journal of Qualitative Studies in Education, 26*(1), 100–17

West, L. (2016). *Distress in the city: Racism, fundamentalism and a democratic education.* UCL Press.

Zsigo, L. (2020). *The rose garden mural at The Corn Exchange.* Rochester. www.lunazsigo.com

Chapter 4

The Feminist Aesthetic and Climate Action: The Roscommon Women's Network

Eve Cobain and Leah Dowdall

Feminist community education groups are at the forefront of consciousness-raising around climate change in Ireland, bringing global ideas and concepts of change to local communities through peer learning and collective action. Through feminist artistic practices, in particular, these groups have become 'powerful catalysts to stimulate imaginative thought, critical dialogue, community mobilisation, personal transformation, and socio-environment' (Clover, 2004, p. 59). This article is a case study of how one community education group, Roscommon Women's Network, uses a feminist aesthetic practice to promote climate action.

Roscommon Women's Network is part of the National Collective of Community Based Women's Networks (NCCWN), a national organization that works directly with and represents the interests of women from communities in rural and urban settings throughout Ireland (2021). As a community education provider, Roscommon Women's Network is also part of a national educational movement in Ireland that harnesses the power of education as a means of social change through a critical pedagogical approach to learning. The work of its CycleUp group, in particular, challenges neoliberal consumer culture through feminist artistic expression, by refashioning used textiles from the group's charity shop into purposeful and decorative objects. Each object features a label with their call to action, which explains the importance of waste reduction and sustainability. The items created as part of the CycleUp process are therefore not only powerful representations of the feminist aesthetic, but also physical representations of the need for urgent discourse around how resources are used and reused. Though their act of rethinking and reorganizing the world and its materials, Roscommon Women's Network manifests the possibility of new 'ways of doing and making' (Rancière, 2004, p. 13), as well as creating new forms of cognition for themselves and their community. As Jacques Rancière asserts in *The Aesthetic of Politics: The Distribution of the Sensible*:

> It is on the basis of this primary aesthetics that it is possible to raise the question of 'aesthetic practices' as I understand them, that is forms of visibility that disclose artistic practices, the place they occupy, what they 'do' or 'make' from

the standpoint of what is common to the community. Artistic practices are 'ways of doing and making' that intervene in the general distribution of ways of doing and making as well as in the relationships they maintain to modes of being and forms of visibility.

(p. 13)

Indeed, the work of Roscommon Women's Network makes visible (and voluble) various forms of inequality within their local community, and on a global scale.

Following a series of interviews with participants (Mary and Laura) in CycleUp and staff (Lisa and John) at Roscommon Women Network, this article explores how the organization uses a feminist aesthetic to promote climate-conscious action through empowering local women learners. To protect the anonymity of these participants, names have been replaced by pseudonyms throughout. By reviewing the organization's key mission and strategic framework, this chapter will explore how these concepts – feminism and climate consciousness – are interlinked and enacted on a practical level. While Roscommon Women's Network serves as a strong example of the ways in which community education organizations are leading the way on climate action through feminist aesthetic activities, their innovation in this area has not been financially rewarded. Moreover, as a community education group in rural Ireland the group have faced their own climate challenges in terms of flooding. As such, the chapter will also explore some of the challenges that grassroots groups like Roscommon Women's Network face in terms of sustainability, in spite of being an example of innovative climate action.

Feminism and climate action in CycleUp

Roscommon Women's Network provides both accredited and non-accredited learning options to learners from a variety of backgrounds, with both male and female learners supported through their courses. With four full-time staff members and one part-time staff member, as well as eighteen volunteers, in the 2018/19 academic year, the Network supported forty-five learners from the local community (*Roscommon Women's Network Strategic Plan*, 2019). While an independent centre, the Network is also part of a broader, community education movement in Ireland. It serves as a strong example of Irish community education's feminist orientation and its rootedness in feminist practices. Walking into the centre itself, one can see various notices scattered across the walls for a variety of support services that are offered at the centre and beyond to ensure women entering receive access to the wrap-around support services they need to succeed. This is, of course, not an uncommon site in many of the community education centres across Ireland, which share a similar ethos and aim.

Community education as it exists in Ireland today owes a debt to the feminist (and aesthetic) practices that call into question prevailing, and often delimiting, discourses and modes of being. Centres of community education see their role as providing a space for both women and men to come together to question and challenge social structures and practices that maintain and perpetuate inequality. As Roscommon Women's Network's Manager, Lisa explains in her interview:

> We believe feminism is about equality. We work through a family model to achieve this. It is not uncommon to see young men, in particular, referred onto our training programmes through their mothers who come into the centre for support. We have one woman who came into our centre and from there her two sons started coming. They love it here. One of the sons is now volunteering in the charity shop.

Women's groups in Ireland have led the way in making various forms of oppression – particularly gendered social and educational inequality – manifest through their collective projects, calling for a radical redistribution of power and resources. The Network's CycleUp Group is a key example of some of these practices and tackles a global issue like climate change directly through small-scale feminist collective action.

By making 'something else [out of] what was to be thrown away' the work of the CycleUp group considers alternative realities that run counter to what has been 'taken for granted' (Greene, 1995, p. 3). Indeed, the group's departure from consumerist modes of production and thinking emerged as a key theme in discussion, with the creative practice taking on a political quality – or becoming what Rancière (2010) might call 'dissensual' – with the capacity to disrupt and give voice to different forms of domination. Not only the act of making (as a community), but the products of this process – fabric owls, toy donkeys, Christmas stockings and, more recently, Covid-19 masks – give rise to new forms of consciousness. The objects are problem-posing, like the critical learning that takes place within CycleUp; they ask the beholder to think about their own practices around consumption.

For Laura, however, this act of revision undertaken in the upcycling process is also about seeing what is already there (returning to and refashioning rather than discarding), articulating the 'common sense' dimension of sustainability and returning to practices that have been modelled by women in the community for many years:

> When I was a child my grandmother was a seamstress and she would get people's clothes and nothing was wasted, every button was reused, every bit of fabric was reused, my grandmother had cigarette boxes, she made us dolls houses from them. I tend to have that attitude, that everything should be used, nothing should be thrown away. I just hate waste. And I think that's mothers, we want the world to be better and we want to get the best out of what we have.

The care with which these productive activities are performed both by Roscommon Women's Network and previous generations of women *makers* gesture to and embody an alternative mode of production, demonstrating how an obsessive preoccupation with material economic growth and overproduction (not seeing the value of *what we have* at hand) undermines the sustainability of the planet and accelerates the climate crisis (Floro, 2012). For the women engaging in the CycleUp group these challenges are not abstract or high-minded but located in everyday experience and everywhere in evidence.

For one of the participants, women were seen as leaders in this regard, in a large part because of their outsized role in care-oriented activities. As Mary noted, 'if you're looking at environmental projects and awareness of global warming and the planet it will be the females that change how they buy things and make lifestyle choices and, you know, how the family reacts around climate change'. This viewpoint highlights the value of social reproduction in terms of shaping responses to the climate crisis (Bhattacharya, 2017; Ferguson, 2019). As Mary noted, 'if you're looking at environmental projects and awareness of global warming and the planet it will be the females that change how they buy things and make lifestyle choices and, you know, how the family reacts around climate change'. In addition, Mary felt she had an important role to play in 'encourag[ing] [her family] not to be consumers'. She outlined how the Network played a key role in empowering not only women in the local community – 'who are more inclined to come in and get the help if they need it' – but also their families. In Mary's view this had a direct impact on the 'males in their family who don't necessarily want to go and get any help'. Supporting women was therefore key to supporting the wider community: 'if the women come out feeling better about themselves they'll be able to support the people that need their support as well, you know'.

At the same time, Roscommon Women's Network provides a holistic learning space, rooted in a feminist praxis of care, for all members of the community, and it was also felt to be a transformative space for men who attended courses there. 'We had a young chap', noted Lisa, 'there was some support he needed holistically that he got here. He got something that he needed that he wasn't getting somewhere else … he would consider himself a feminist and I think that's a great thing!' Discussing the psychosocial challenges within the community at large, the women were keen to point out the intersectional nature of feminism that their practice interrogates. As Laura summarized, 'discrimination isn't just a gender thing; if you fall into a certain economic bracket you're also discriminated against … we want equal rights for everybody … a level playing field'. Male learners, however, remain largely on the training side of Roscommon Women's Network's provision. The community education programmes and courses the Network offers, such as CycleUp, remain largely female spaces.

The way in which Roscommon Women's Network responds to the needs of the community is also evidenced by the flexibility within the group and participants' ability to quickly react to the changing needs of the times. For instance, even before the Irish government had mandated the wearing of facemasks in public settings, the CycleUp group had refocused their energies on producing cloth face masks made from recycled materials. The decision to do this came from learners themselves who saw a need and quickly responded to it intuitively.

Interestingly, participants in the CycleUp group noted that they did not make environmentalism a key focus of every meeting, but rather preferred to allow these conversations to happen organically. Laura, who said she did not see herself as a climate activist, described instead enjoying a return to what she described as a traditional outlook on material goods – an appreciation of everything having a use and therefore a rethinking about waste. While concern for an environmental agenda may not have been a motive for joining the programme, or even a focus in the meetings, participants did agree that one outcome was a greater appreciation for climate-conscious action. As Susan noted, 'my participation in this course has helped transform my thinking into broader healthy life choices on things like food and consumer purchasing. I am learning to make small changes every day'. While not driving the discourse of each meeting, therefore, the sheer act of doing led to a deeper inner questioning about personal practices and global challenges of the modern day. This reflective practice did not end with participants on the course. Indeed, for many, involvement in the programme led to conversations with family and friends about current environmental challenges and female empowerment. For instance, Laura described chatting with her granddaughter about climate action. In some instances, however, the ideas and changes set in motion by participating in the group were felt to pose a challenge for a number of women. Lisa noted how one woman in particular came to her to share that a participant in CycleUp 'had very difficult conversations with her family. She said she'd learnt so much on the course it had caused trouble in her family'. These conversations, in response to understanding gained through participating in the CycleUp group – whether positive or challenging – opened an important space for critical discourse.

It is clear that raising awareness about climate action is at the heart of the CycleUp Programme's mission, yet for learners, this aspect of the programme is not the only or indeed the foremost reason for participation. The social aspect of the group's work was incredibly important to the continued investment of participants, with Laura further emphasizing, 'if I didn't have a great group of women to come into every Friday, I wouldn't have been able to do it'. Women entered the group, bringing with them sometimes painful past experiences, ranging from personal challenges to health issues. For one participant, who had left her husband and was recovering from serious ill-health, the course brought a renewed sense of purpose, belonging and self-confidence. The profile of women in the group ranges, with women spanning different age groups and backgrounds, yet in the group operate as a collective. The women are learning together and experiencing individual growth through collective action. In a rural community, where distance breeds isolation, this social aspect of the course was seen as an equally important, if not a more important, benefit to the group's overall mission.

CycleUp as an example of transformative, aesthetic feminist learning

Like many Irish community education courses, CycleUp takes a Freirean pedagogical approach to education, meaning the group employs a critical approach as outlined in Paulo Freire's *Pedagogy of the Oppressed* (1970). In practice this means that learners are encouraged to learn from each other by raising questions and engaging in critical dialogue. This method of learning gives way to a process of conscientization (conscientização) that is marked by a deepened or more acute understanding of the world, existing power structures and our relationship to one another. While this process underpins all of the programmes that Roscommon Women's Network offers, the CycleUp group does this by focusing on the key issues of feminism and environmentalism through collective action, allowing a Freirean critical dialogue to emerge organically through the consciousness-raising work they are doing. The very act of creating art through repurposed materials, as such, becomes a catalyst for critical conversations about individual and collective responsibility for social and environmental change (Slevin et al., 2020).

The interest in CycleUp is in part connected to the growing interest around sustainable environmental action, but it is also undoubtedly connected to the group's holistic approach to learner development – one that has earned the group and the Network more broadly a glowing reputation in the local community. Throughout discussions with learners and tutors, 'trust' emerged as a value underpinning all of Roscommon Women Network's work. As manager Lisa stated, it is

> that holistic support … it's knowing if [participants] offload that it's confidential. It might only be listening, there might be nothing we can do but it's someone to rant to and you might get a steer or a signpost. We know services out there that's part of our role.

Similar themes emerged in conversation with Laura and Mary who pointed to the relationships they had built with staff and tutors as reasons for continued participation and, more importantly, a reason for referring others to the Network.

The benefits that learners experienced through participating in the CycleUp group were described as transformative by both Mary and Laura. While the programme is non-accredited, participants learn a variety of practical skills such as design, sewing, marketing and promotion. Crucially, participants also bring a lot of pre-existing knowledge and experience to the programme, making peer learning a key facet of the group. In their interview, the women engaging in CycleUp emphasized the unique contribution that each woman brings to the group, and how it has paved the way for personal and collective growth. The women who take part in CycleUp come from a variety of different backgrounds, with some bringing sewing or arts and craft skills and others an interest in environmental issues and activism. Whatever their prior experience, learners note their initial encounter with upcycling as something that put them in unfamiliar territory and into a space of learning. As manager, Lisa, further described:

> Walking into a fabric shop and buying a yard of material is nothing like having to go into a stuffy room with bags of clothes, going through them, washing them, sorting them. They [the women on the CycleUp programme] said to me it's a lot easier to walk into a shop. They're complete converts now. It's really changing attitudes and really changing awareness.

Explaining the sorting process involved in their upcycling projects, Laura described it as an act of 'see[ing] potential'. 'It's amazing to look at the stuff and see what you can do with it, like an artist looking at a piece of stone to make a sculpture, you have to see the potential there.' The capacity to see 'potential' could be said to extend to all activities of the group, whether it be the potential to effect change within the self, the community or in response to the climate crisis. As such, the imaginative process involved in this sorting and making creates the conditions for other kinds of imagining. As Greene (1995) notes:

> Imagination is what, above all, makes empathy possible. It is what enables us to cross the empty spaces between ourselves and those we teachers have called 'other' ... imagination ... permits us to give credence to alternative realities. It allows us to break with the taken for granted, to set aside familiar distinctions and definitions.
>
> (p. 3)

The programme combines elements of artistic production, collective action and critical discourse in a way that allows learners to experience greater personal benefits beyond the hard objectives of the course. As Laura describes in her personal reflection on becoming engaged with Roscommon Women's Network:

> I was at a very low ebb of my life; my marriage had broken down and I was very sick. They couldn't find anything wrong with me and my doctor suggested I come over to RWN ... I gradually started taking control of my life. I split up from my husband and then I had a very serious heart attack and I joined the Women's Group here – I was coming in in my wheelchair. I used to help out doing arts and crafts. I got involved with the WINDOW project [Women Initiating Development Opportunities for Women] and there were 10 of us. Most of the women would have been through bad experiences, with low self-esteem. We started doing the training and most of the women got jobs. I went to college and I got a degree in Fine Art and I thought I'd never do it. It has changed who I am because to me my lack of education had held me back my entire life.

The feeling of social belonging plays a powerful role in the success of the group in bringing people along and providing a safe space for critical discourse around the large-scale global issues which they are tackling.

Challenges faced: Rural learning, climate change and funding

Access to education, particularly full-time education, remains a challenge for Irish women, and community education groups like Roscommon Women's Network and its CycleUp programme play a critical role in enabling lifelong learning opportunities for women at a local level. This is important because on a national scale these types of learning opportunities remain underdeveloped and under resourced. The 2017 Adult Education Survey (Central Statistics Office) on adult learning in Ireland found that females are more likely to report some form of unmet demand for lifelong learning. This survey found that 36 per cent of females reported a gap in available learning options compared with 29 per cent of males (CSO, 2017). Concern surrounding female participation in education has only increased in recent times as a result of Covid-19, with international studies showing that women are facing even greater levels of disadvantage as a result of the crisis (OECD, 2020). Roscommon Women's Network has confirmed this impact at the local level, with John, Local Training Initiative Coordinator at Roscommon Women's Network, explaining that 'the distance to the centre, the lack of childcare options available, and the limited access to necessary broadband requirements for remote learning' remain a challenge for learners, particularly women, with these issues posing a significant risk of decrease in learner participation over time. While the Network has tried to address these challenges head on, financial limitations have been a continuous barrier.

Financial challenges arose a number of times in interview with staff and learners, who were particularly frustrated that programmes such as the CycleUp were not held in equal regard to that of more traditional learning options. Of course, community education in Ireland has consistently struggled for parity of esteem with the formal educational sector and has been significantly under-funded, while facing increased financial cuts during years of austerity (Harvey, 2012). In 2018, the difference in investment between a community education learner (€221.89) and a more traditional further education and training learner (€1052.77) stood at €830.88 (SOLAS, 2018). Tutors working at community centres like Roscommon Women's Network, who receive salaries via external funding from government support structures, have not had a pay increase since 2011, despite pay raises being awarded to teachers and tutors in other educational sectors. These differences are notable when considering that the majority of community education learners are indeed women, meaning that these policies are serving as further structural barriers denying equal educational access to women – an impact that groups like Roscommon Women's Network are forced to deal with in spite of receiving public praise for their innovation in the areas of gender equality.

Like many other community education groups, Roscommon Women's Network has faced this challenge by transforming itself partially into a social enterprise, using revenues from its charity shop and the art it produces from its CycleUp programme to cover the deficit. There are, however, limits to even what this can achieve. As Lisa reported, the demand for the CycleUp products 'far exceeds our capacity as a small provider'. She described having to turn away a large-scale order from a local business who was looking to make a large and sizeable purchase of products due to the lack of space and industrial equipment. Creative potential is instead curtailed by the limited investment on the part of funders who favour courses on employment activation over climate action, rural development and gender equality.

Being located in the west of Ireland, in the small rural community of Castlerea also poses a great deal of challenges not only in the group's ability to sell products, but in their ability to support learners. CycleUp can only run one group out of the centre and it is currently full, with eighteen learners on a waitlist to participate. While admitting more people to the group would be ideal, the group pace significant structural challenges including access to equipment, classroom space and available tutor support. These challenges stifle the group's true potential for success in a community they feel would benefit from greater access to lifelong learning opportunities and stronger awareness of the global challenges we face. LTI Coordinator John describes the community in which Castlerea operates as characterized by 'economic, social, or educational disadvantaged', noting that those who engage with their programmes are also 'geographically disadvantaged'. By virtue of its location, therefore, Roscommon Women's Network offers many opportunities for learning that would not otherwise be available to the local community. Importantly, through its CycleUp group, it is facilitating conversations and learning in a very practical way while also challenging larger global issues such as climate change.

Despite being at the forefront of climate conscious action, ironically climate change has had a significant impact on the group's development. The beginning of 2020 in Castlerea, along with much of Western Ireland, was marked by unprecedented levels of flooding. Rural communities felt that the challenges of flooding were only compounded by the lack of a national response (*Irish Times*, 22 February 2020). For smaller centres like Roscommon Women's Network, flooding meant a complete shutdown of services. These challenges only add further strain to an already under-resourced community education centre, struggling to meet current financial demands. As Lisa described:

> All our flooring had to be taken up. We are suffering severely from ongoing flooding since before Christmas. Funders are great and its absolutely brilliant to have but when you are in your wellies and on the ground, you are depending on volunteers and people working here late at night trying to keep the water out.

Seeking support from the larger education sector, and hoping that its recent national success may help in this endeavour, instead the group was left to find a solution to the crisis independently or face a temporary cut in funding. As Lisa further described, 'we had to worry about our learners. They each receive a payment from the local education and training body to come here and complete their courses. If we did not open, they were not going to get that payment'. The challenge was left to volunteers and the local community to fix. The response from the state funders appeared to be in complete contrast to the praise the organization was receiving for its climate action, with CycleUp's products being hailed by educational funders as example of innovation within the sector. Interestingly, the lack of support around the legitimate environmental challenges posed by the flooding stood in stark contrast to the support the Network later received in response to Covid-19 – a clear, nationally shared experience of disadvantage. As Lisa explained, 'during the shutdown of the centre during Covid-19, there was no question about the learners receiving their payments. The response was so different than it was for the flooding. It is the difference between a local and global challenge.'

Despite climate change being a global issue, the fact that the impacts of it are not experienced equally and simultaneously meant that, unlike Covid-19, the flooding was a challenge that funders could simply ignore. This lack of response captures some of the challenges that rural providers like Roscommon Women's Network face, even when they are seen as at the forefront of climate conscious action.

Conclusion

CycleUp shows us how feminism and climate action can come together, through aesthetic and critical pedagogical processes, into a powerful programme for change. The group is leading the way in social change through art by challenging modern consumer culture and traditional gendered power structures. It is also opening a dialogue around potential solutions to large-scale global crises at a local level. Nevertheless, this cutting-edge work remains stifled by external challenges which largely stem from being a small, under-funded, rural community education provider. Unfortunately, the challenges outlined above, including financial precarity and a struggle for recognition, are not unique to Roscommon Women's Network; there are many more Irish community education groups who share similar experiences. Rather than harnessing the powerful solutions being crafted at the local level, national public policy tends to favour large-scale neoliberal 'solutions' that continually fall short of making any meaningful, tangible or sustainable change. One of the most important lessons gleaned from the example of CycleUp is that despite all of the gendered barriers and structural setbacks faced by small under-funded community-based organizations, there is more than a glimmer of hope that sleeping giants lie within local communities, ever ready to envision and enact viable solutions for change.

References

AONTAS (2001). *Women at the forefront the role of women's community education in combating poverty and disadvantage in the Republic of Ireland.* https://www.aontas. com/assets/resources/AONTAS-Research/Women-at-the-forefront.pdf

Bhattacharya, T. (2017). *Social reproduction theory: Remapping class, recentering oppression.* Pluto Press.

Central Statistics Office (2017). *Irish adult education survey.* https://www.cso.ie/en/ releasesandpublications/er/aes/adulteducationsurvey2017/

Clover, D. (2004). Public space and the aesthetic-politic of feminist environmental adult learning. *Counterpoints, 230,* 59–70.

Department of Education and Science, Government of Ireland (2000). Learning for life: White paper on adult education. *Dublin Stationary Office.* https://www.education.ie/ en/Publications/Policy-Reports/fe_aduled_wp.pdf

Ferguson, S. (2019). *Women and work: Feminism, labour, and social reproduction.* Pluto Press.

Floro, M. S. (2012). The crises of environment and social reproduction: Understanding their linkages. *Working Papers*. American University, Department of Economics. https://dra.american.edu/islandora/object/auislandora%3A70504/datastream/PDF/view

Greene, M. (1995). *Releasing the imagination: Essays on education, the arts, and social change*. Jossey-Bass.

Harvey, B. (2012). *Downsizing the community sector: Changes in employment and services in the voluntary and community sector in Ireland*. Irish Congress of Trade Unions, Community Sector Committee.

National Collective of Community Based Women's Networks (2021). *Our history*. https://nccwn.org/about-us/our-history/

OECD (2020). Women at the core of the fight against COVID-19 crisis. OECD Publishing, Paris. https://read.oecd-ilibrary.org/view/?ref=127_127000-awfnqj80me&title=Women-at-the-core-of-the-fight-against-COVID-19-crisis

Rancière, J. (2004). *The Aesthetic of Politics: The distribution of the sensible*. Continuum.

Rancière, J. (2010). *DISSENSUS: On politics and aesthetics*. Continuum.

Roscommon Women's Network (2019). Connecting women, building communities strategy statement Roscommon Women's Network, 2019–2024. https://rwn.ie/wp-content/uploads/2019/04/RWN-Strategic-Plan-Print-Ready-compressed.pdf

Roscommon Women's Network (2020). www.rwn.ie

Slevin, A., Elliott, R., Graves, R., Petticrew, C., & Popoff, A. (2020). Lessons from Freire: Towards a pedagogy for socio-ecological transformation. *The Irish Journal of Adult and Community Education: The Adult Learner*, 73–95.

SOLAS (2018). Annual reports and accounts 2018. https://www.solas.ie/f/70398/x/d21ad1190d/annual-report-english.pdf

Chapter 5

Wasteland: A Feminist Public Pedagogical Response to Climate Anxiety

Kathy Sanford, Darlene E. Clover, Kay Gallivan, Kate Brooks-Heinemann and Heidi Pridy

Rising sea waters, fire storms, hottest year on record, displaced persons, resource inequalities, melting polar ice caps, deforestation, food insecurity, freshwater shortages, pestilence. These are but a few of the major ecological issues with which we are bombarded on a daily basis through mainstream and social media. Some people live in a state of denial, believing these environmental occurrences are either natural, exaggerated or will be fixed by technology (Kagawa & Selby, 2010). Others experience an acute sense of 'green fatigue', a belief that their individual, isolated actions are largely irrelevant when set against the enormity of the global climate crisis. Still others, particularly youth and younger adults, are frightened. They live in a state of 'climate anxiety' brought about by the 'juggernaut of self-perpetuating and self-reinforcing systems of power and exploitation' which, by placing the entire planet in jeopardy, may rob them of a future (Evans, 2012, p. 3). There is also another group of people; a cadre of feminist artists, activists and educators who refuse to accept, to ignore, to remain silent or to disappear into fear. This group mobilizes their creativity, imagination and aesthetic practices into deliberate, provocative acts of public protest and pedagogy. Through collaborative arts-based endeavours they translate complex environmental issues and concerns into powerful visual responses (Clover & Hall, 2009; Varney, 2018). At a time when the world is beset by ecological crises, these public ecological art practices take action and offer a critical insight into reality as well as inspiration through an imagination of the possible.

Our chapter focuses on one such group. We tell the story of three feminist artist-activists-educators who, working in collaboration with youth from local secondary schools and other community artists, created an extraordinary community installation of ecological dissent entitled *Wasteland: A Climate Anxiety Haunted House* (Figure 5.1). Conceived in the spirit of feminist activism and public pedagogy, the project began as part of a pre-service teacher education course at the University of Victoria, Canada. Students were tasked with developing multimodal enquiry projects with groups of secondary school youth at Esquimalt High School in Victoria. Working with the youth, two pre-service teachers and feminist artists settled on the theme of climate anxiety. Serendipitously, Kay, one of

Figure 5.1 *Wasteland: A climate anxiety house.* Photo by Kathy Sanford.

the pre-service teachers, was at that time working with a local housing developer to create an art instillation in a pre-demolition house in the local community. That demolition site became *Wasteland*. This poignant, visceral project caught the attention of community members, local government and the media. It served to demonstrate to young people in particular that they could use their voices and creativity to speak aloud their fears and concerns as ecological citizens.

This chapter is written by two feminist scholars and researchers. Kathy Sanford was the instructor of this creative teacher education course and project, and Darlene Clover is an adult educator who has focused on environmental issues since the early 1990s. This chapter is shaped by and around the visionary activism of three pre-service teacher candidates and feminist artists, Kay Gallivan, Kate Brooks-Heinemann and Heidi Pridy. All of our perspectives intertwine to tell the story and record the experience.

Feminist activist art and the installation

Over the decades, the arts have played a key role in the service of activism. In general, using the arts in activist contexts is understood to have numerous benefits. For example, arts have the power to speak to multiple and diverse communities in ways that can better be heard and that resonate with both feeling selves and thinking selves, what Beyer (2000) calls our structures of feeling. In addition, the arts are perceived as being able to open new avenues of connection between individuals, enabling them to explore and share common concerns, solutions or possibilities.

There is no singular definition of feminist activist art, just as there is no singular definition of feminism. Aagerstoun and Auther (2007) remind us that 'feminist activist art has consistently exhibited a diversity of subject matter and form that defies attempts to pigeonhole the practice. Feminist artists have pursued activism around a wide range of issues pertaining to race, gender, and sexuality and their intersections with social, political, and cultural forms of oppression' (p. vii). However, central to feminist activist art is the quest for gender equity by rendering visible hegemonic patriarchal norms that exclude, marginalize, oppress, stereotype and of course, have brought us to the brink of environmental catastrophe. Another important dimension of feminist aesthetic activist practice includes recognizing and allowing for emotions, for feelings that come from being oppressed or, in the case of this project, from a fear that your dreams will never become a reality and you must simply suffer in silence (Clover & McGauley, 2016; Foster, 2020).

Feminist and environmentalist critiques have been strongly interrelated since the 1970s. Ecofeminist Shiva's (2013) work in particular illustrates an important 'relationship between women's liberation and a struggle for the liberation of life on earth' (p. 49). Within the context of global climate change, feminist art activists are among those fighting to alter the way in which the Western patriarchal world currently uses resources, seeking to replace corporate ideology with more holistic and respectful ways of living well in the world. For many feminists, the challenge of the problematic ecological situation necessitates an emphasis on public education and the imagination. Based in this belief, feminists have used a variety of artistic practices, including quilts, visual arts and documentaries (e.g., Clover & McGauley, 2016; Foster, 2020; Lari & Newlands, 2017). The imagination is about the stories people tell, perceive and frame a problem, and the avenues for collective revisioning and action these open up.

Wasteland is an example of 'installation art', a large-scale public project in which the whole space becomes a single unified artwork. Installation art has a number of common elements. One is the use or inclusion of more than one art medium. *Wasteland* included near life-sized papermache figures, trees, large-scale murals and a diorama entitled 'fort garbage' that one could enter. Another aspect of installations is that they incorporate found objects. Almost every aspect of *Wasteland*, including branches, plastic sculptures, garbage or magazine photographs, was a found item from our social and/or natural environments. Installations also frequently use audio or video components, as well as light and other technologies. The lighting for Wasteland was done by Limbic Media, a Victoria-based interactive light technology company. The eerie sounds were drawn from the soundscape called *The stairway of whispers* created by Esquimalt High School students. The recorded sounds were composed of layers upon layers of the artists' voices eerily speaking about climate change and anxiety. Some installations involved different actions or activities, including music shows spanning a variety of genres, a Metis beading workshop by contemporary artist Audie Murray, and a smudging ceremony by

Cowichan Elder Della Rice. Another characteristic of installation art is that when it is over, the physical work disappears, although it is often documented in photos or video. *Wasteland*, as noted above, disappeared when the building was demolished. However, it lives on in videos and a virtual 3-D tour which can be found at https://waste-land.webflow.io/. Finally, central to installation art is an embodied experience because people are actually physically immersed in it. Clark (2005) reminds us that one way that hegemonic patriarchy is expressed by 'privileging the mind over the body' (p. 210). Embodied learning in a feminist ecological context is therefore an important strategy because the environmental crisis is felt in the body; it affects not just what we think, but how we feel and act (Drew, 2014). Visitors to *Wasteland* experienced the many artworks/stories of climate anxiety by walking through them, by being surrounded and immersed in them.

Starting off …

The *Wasteland* project began, as noted above, as an attempt by teacher education instructor Kathy, in collaboration with two practising secondary school teachers, to bring their groups of students together in a meaningful interaction that would lead to a culminating project that would be determined by the students. The parameters of the project were left open. As Kate recalled, 'I guess it started at Esquimalt High School, when we were working with kids there and were given a project to work on.' Kay continued, 'It's such a sweet memory to me because Kate and I didn't even know each other that well at the start, but early on we caught each other's eye from across the room' and their ideas synched. Their first idea for their project was to make a type of 'garbage man' which was a steadily growing man made out of garbage that the students would add to as more garbage was produced. However, this idea shifted when a new opportunity arose. At the same time as this project was developing at the school, Kay was in discussion with a development company about using a pre-demolition house as an art space. She recalls,

> we went for coffee with this developer and you know, the first thing I said was that I had this idea that I wanted to pitch to him. And then Kate and I get to the meeting and we're ready to really argue our case and I say, 'here's what I have in mind we want to make a climate anxiety haunted house'. And the first thing he says is 'I have the perfect house' and it was that easy … it all happened so fast.

There was a fusion of ideas, and they pitched the idea to the instructors about creating a community space to share their projects and to include the work of local artists as well.

Wasteland provided a space for social criticism that was inherent in the whole pre-demolition art space and a social reimagining. Kay describes a really deep sense of consciousness for herself where she could tie her art practice to social justice. 'I am really sensitive to whatever is going on in the world and it really comes out in my art practice which often has a very public component.' However, she had not been able to tackle climate change because of an overwhelming sense of hopelessness about it. It was not until this collective community art project that she felt able to focus on climate change and address her own anxiety, involving the community and the public in creating a visceral and poignant response to the general ignorance of us all. She commented, 'it just became about all of us being present with and expressing what we're feeling about it.'

Kay and Kate, as intersectional feminist educators and artists, were influenced by their previous work as public muralists and painters and became more and more excited as they considered the possibility of the *Wasteland* project. They define *Wasteland* first as a domestic space because it was an actual house. The space influenced the work that they did in facilitating an environment where people could come in and be welcomed. They created a space that was nurturing and community building, including both novice and experienced activists and artists in the project, noting that this work has been traditionally viewed as women's work which, they noted, isn't really valued. And when people think about activism they don't necessarily think about that type of 'domestic' work, which is overshadowed by the 'warrior' image of standing up and being heard – this wasn't that!

The *Wasteland: A Climate Anxiety Haunted House* installation project provided ways for intergenerational groups of people to engage in previously held assumptions about the power of colonial patriarchy and our place/role in the world. As Kate described, art has multiple roles:

> First there's art as therapy, so art is a mental health tool and also a way to connect back to nature. I think that if you connect people through art to nature, they get to see it in a different way and when you spend more time observing it and really immersing yourself in it, it becomes more real and personable – it's a way people can get closer to nature and kind of start to see that it is alive, it is beautiful and it's very important to them in that moment, and for all of us for so many different reasons it is significant, its' really important and we need to make sure that we treat it better.

In this project, all of the community artists used their work as a 'gentle way to confront difficult things', both in the creation of the works and the visitor engagement. As Kate describes, 'it was a space where people could be present with their feelings and be gentle with themselves.' Climate issues are very real, and we must challenge them head on, but they can, as noted in the introduction, be overwhelming and frightening. Kate spoke therefore of art as giving people a soft space where they face something scary and dark together.

Public pedagogy and art collectives shaping of educational spaces

Tavin and Erdman (2015) argue that public pedagogy is created by citizens with the public's interest in mind. The *Wasteland* installation clearly addressed public interest, developing from the desire for community artists and students to make a statement about climate and the environment. Public pedagogy is a way to 'include the public, an individual or group of people interested in the common good, disrupting space, and focusing on educational practices outside of the traditional schooling environment' (p. 288) – the *Wasteland* project served to disrupt and bring educational encounters to the community. Viewed through a feminist equity lens, 'teaching and learning in these settings can be viewed as activist work, focusing on that which is culturally and socially relevant' (p. 288). Public pedagogy, Dewhurst observes (2014), 'is important as a space of resistance to institutions – schools, museums, popular culture, government – which are seen as reproducing a hegemonic discourse of capitalism, materialism, white supremacy and neoliberal politics' (p. 289). Education for young people becomes more than competing for good grades – it becomes a way to engage with important societal issues meaningfully in the public sphere.

Most importantly, public pedagogy and socially engaged art can help us confront social inequities (Dewhurst, 2014) and use arts-based practices to take action. Schools, in collaboration with community, can 'play a productive role in educating students to think critically, take risks, and resist dominant forms of oppression as they shape their everyday classroom life' (Giroux, 2013, p. 7). The installations were showcased both in the Wasteland Haunted House and in the halls of the school, drawing attention to the climate issues and offering opportunities for teachers and students to engage in meaningful dialogue. In the interplay between school, feminist practice, community activist artists and political leaders, we can challenge and take up new ways of learning, communicating, collaborating and shaping a different approach to education as well as to value the arts as a powerful and integral aspect of community.

Wasteland, as a public pedagogy installation project, was empowering for many of the participants. As Heidi describes below, the project enabled them to identify as an artist, activist and feminist, providing them with voice and choice about what they wanted to say and how they were going to express their views. Kay describes the opportunity to engage in this public pedagogy project as 'a really empowering thing and the fact that we were given that role and the free inquiry project really gave us the space … you know, you kind of gave us and we took a mile but you really did give us that space'. She noted feeling a 'real increased sense of confidence that there's space for me within education. And that I can also make that space for myself and that's really nice'.

Public pedagogy can enliven and engage learners, creating a space for energy and enthusiasm (Sandlin et al., 2010). Kate commented, 'I felt like I was shooting off into outer space in a rocket, like I was so excited. It was just like we were kind of in school and it was interesting and I felt engaged and then I just felt like a huge wave of inspiration and just ready to get to work'. When she had the opportunity to focus her interest she felt that there was hope for education that she had experienced as boring and not engaging. And when they actually said that it was okay to do that it was like, 'okay I feel like there's hope for education'. As social justice education, the Wasteland project drew attention to a deeply troubled world where inequity and destruction prevail. It interwove the principles of equity, activism and social literacy (Dewhurst 2014), creating a space for shared power and equity rooted in people's experiences, combining reflection and action together and seeking to dismantle systems of inequality to create a more humane society.

The *Wasteland* project provided an opportunity for participants to, as Kay noted, 'step outside of capitalism just a little bit and focus on ideas and educate yourself.' As Dewhurst (2014) commented, 'Artmaking and public performances can be used as counter-narratives to fight oppressive forces' (p. 290). The aim of public pedagogy projects is to 'engage and inspire the community by surprising them with projects in spaces they would not normally encounter such interactive and collaborative works of art or events' (p. 291). As Kay stated,

> It's a great place to introduce these ideas to the public and can also be a shift away from the dynamics that in a normal classroom in the sense that there's a teacher who is the knowledgeable one. That creates a binary and in this project there was an elimination of the binary between audience member and artist ... and also between teacher and student, knowledge and experience.

Kay had learned about collective organizing largely through intersectional feminist movements, developing the skill to create this large-scale *Wasteland* project in three weeks. Additionally, Kay and Kate offered local artists and activists an opportunity to contribute to a rich community and develop their voices and their talents in the creation of a common project.

The Ghost Woods room

Heidi Pridy's (pronouns they and their) contribution to *Wasteland* was particularly memorable – The Ghost Woods. This room on the top floor of the house was visually powerful (see Figure 5.2) as a contribution on its own to the installation, but also in relation to the work of the other artists whose work was represented in the room. For Heidi, *Wasteland* was an opportunity to come out as an artist in public and to share their vision alongside and interwoven with three other artists.

Heidi was a self-identified activist, having worked on many activist projects as a child and an adult. However, surprising, despite engaging in art practices for most of their life, they did not identify as an artist until the opportunity came to contribute to the *Wasteland*. In their 'artist statement', they noted:

> As I grew, the love I felt for the Earth became overwhelming, as did my grief and outrage at the violence and destruction enacted upon it. I threw myself into activism, panicked by the fear of impending loss. I struggled with my own complicity in harmful systems, and in my guilt, I became avoidant and disconnected from nature. Overwhelmed with sadness and despair, I turned

inward and tried to disappear. After years of running away from these feelings, I came to understand that the only release for this anguish was to re-engage with the land on an emotional and intimate level.

Heidi not only became an artist through this project but they came to understand their own relationship with art as a fuel that could keep them engaged in the organization and in activism and other ways they are working to make social change. For Heidi, art is an individual healing process, but they also believe it has a much greater political and social impact when they are a collaborative, collective, process of sharing. It is the sharing of making art that enables Heidi, and similarly Kay and Kate, to be able to address climate anxiety and build an intimacy with others to talk through things that people are experiencing. Even though it's really hard to talk about climate anxiety, this shared *Wasteland* experience provided a platform for sharing and coming together over something that impacts so many people very deeply on a daily basis. The Ghost Woods room offers a kind of sanctuary, away from the eeriness, the blood and garbage central to the lower ground floors. It is an ephemeral space for reflection on what we have, and we have lost or are losing. Indeed, Heidi wanted to create something with light and shadows that gave the impression of a ghost or a memory of a forest. They were drawing upon their own memories as a child of being in the woods and all the different places they loved and felt connected to, but they always wanted to create a space to acknowledge the loss and grief. The other artists who contributed to the room worked collaboratively with Heidi to interconnect their work into a unified piece. Collectively they created the feeling of a burned-out forest, with Heidi's work in the centre of the room and the others creating stencils of trees that were also hands and silhouettes of trees on the windows. Heidi wanted to give the impression that visitors were walking into a ghost forest, so set up lights so that, when a person walked into the room, there was light behind so they saw their own shadow and became part of that ghost forest. The bed sheet (see Figure 5.2) in the centre of the room created the moving shadow effect, using recycled or found objects to get the balance just right.

Figure 5.2 *Ghost Forest exhibition room.* Photo by Kathy Sanford.

Heidi found that there was something really important about being flexible to work with the materials and the context in collaboration with others. Heidi's artwork became something more than personal, something they wanted to share, something more than a therapeutic activity but a type of activism that reached a broader community.

The feminist activism that this work represented, Heidi likened to doing the washing up, work that is needed to maintain any sort of an organizing community. Not only is the art important, or being on the front lines of a protest, which is often as far as the patriarchal glamorous notion of activism, but the behind the scenes work, taking minutes, sending emails, building relationships and care work – work that does not get seen – is important. The art was the public face of the activism, but Heidi's involvement in the *Wasteland* project with other artists was the care work for themself as well, balancing the outward-facing political messages through the art, but also the inward-facing community-building and sharing. The collective allowed for an intimacy to develop that is often very difficult to achieve and ultimately, Heidi believes, relationship building and relationships are the most important thing in making changes in the world. The process of making art, considering how it makes the creators feel and recognizing that everyone is entitled to be creative and express ourselves – was a significant aspect of Heidi's involvement in *Wasteland*.

In becoming a school teacher, Heidi is able to support adolescents to identify a purpose, create a space for themselves and use their voices for work they see as important, collectively sharing a vision to address societal inequities and redress injustices. Not only do spaces like Wasteland show them what they are capable of, but also that they have a responsibility for each other in the community and a responsibility to have their voices heard. As Giroux (2013) noted, public pedagogy helps in 'identifying the link between learning and social transformation, provide the conditions for students to learn a range of critical capacities in order to expand the possibilities of human agency, and recover the role of the teacher as an oppositional intellectual' (p. 7).

Ripples of influence and power

Community artists contributing to the *Wasteland* project found it to be an immersive experience, one that brought power to people when they got together to paint a mural together and contribute to a bigger initiative. Other artworks that contributed to *Wasteland Climate Anxiety* included a post-apocalyptic family positioned in the kitchen, a tidal wave made from discarded pop cans and sheets of plastic, a bloody farm salmon carcass exhibit, a split face of a tiger and its skull, and myriad other artistic activist statements that can be found at https://wasteland.webflow.io/3d-tour, all adding commentary to the destruction of the world as we have known it. For Kate, not being able to express ourselves authentically is a huge source of anxiety, and thinks that the issues that you are having with anxiety stems in part from being silenced and ignored. We need to teach youth, and ourselves, to be real and authentic, to be present with our feelings so we can act in the world from a place of authenticity. Contemplative sadness, suggests Kay, is something we all need to provide space to experience and to find words to express and share with others. It is more important than ever, comments Giroux (2013), 'that educators and all those concerned about democratic public life provide an alternative vision of schooling that supports democratic forms of political agency and a substantive democratic social order' (p. 8). By involving community activist artists and high school youth in a common project, using a feminist and collaborative frame of reference, we provide a collective vision and purpose for education and a way of moving forward with vision and purpose. *Wasteland* helped people understand that their experiences are shared, it helped everyone involved to lift the shame and start vocalizing things, to admit that they have climate anxiety. Throughout the project people came together, young and old, to reach out to others who were anxious and afraid. This is what Giroux calls education at its best, teaching and learning 'connected with the imperatives of social responsibility and political agency' (p. 9). *Wasteland*, however, takes this a step further as a collective public pedagogical project in which many people were allowed to participate or to experience. Kay and Kate made sure that the application process to contribute to the project was not complicated, thereby providing access to many community artists. The pre-demolition house was located accessibly, and the hours – even though only open for two weekends – enabled visitors to attend during the day or evening. There were activities for all ages, including spoken word workshops, music events, and poetry readings, and multiple floors of exhibits. The project was a collective, creative and powerful wake-up by the educators, artists and youth about a common concern and goal. The art told important stories to visitors as they walked through the rooms, as they were immersed in this large-scale envisioning of often unspoken climate anxiety. The location in a pre-demolition house made, as feminists call it, the personal political and the ecological, a feminist concern. For Kay and Heidi, it connected the domestic of everyday life with the array of environmental disasters in a shockingly realistic portrayal of what it will mean if we carry on with the status quo.

Conclusion

Feminist installation pedagogies of activism such as *Wasteland* draw attention powerfully to the environmental crisis and its impact on futures in ways both concrete and ephemeral. Community artists played the role of public pedagogues, educating through their work, and connecting the pedagogical with the political with the personal. For Giroux (2013), the 'fundamental challenge facing progressive educators within the current age of neo-liberalism is to provide the conditions for students to address how knowledge is related to the power of both self-definition and social agency' (p. 11). Although temporary and emergent, the memory of *Wasteland* has long-lasting impact on the community, the artists, the teachers and the students, changing our understandings of 'education' as pedagogy interweaves with activism and social change. The feminist collective worked together to emphasize the 'human aesthetic dimension [that] politicises arts practices and the women involved in such practice by altering systems of participation, decentring power, and binding the world to larger social, cultural, and political realities' (Clover & McGauley, 2016, p. 200). The education of all contributors – and visitors – became so much more than a community project or a school activity. So, while it has been demolished, the Haunted House and all of the activist art that comprised *Wasteland* continues to reverberate in the memories of the thousands of people whose lives it touched.

References

Aagerstoun, M., & Auther, E. (2007). Considering feminist activist art. *NWSA Journal,* *19*(1), vii–xiv.

Beyer, L. (2000). *The arts, popular culture and social change.* Peter Lang.

Clark, M. C. (2005). Embodied learning. In L. English (Ed.), *International encyclopaedia of adult education* (pp. 210–13). Palgrave.

Clover, D. E., & McGauley, L. (2016). Imagining the possible: Feminist arts-based adult education, leadership and enquiry. In D. E. Clover, S. Butterwick, & L. Collins (Eds.), *Women, adult education and leadership in Canada* (pp. 191–204). Thompson Educational Publishing.

Clover, D. E., & Hall, B. L. (2009). Critique, create and act: Environmental adult and social movement learning in interesting times. In F. Kagawa & D. Selby (Eds.), *Education and climate change: Living and learning in interesting times* (pp. 161–74). Routledge.

Dewhurst, M. (2014). *Social justice art: A framework for activist art pedagogy.* Harvard Education Press.

Drew, L. (2014). Embodied learning processes in activism. *Canadian Journal for the Study of Adult Education, 27*(1), 87–101.

Evans, T. (2012). *Occupy education: Living and learning sustainability.* Peter Lang Publishing.

Foster, V. (2020). A community of imaginations: An account of an ecological arts-based practice. In D. E. Clover, S. Dzulkifli, H. Gelderman, & K. Sanford (Eds.), *Feminist adult educators guide to aesthetic, creative and disruptive practice in museums and communities* (pp. 138–44). University of Victoria.

Giroux, H. (2013). Public pedagogy and the politics of resistance: Notes on a critical theory of educational struggle. *Educational Philosophy and Theory, 35*(1), 5–16.

Kagawa, F., & Selby, D. (Eds.). (2010). *Education and climate change: Living and learning in interesting times.* Routledge.

Lari, L., & Newlands, M. (2017). Knitting nannas and frakman: A gender analysis of Australian anti-coal seam gas documentaries and implications for environmental adult education. *The Journal of Environmental Education, 48*(1), 35–45

Sandlin, J., Schultz, B., & Burdick, J. (2010). *Handbook of public pedagogy: Education and learning beyond schools.* Routledge.

Shiva, V. (2013). Thinking eco-feminism. In *Talking environment: Vandana Shiva in conversation with Ramin Jahanbegloo* (pp. 46–66). Oxford University Press.

Tavin, K., & Erdman, L. (2015). Arts-based interventions into normative practices: What it is and What should never be. *Conference paper from 3rd conference on Arts-Based Research and Artistic Research*. Faculty of Fine Arts, University of Porto.

Varney, D. (2018). Climate guardian angels: Feminist ecology and the activist tradition. In L. Stevens, P. Tait, D. Varney (Eds.), *Feminist ecologies* (pp. 135–53). Palgrave Macmillan https://doi.org/10.1007/978-3-319-64385-4_8

Websites

https://waste-land.webflow.io/about
https://waste-land.webflow.io/3d-tour

Part II

STORYING AND THE FEMINIST IMAGINARY

Chapter 6

Feminist Fiction-based Research in the Context of War and Military Museums: Fostering Imagination, Engagement and Empathy

Nancy Taber

It's not only desirable but utterly necessary to *inhabit* the past rather than simply portray it.

Annabel Lyon, *Imagining ancient women*

I have always been entranced by fiction. As a child, I liked nothing better than to browse the stacks of a library. I can still feel the smooth texture of the laminated covers and hear them crackle as I opened book after book. My parents were amazed at my ability to lose myself in a story and shut out the world. Luckily, I was also good at unconscious multitasking, so I managed to walk from the bus stop while reading and still make it home safely. I'd look up and think, 'Oh, I'm here. How did that happen?' As a teenager, I even tried my hand at writing fiction, getting so far as writing a few short stories and mapping out an adventure novel that eventually went nowhere. When I attended military college, I had to fight the pull of a novel in order to focus on studying. If I was swept up in a particularly good book during exam time, I traded mine with a best friend's; we were supposed to secure the other's in our lock boxes and not give it back. Over the years, with work and family, my free time to read waxed and waned. When I completed my MEd and PhD, and then accepted a university tenure-track position, my reading time focused on journal articles and academic texts, as did my writing. I enjoyed it but missed fiction.

In the summer of 2014, I was reading a non-fiction book (Gossage, 2012) about a Canadian woman who was travelling on a civilian ship with her children during the Second World War when it was attacked by a German raider. As a citizen of a British Commonwealth country, she (and several other women) was treated as a prisoner of war and was to be transported to an internment camp. Two missionaries offered to take her children to America until the war was over. She decided to keep the children with her, but the context of the decision intrigued me as there was very little about it in the book. I immediately put the book down and picked up a pen, thinking that this was a perfect opportunity for fiction to explore this tiny fact that was all but hidden in this larger narrative of women's experiences, which was in itself all but hidden in the larger context of Second World War non-fiction. I registered for a series of creative writing courses, joined a local fiction writers' group, started writing and dove into fiction-based research.[1]

In this chapter, I argue that fiction-based research is a creative feminist aesthetic which allows for political possibility by engaging readers' imaginations in ways that can challenge assumptions and generate empathy. In so doing, fiction-based research holds great potential for social justice; in order for people to work for societal change, they must first understand there is a need for it. Telling stories of underrepresented lives is a powerful way to open readers' minds to historical and contemporary injustices. I explain my research context of war and military exhibits, museums and heritage sites. I detail my use of feminist antimilitarist theory as well as my data collection process of feminist discourse analysis and visual methodologies. I describe the main tenets of fiction-based research and explain how I applied it in ways that transformed my data into narrative. I give examples from two stories in a collection about women, war, museums and heritage sites as well as from a historical novel about Acadian women in three different centuries, using museum photographs (my data) and narrative excerpts.

Research in war museums, military museums and heritage sites

War and military museums both glorify war and question it (Loxham, 2015; Taber, in press; Winter, 2010, 2012). They are contested sites of learning and of historical significance, with conflict over what is displayed, how and by whom (Daugbjerg, 2017; Dean, 2009; Thivierge, 2016; Zolberg, 1996); they often centre on male heroism, nationalism and sacrifice (Taber, in press; Winter, 2010, 2012). Heritage sites tend to focus on an exclusionary version of history (Levin, 2010; Lowenthal, 2003) that fails to problematize the military and war as well as makes little connections to the present (Taber, 2020).

My research at these sites uses a feminist antimilitarist learning lens, informed by Enloe's (2016) exploration of the ways in which militarism and patriarchy intersect in militaries and in society. Men and women are often viewed in binary ways, with men as military masculine protectors and women as civilian feminine protected (regardless of the multiplicity of ways in which gender is enacted), with life as a zero-sum game won by violence against enemy others. In museums, war and the military are often viewed as sacred and beyond critique due to the deaths of honourable heroic men (Taber, in press; Thivierge, 2016; Zolberg, 1996).

In order to explore gendered representations in war and military exhibits, museums and heritage sites, I use feminist discourse analysis (Lazar, 2005) which 'demystify[ies] the interrelationships of gender, power, and ideology' (p. 5) and visual methodologies (Rose, 2016), in order to understand how 'a specific visuality will make certain things visible in particular ways, and other things unseeable' (p. 188). As I tour war museums and exhibits, I ask questions such as: How/is war/the military glorified and/or problematized? How are military personnel and civilians/friend and foe/men and women represented? Who is present and who is absent? What stories are told? How/does the museum/heritage site interact with its national/local context?

I then use the methodology of fiction-based research, which, in my war and military museological focus, aims to provoke readers and stimulate discussion, demonstrating that museums, often perceived as isolated institutions, have societal importance. The research discussed in this chapter utilizes fiction to help readers explore how war and militaries intersect with their own lives, in often unseen ways. It derives from two sources: excerpts from my short story collection focusing on the intersection between women, war, museums and heritage sites; an excerpt about the Seven Years War from my historical novel.[2]

Fiction-based research

Fiction writers and scholars from a variety of disciplines have long argued that humans learn best through story form because humans understand the world narratively (i.e., Cron, 2012; Clandinin & Connelly, 2000; Czarniawska, 2004; Ellis, 2004; Riessman, 1993). For example, Cron explains, 'story is what enabled us [early humans] to imagine what might happen in the future, and so prepare for it' (p. 1). Furthermore, 'a powerful story can … help instill empathy' (p. 2) in a reader. She claims that fiction writers are amongst

> the most powerful people in the world [because they] can change the way people think simply by giving them a glimpse of life through their characters' eyes. They can transport readers to places they've never been, catapult them into situations they've only dreamed of, and reveal subtle universal truths that just might alter their entire perception of reality.
>
> (p. 2)

It is this power that I strive for in my own fiction-based research. The work of Patricia Leavy (2013, 2018; Harris & Leavy, 2019) is also particularly helpful in understanding and utilizing fiction-based research. She builds on the rich history of pedagogical storytellers to cohesively argue how and why fiction-based research is a strong, useful and unique methodology.[3] Leavy (2013) situates fiction-based research within the larger context of arts-based research as it is a creative practice that intends to make research accessible to general audiences in engaging ways. Literary techniques such as plot, dialogue, scenes, visuals, character development and access to the inner lives of characters are used to draw readers into the narrative. Researchers become storytellers (Leavy, 2018).

Nayebzadah (2016) outlines four strengths of fiction-based research: '(i) fiction creates innumerable possibilities; (ii) fiction is engaging and engaged; (iii) fiction reaches a wider audience; and (iv) fiction allows one to bear witness' (p. 55). Furthermore, as Leavy (2013) explains, fiction-based research is useful for:

1. Portraying the complexity of lived experience or illuminating human experience (linking the particular and the universal, or micro and macro levels); 2. Promoting empathy and self-reflection (as part of a compassionate, engaged, or social justice approach to research); and 3. Disrupting dominant ideologies or stereotypes (including building critical consciousness and raising awareness).

(Leavy, 2013, p. 38)

Leavy (2018) further argues that 'through our imaginations fictions grants us entry into what is otherwise inaccessible' and 'allows us access to imaginary or possible worlds, to re-examine the worlds we live in, and to enter into the psychological processes that motivate people and the social worlds that shape them' (pp. 190, 191). Fiction-based research is therefore ideal for critical feminist research with social justice aims (Harris & Leavy, 2019; Leavy, 2013, 2018; Nayebzadah, 2016).

Fact and fiction are inherently related. Crummey (2019) explains that there is a 'symbiotic relationship between the real world and the mirror of fiction' (p. 10). Leggo and Sameshima (2014) explain that fiction can 'hold [facts of] the past in a certain light in order to interpret' the present (p. 540). Leavy (2018) points out that fiction is, after all, often 'grounded in reality', particularly historical fiction which demonstrates the 'interplay between fiction and nonfiction' (p. 191). Additionally, many types of qualitative research use non-fiction story elements in data collection and dissemination, such as autoethnography, biography, ethnography, life history and narrative, with researchers always 'bring[ing] their assumptions and experiences to bear on their projects' (Nayebzadah, 2016, p. 51). This qualitative research is assessed through transparency, reflexivity, thick description, saturation, triangulation, member checks, consistency and reliability (Merriam & Grenier, 2019).

Fiction-based research is assessed through related means: resonance (is the story plausible), aesthetics (literary tools), narrative congruence (story structure), empathetic engagement, ambiguity, resonance, verisimilitude (does the story come alive in a reader's imagination) and authorial voice (Leavy, 2013). Furthermore, there must be a balance between literary artfulness and social usefulness (Leavy, 2013). For feminist adult education, the social usefulness is a pedagogical one: What can readers learn from fiction that will help them understand themselves, others and the world in socially just ways? The hope is that these understandings translate into action, in some way, in readers' lives.

Fiction-based research in war and military exhibits, museums and heritage sites

In order to create the stories in my collection and novel, I selected and combined my findings (Leavey, 2018; Nayebzadah, 2018) from each museum, focusing on one key point that inspired a plot, character, scene and/or setting and then combining other points to create a narrative. I supplemented my research in museums with other sources to ensure that the details were correct. I also considered what facts could not be changed and which could not. In 'The Lifespan of a Fact', D'Agata and Fingal (2012) argue about this very issue with respect to creative non-fiction. D'Agata (author) was concerned with the overall truth of a story, changing what he saw as inconsequential facts to accommodate the narrative, create an image and engage emotions. Fingal (fact-checker) concentrated on absolute accuracy for dates, timings, events, numbers and locations.

In my short story collection, I changed what I felt was relatively inconsequential and kept what was important as needed for narrative reasons. For instance, in one story, I moved a Portuguese census up a few hundred years and increased its demographic detail. It was necessary to suit the plot and whether the first census was in the 1300s or 1500s is of not much import in contemporary people's lives. In my historical novel, I changed the British occupation of a French island from 1761–3 to 1755–6 because I needed to get my characters there earlier. While when the island was occupied was important for those who lived there in the eighteenth century, the change of a few years is not of much consequence now. Additionally, these dates are not widely known so my changes were not likely to pull a reader out of the story, and I acknowledged them in my Author's Notes.

All of my characters are complex strong women who resist being stereotyped and shoved into traditional roles. As women throughout history have rebelled against their oppression, my characters are certainly realistic. Nevertheless, I was careful to situate them in their own time, giving them thoughts and actions that fit their context. Though the stories were inspired and influenced by my museum research, they take a feminist antimilitarist twist, with plots and characters that re-imagine gender and violence in ways that challenge the presented narratives. Indeed, this is where fictionalization was particularly useful because the stories of women are typically given short shrift in war and military museums, where they are often underrepresented and stereotyped (Brandon, 2010; Taber, in press).

Using Leavy's (2013) criteria, in my stories, I aimed to create a 'virtual reality' with thick descriptions, appropriate tone and the five senses; use the narrator's point of view, character interiority, and character development to build empathy and engagement; build narrative coherence; allow for 'a multiplicity of meanings to emerge' (p. 84) through ambiguity; include thematic content that contributed to 'understanding about a historical event or time, a culture or subculture, a certain kind of experience' (p. 85); and, aesthetically engage readers with rich language, specificity and literary tools.

Fiction snippets

In this section, I explain how, where and why I got my ideas, include photographs of relevant exhibits, and provide fiction snippets to demonstrate how I proceeded from data to narrative.[4]

In Flanders Fields and Canadian War Museum: Bessie's Ghosts

I was inspired to write 'Bessie's Ghosts' after a visit to the In Flanders Fields museum (Ypres, Belgium) because there is surprisingly little about nurses (and women in general) in the otherwise critical museum, with little more than an empty uniform lying in a display cabinet (Figure 6.1). In the Canadian War Museum (Ottawa, Canada), an empty uniform of a Bluebird (Figure 6.2) is situated beside a diorama of a muddy Ypres battlefield. I was struck by the disembodied nature of the exhibits. A book about Prince Edward Island Nursing Sisters (Dewar, 2014) helped give me a more in-depth understanding of the experiences of nurses in the First World War.

'Bessie's Ghosts' takes place in 1968 and begins in Prince Edward Island (PEI), Canada. The main character is a 77-year-old woman, Bessie, who is haunted by the ghosts of her past. When a reporter interviews Bessie about her time as a nurse at Ypres in the First World War, the reader learns about her service through flashbacks, which each focus on a death and a ghost that attaches itself to her. The following excerpt introduces the first ghost, an Allied soldier whom Bessie treated, a casualty of a chlorine gas attack in 1915.

> *When Bessie stumbled out of the surgery and gulped the cold night air, she glimpsed a man over her shoulder. She turned to see who he was, but no matter how she spun or twisted, she couldn't focus on him.*
>
> *'Who's there?' Pricks of fear emerged as goose bumps on her arms.*

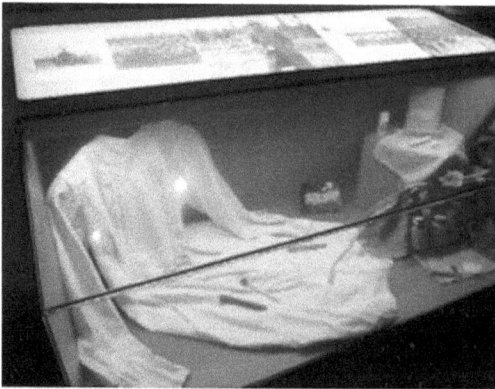

Figure 6.1 *Nurse's uniform.* In Flanders Fields.

Figure 6.2 *Bluebird uniform.* Canadian War Museum.

The man morphed into her line of sight. He had blond curly hair and there was a mole on his cheek. It was the soldier she'd watched die. She backed away.

She shook her head to clear her thoughts and her eyesight. The Matron, the nurse in charge of the nursing sisters, had warned her stress and fatigue could play tricks with your mind.

The soldier disappeared.

She stared into the darkness. When he failed to reappear, she stumbled towards her sleeping tent, fell onto her cot, and was asleep without another thought.

As the story continues, readers learn more about Bessie's experiences, how she coped with them and how they affected her subordinate place as a woman. Neither the In Flanders Museum nor the Canadian War Museum were built during Bessie's lifetime, but as the collection of objects for possible museums was ongoing during the war, Bessie's thoughts of the meaning of remembrance are threaded through the story. In one instance, in another flashback, she and her best friend Ellie have just arrived in Poperinghe in 1918.

The only thing available to eat at that time of night was toast and beans. And, of course, tea. They loaded their metal trays and carried them to a wooden table, within earshot of a group of men in a heated discussion. They were arguing over the upcoming arrival of a British Member of Parliament who was trying to establish a war museum.

Bessie poked at her food. 'Who's going to think about the war when it's over?' she asked. 'Not me.'

'You wouldn't forget me, would you?' Ellie teased.

'Never.' Bessie reached out and squeezed Ellie's hand. 'Friends forever.'

The story continues with Bessie travelling back to Ypres (the city itself is a heritage site) in 1968, where she puts her ghosts to rest.

Air Force Space & Missile Museum and Kennedy Space Center: Dani and the Far Side of the Moon

My process for the Air Force Space & Missile Museum and the Kennedy Space Center (Cape Canaveral, USA) was slightly different in that I had a general idea for the story first and then visited the museum to get context and detail. The story, 'Dani and the Far Side of the Moon', is about a woman mourning her mother who died in an astronaut training exercise decades ago. The accident is modelled on the one that killed Gus Grissom. Dani is a conspiracy theorist who searches for clues at the Kennedy Space Center (Figure 6.3) and the Air Force Space & Missile Museum (Figures 6.4–6.6).

Dani strode into the Forever Remembered section, a short hall with seven glass cases on each side. Challenger crew members memorialised on one, Columbia on the other. All dead. Gave their lives for space exploration. There was a soft

Figure 6.3 *Forever remembered.* Kennedy Space Center.

Figure 6.4 *Monkeynauts & Astrochimps.* US Air Force Space & Missile Museum.

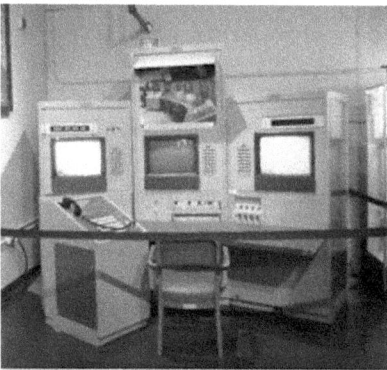

Figure 6.5 *Flight termination console.* US Air Force Space & Missile Museum.

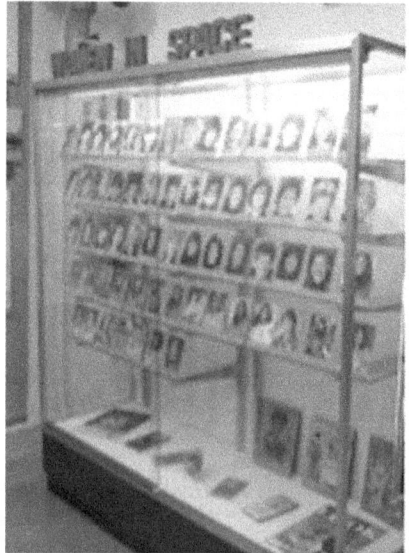

Figure 6.6 *Women in space.* US Air Force Space & Missile Museum.

yellow-bluish glow to the quiet area. A quotation from then-President Ronald Reagan was projected on the back wall. It read, 'The future doesn't belong to the fainthearted, it belongs to the brave.' Easy for him to say. He didn't lose his mother.

Later, Dani ends up at the Air Force Space & Missile Museum because she thinks one of the volunteer docents, Carol, who served with her mother as an astronaut, has information about her mother's accident.

On the far facing wall was a large exhibit about monkeynauts and astrochimps. On the back was a small case labelled, Women in Space, *with rows of photographs of women astronauts. There she was. Dani's mother. In an orange jumpsuit, white helmet under her arm. There was a Daisy and Donald Duck comic book in the bottom of the case, both in space suits. Dani's itched to reach in and snatch it out. Her mother would have hated being equated with cartoons.*

Later in the tour,

Dani followed the group out of that building and into the adjacent blockhouse. Carol stood in front of three yellow steel cabinets with cathode monitors, buttons, and a black telephone with a cord. 'This was the Flight Termination Console. One person had the responsibility of detonating explosive charges on a rocket if it appeared to be heading towards a populated area. Not for the faint of heart, this job. Any questions?' Dani resisted throwing her hand up to ask if someone had terminated her mother.

As the story progresses and a hurricane barrels towards the coast, Dani finally learns the secret of what happened to her mother.

Acadian Museum of Prince Edward Island: Ancestral Echoes

My final example comes from my research about the Acadian deportation from Prince Edward Island in 1758. The Acadians were descendants of French settlers in Acadia, which is now New Brunswick, Nova Scotia, Prince Edward Island, and parts of Quebec, Canada, as well as Maine, USA. They were expelled by the English from 1755 to 1764. Many were transported to France and Britain. Some hid from the English, others later returned to Canada, and some migrated to places such as the Caribbean. My historical novel has three protagonists, Raina in present day, Celeste in the late nineteenth century and Madeleine[5] in the mid-late eighteenth century. My data collection at the Acadian Museum of Prince Edward Island (Miscouche, Canada) informed three scenes in particular: two where Madeleine and her family are locked in a hold of a ship crossing the Atlantic and one where Raina learns about Madeleine (her ancestor) during a museum visit (see Figures 6.7–6.9).

In one of the first scenes with Madeleine, she is thinking of her home and her children.

Je me souviens de ma mère. Je me souviens de chez moi. Je me souviens de la sécurité. I remember my mother, home, safety. Madeleine repeated the words, the rosary in her chilled hands, as she moved from bead to bead. She couldn't remember when she'd shifted from Our Fathers and Hail Marys to these three phrases. It must've been sometime after Joseph vomited up the rotten biscuits and maggoty salted meat that'd served as a miserable excuse for dinner. He'd fallen into an exhausted sleep soon after. Marie-Blanche, who'd only nibbled at her food, at least kept her portion down, slipping into her dreams with frightening ease, she had so little energy.

Figure 6.7 *Acadian deportation and Marie-Anne Oudy.* Acadian Museum of Prince Edward Island.

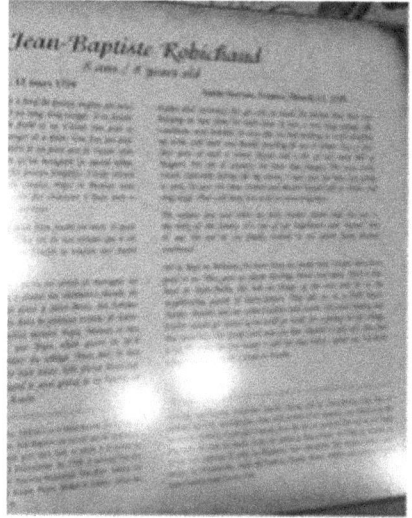

Figure 6.8 *Jean-Baptiste Robichaud.* Acadian Museum of Prince Edward Island.

Figure 6.9 *Madeleine Doiron (née Bourque).* Acadian Museum of Prince Edward Island.

A few days later, the first child dies on board.

> *Someone handed Madeleine an almost clean piece of cloth that became a shroud as they wound it around the small body, moving upward from his tiny toes, to his knobby knees, to his thin chest. They paused when it reached his chin. Madeleine kissed his lifeless cheeks. They continued until he was entirely encased. A hush fell over the hold as she walked to the hatch. When a sailor unlocked and opened it, the clean chill of the evening air rushed over her. She raised her eyes to the moon, alone in*

*the sky with only the stars for company. With a deep breath, she prayed over the boy,
lifted her arms out the hatch, opened her hands, and let him fall to the cruel sea below.*

Near the middle of Raina's story (told in first-person point of view), she and her cousin, Simone, visit the museum in order to learn more about Madeleine.

*I strode past the first panels into the array of exhibits that snaked this way and that.
Simone stopped in front of one describing the origins of Acadia. 'Slow down.'*

*'You can look if you want. I'm going straight to Madeleine,' I said over my
shoulder. She hurried to keep up. There was our great-great-something-great
grandmother. A paper-maché looking sculpture, wearing a white dress and brown
shawl, her head covered with a kerchief, sitting in front of a spinning wheel. She
was surrounded by cut-out figures and paintings of other historical figures, but
my gaze was only for Madeleine. It was the first time I'd considered her as a real
person, not just a long-dead ancestor, but a living breathing feeling human. The
centuries between us collapsed.*

*'She was fifteen when she got married?' Simone gasped as she read the
accompanying panel. 'To a widower who was 30? Gross.'*

*I scanned the words. Noted dates and places. Recognised the connections.
Madeleine, born in the 18th century, in Rustico, followed generations later by
Celeste in the 19th, then me in the 20th, and Simone in the 21st. 'Not much about
Madeleine herself here, is there?' I said.*

*'Nope, but I didn't realise it was the Treaty of Utrecht between Britain and
France in 1713 that set the stage for the expulsion decades later. Imagine, kings in
two different lands you've never even set foot on forcing you out of your home and
across the ocean.'*

*'Not much has changed over the centuries. Kings and queens, maybe, but
refugees ... ' I let my words trail off as I stared at my ancestor.*

As the novel progresses, the stories of Raina and Madeleine merge and come to a resolution in the present.

Conclusion

Although some of my characters are based on real people and real events, some are composite characters, and some are completely invented, all of them are fictionalized. What engages my imagination and, hopefully, my readers, is that they *could* be real people and their stories *could* be real. My stories are grounded in factual data and communicated through rich fictional narratives. Fiction-based research and aesthetic literary techniques give readers a window into a specific time period and a particular situation, into the experiences of a complex woman. On the page, a character can come to life in a way that evokes pedagogical empathy and understanding, which may then translate into a reader taking positive action in reality, blurring the line between fact and fiction in a most satisfactory way.

Notes

1   It took me several years, but I finally published a short story about the mother's decision, *Precarious Passage,* in 2020.
2   Working title of my short story collection is *Secrets and Stockings: Stories.* This research was supported by an SSHRC Insight grant, SSHRC Connections grants, Brock Faculty of Education Research and Development grants, and personal travel. *Born an Islander* working title of the historical novel is *Ancestral Echoes.* This research was supported by Brock Faculty of Education Research and Development grants as well as personal travel.
3   Leavy is also the editor of the Brill/Sense Social Fictions book series.
4   All photographs taken by the author. All snipped and edited to fit the purpose and scope of this chapter.
5   My ancestor from eleven generations ago.

References

Brandon, L. (2010). Looking for the 'total' woman in wartime: A museological work in Progress. In A. Levin (Ed.), *Gender, sexuality, and museums: A Routledge reader* (pp. 105–14). Routledge.

Clandinin, D. J., & Connelly, F. M. (2000). *Narrative inquiry: Experience and story in qualitative research.* Jossey-Bass Publishers.

Cron, L. (2012). *Wired for story.* BTen Speed Press.

Czarniawska, B. (2004). *Narratives in social science research.* Sage.

Crummey, M. (2019). *Most of what follows is true: Places imagined and real.* University of Alberta Press.

D'Agata, J., & Fingal, J. (2012). *The lifespan of a fact.* W. W. Norton & Company.

Daugbjerg, M. (2017). The 'distant war' up close and personal: Approximating Afghanistan at the Danish Arsenal Museum. *Critical Military Studies, 3*(1), 50–68.

Dean, D. (2009). Museums as conflict zones: The Canadian war museum and bomber command. *Museum & Society, 7*(1), 1–15.

Dewar, K. (2014). *Those splendid girls: The heroic service of Prince Edward Island Nurses in the Great War, 1914–1918.* Island Studies Press.

Ellis, C. (2004). *The ethnographic I: A methodological novel about autoethnography.* AltaMira Press.

Enloe, C. (2016). *Globalization and militarism: Feminists make the link.* (2nd ed.). Rowman & Littlefield Publishers, Inc.

Gossage, C. (2012). *The accidental captives: The story of seven women alone in Nazi Germany.* Dundurn.

Harris, A. M., & Leavy, P. (2019). *Contemporary feminist research from theory to practice.* The Guilford Press.

Lazar, M. (2005). *Critical feminist discourse analysis: Gender, power, and ideology in discourse.* Palgrave-MacMillian,

Leavy, P. (2013). *Fiction as research practice: Short stories, novellas, and novels.* Routledge.

Leavy, P. (2018). Fiction-based research. In P. Leavy (Ed.), *Handbook of arts-based research* (pp. 190–207). The Guilford Press.

Leggo, C., & Sameshima, P. (2014). Startling stories: Fiction and reality in education research. In A. D. Reid, E. P. Hart, & M. A. Peters (Eds.), *A Companion to Research in Education* (pp. 539–48). Springer.

Levin, A. (2010). Introduction. In A. Levin (Ed.), *Gender, sexuality and museums* (pp. 1–12). Routledge.

Lowenthal, D. (2003). *The heritage crusade and the spoils of history*. Cambridge University Press.

Loxham, A. (2015). Shaped by familiarity: Memory, space and materiality at Imperial War Museum North. *Museum & Society, 13*(4), 522–38.

Lyon, L. (2012). *Imagining ancient women. Henry Kreisel Lecture Series*. University of Alberta Press.

Merriam, S. B., & Grenier, R. S. (2019). *Qualitative research in practice: Examples for discussion and analysis*. Jossey-Bass.

Nayebzadah, R. (2016). The truth behind fiction-based research. *Journal of Humanistic and Social Studies, 7*(2), 49–61.

Riessman, C. K. (1993). *Narrative analysis*. Sage.

Rose, G. (2016). *Visual methodologies: An introduction to researching with visual materials* (4th ed.). Sage.

Taber, N. (2020). Whose (military) heritage: A feminist antimilitarist analysis of heritage sites in Canada, England, and Europe. In K. Sanford, D. E. Clover, N. Taber, & S. Williamson (Eds.), *Feminist critique and the museum: Educating for a critical consciousness* (pp. 137–55). Brill Publishing.

Taber, N. (2020). 'LCol Smith with unknown bomb girl': Problematizing narratives of male battlefield heroism in Canadian military museums. *Critical Military Studies, 6*(3–4), 243–53.

Thivierge, J. (2016). Exhibiting dark heritage: Representations of community voice in the war museum. In D.E. Clover, K. Sanford, L. Bell and K. Johson (Ed.), *Adult education, museums and art galleries: Animating social, cultural and institutional change* (pp. 153–63). Sense Publishers.

Winter, J. (2010). Designing a war museum: Some reflections on representations of war and combat. *At the Interface/Probing the Boundaries, 71*, 1–19.

Winter, J. (2012). Museums and the representation of war. *Museum & Society, 10*(3), 150–63.

Zolberg, V. L. (1996). Museums as contested sites of remembrance: The Enola Gay affair. *The Sociological Review, 43*(1), 69–82.

Chapter 7

Dark Realism: An Auto/biographical Enquiry into Creative Strategies of Queer Resilience

Ivan Kirchgaesser

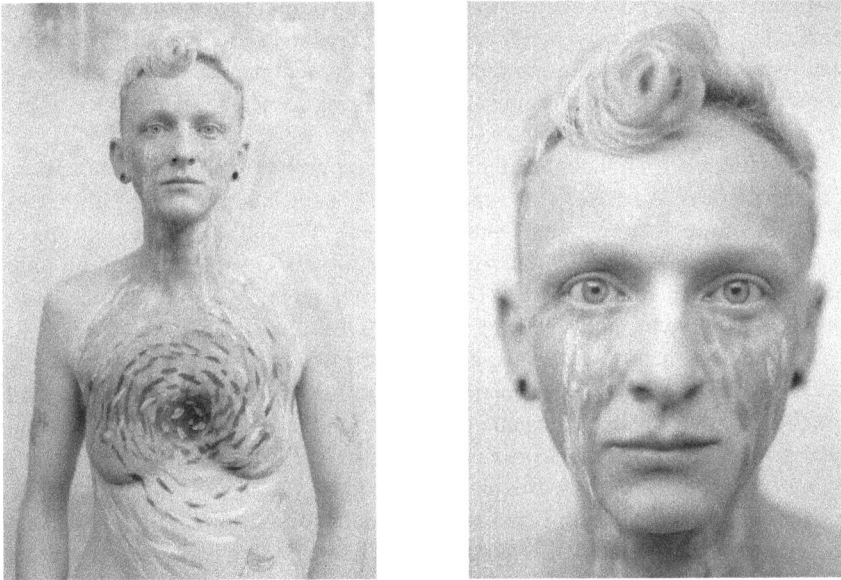

Figure 7.1 *For all the tears I cannot cry*. Ivan Kirchgaesser. Photos by Allan Laurent Colin (2021).

Portugal, October 2020. A story about almost dying

Note: Trigger warning: homophobic violence.

We are in the Portuguese countryside. A retreat for queer people. Here, you can invent a new name for yourself every day. The others will call you by it. No questions asked. When I step out of the house, I look down a scorched valley. Wildfires turned the green land black. Large rocks and boulders are strewn around. They light up golden this late afternoon in October. I scan the horizon. Because of the clouds' reflection, it looks as though the sun is setting in six different places. We are quiet for a moment and drink it in.

The day before. A friend and I are doing push-ups outside. He presses down between my shoulders to make it harder, hovering over me. Suddenly a 'whooshing' noise. Something whizzes past, right between our heads. Time slows down. The instant stretches out. Someone is shooting bullets at us, my friend shouts. We run inside. This place has a neighbour who is scared of us. Our queer existence – so triggering that he wants us dead.

We don't leave. Not immediately. The police are hardly helpful. They tell us to come and file a complaint. But we look after each other. That is more important than getting away from the danger. I refuse to respond to fear with fear. That night, three of us sleep downstairs in front of the fireplace. We guard the frontline in case something happens. I feel safe between two people.

In the car to the police station, we check our accounts of what happened against each other. Some of us can barely remember. I retained a lot of details. We realize that we must tell the story using each other's document names. Not the names we know each other by. Those beautiful, fluid, shifting names. I feel paralysed. Can't get it out of my mouth. We listen to Queen.

The officer is friendly but cannot take our reports. He is alone at the station. Come back later. We drive to the supermarket. Usually, we have a plan for what we need. This time, we gravitate to whatever appeals. We end up with a huge pile of pastries, crisps and liquor. When we get home, we eat. One of us brings out their accordion. Another prepares a bowl of Dead Sea facial mask. We all help ourselves. Five queers surviving and still being fabulous. I love these people so much.

On our last night together, we decide to throw a party and dress up for the occasion. This place has a transformation room full of costumes, wigs, shoes and jewellery. I ask for help picking an outfit. I am handed a body suit with green and blue flowers and rhine stones over a netted pattern. It has been worn by many members of the community. This skin feels good.

The next morning, I ask if I can borrow the suit. I want to be able to slip back into this feeling of being held in the right place. I pack some stale pastries for sustenance. On the plane back home, I make my first notes for what is to become this text.

Three months later. I ask my friends: was it irrational of me to stay? The danger was real. I could have been killed. People I talked to after the shooting urged me to leave. I didn't. As one of us said: I am tired of running away. Out there, we created a retreat for ourselves where we could be on our own terms. Where we could live according to our values without being questioned by a heteronormative society. A little parallel queer universe. We weren't prepared to let that be taken away by one scared individual.

My one friend responds: 'I think you were rational. Risk-aversion shouldn't be the only factor in decision making.' The other adds, 'I didn't understand at the time why you weren't leaving. But now that you've told this story, I see why you stayed.' Processing is required for healing. And you couldn't have done that to the same extent if everybody had fled.

Figure 7.2 *The day after the shooting.* Photo by Eyal Alef Ophir (2020).

On the value of aesthetic practice for learning, growing and healing

In this auto/biographical text, I reflect on the question of feminist aesthetics in terms of how queer people make life worth living, how they create beauty, relationships and art in a world where their safety and flourishing of this community cannot be taken for granted. Meandering through three examples – the retreat in Portugal, the Berlin drag scene, and an artistic collaboration and love story in Mexico – I unpack manifestations of aesthetic practices and their value for learning, growing and healing in a communal setting. Furthermore, I explore how telling these stories – embedded in a research context – can itself become an 'aesthetic' process.

Learning from life

The situation in the Portuguese case story above is one of trauma and resilience in the context of queer life. My queer life. By writing, I try to make sense of what happened and distil new insights from it. This is my life research. By sharing it, I hope you can learn something, too. Auto/biographical enquiry may not be generalizable in the traditional sense. However, what speaks for this personal approach is that I have unique access to my experience, and I can get to a depth that is hard to attain otherwise (Merton, 1988). Also, listening in to someone's story can be a beautiful organic way to learn. It is more than conveying information, it evokes care. Giving you a glimpse into my life may enable you to recognize yourself in me, or to live into an experience that is unfamiliar. This is how perspectives can be expanded beyond the individual bubble: we don't have to be the same in order to relate. We can draw on the intersubjectivity given to us by the grace of living as human beings in a shared world. Clearly, we all inhabit this shared reality in different ways. We experience it from different social, geographical and temporal locations. Sometimes, it may seem as though our life worlds are too separate to ever meet. But we need to connect to make it work together! Therefore, the least I can try is to build bridges by sharing my experiences. Between queers and non-queers. Between traditional and progressive academics. Between Familiars and Others.

Aesthetic turns

What I need in order to learn about human experience is not an objective, distant observer's perspective. I need for the phenomena to come alive. Feminists and auto/biographical narrative researchers have been working from this insight for decades (Clover, Sanford & Butterwick, 2013; Cixous & Calle-Gruber, 2003; Formenti, West & Horsdal, 2014; Formenti & West, 2018; Freedman, 1992; Stanley, 1992; Tompkins, 1987). They have created countless precedents that make a case for more relatable and participatory (academic) practices – using presentational methods, bringing in different types of voices, dissolving traditional researcher-participant hierarchies and taking experience seriously. Interestingly, in the early days of science, criteria for validity had not yet settled in favour of objectivity, generalizability and replicability. In the eighteenth century, when philosophy, literature and science were still more intimately connected and embedded in life, 'the vividness of evidence, or the immediate sensuous appeal of the fact itself' (Jackson, 2003, p. 126) was thought to be essential in conveying knowledge about human experience; an aesthetic turn *avant la lettre*, if you consider that aesthetic can be understood in an expanded sense 'as that which enlivens our being in contrast to the *anaesthetic* or numbness' (Sacks, 2018, p. 175). It is akin to the pragmatic perspective on beauty as a quality that can be experienced when reasoning and imagination are unified to get to an embodied truth (Leddy, 2016).

The feminist or gendered aesthetic, framed in this expanded way, can be seen as a crucial factor in learning *from* and *in* life, as well as in processes of growth and healing. Feminists remind us that experienced oppressions, exclusions and violence must be healed, we must take care of our own bodies and minds. But they also argue that we are never simply 'victims' of the powerful because we have the power of story and self and social reflection. Let me unpack this further in the light of the case story. What were the dynamics at work? First of all, it is interesting to note how life can appear more vivid in the proximity of death. Secondly, that which made life worth living in the face of violence and fear was the way we responded as a community – and how we established this sense of community in the first place. None of us knew each other particularly well when we met. However, we

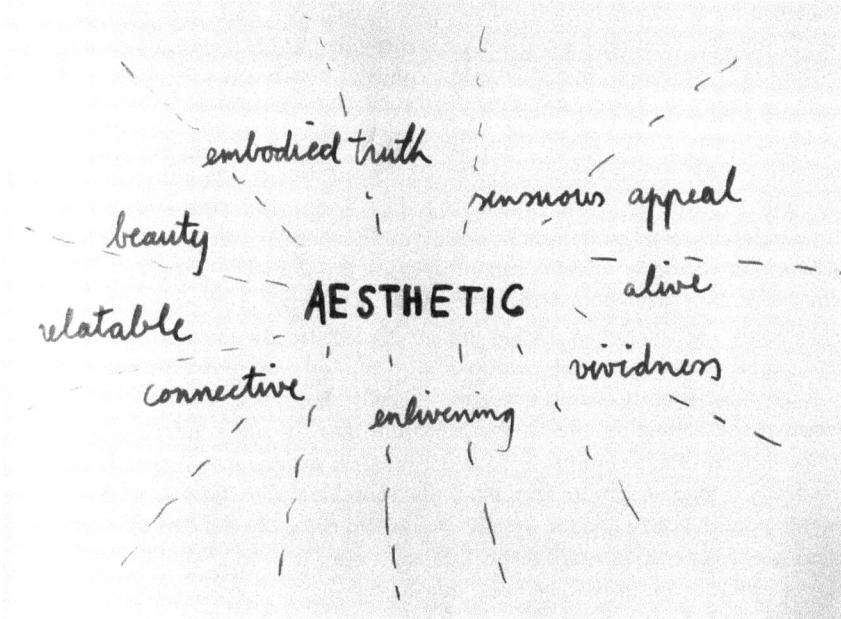

Figure 7.3 *Mapping the gendered aesthetic.* Photo by Ivan Kirchgaesser (2021).

were able to tap into practices that have a long history in queer culture, and, more specifically, in the international network of non-assimilationist gay people that the retreat place belongs to. They include the permission to experiment with identity through the daily name-stating ritual and regular dressing up, the creative processing of various life experiences through performing for each other, as well as a shared appreciation of music, nature, good food and personal care. Each of these things has a positive effect on the quality of life. They are connective in the sense that they bring people closer to themselves, each other and the place.

Queer resilience

Being resilient means claiming my life. It's the antideath.
Transgender participant Jay (Singh et al., 2011, p. 24)

Resilience, seen as the capacity to deal creatively with novel, potentially challenging situations, as well as the capacity to heal from trauma and to grow as a person, gets strengthened in a rich social context like my queer community. Note that I am taking a relational perspective as put forward by feminist psychologist and scholar Judith Jordan (1992), rather than an individualistic one that conceives of resilience as a skill that only some intrinsically tough people happen to have. As therapist Linda Hartling puts it, 'Jordan ... opened the way to understanding resilience as a human capacity that can be developed and strengthened in all people through relationships, specifically through growth-fostering relationships' (2010, p. 52). Studies in the LGBTQIA+ community (Bartoş & Langdridge, 2019; Singh & McKleroy, 2011; Singh et al., 2011) confirm the relevance of such an ecological perspective. This body of research challenges the use of the picture of 'bouncing back' as returning to a prior state of normality – assuming that this is desirable and that there was normality to begin with. Knowing what it feels like to be different raises some salient questions about the power dynamics involved in so-called normality – which can only signify the comfort of familiarity to those who 'fit in'. Because who gets to define what is normal? And who gets to define what needs 'fixing'? For all I know, my creative agency to name and position my own experiences is one that I worked hard for, and I am not planning to let go of it any time soon. Coming out as a gay trans man has made me more acutely aware of the damaging effects of (hetero)normativity and gendered oppression in its various manifestations – even in so-called progressive Western societies. Ironically, it made me more feminist in the sense that my solidarity with women's ongoing political struggle for equality has grown since I began experiencing first-hand how I get treated more respectfully as a man than as a woman. Hence, my aim is certainly not to bounce back, but if anything, to bounce into a new place, and bring you along with me.

In the spirit of relational resilience and bouncing forward, I can confirm that the communal culture of aesthetic practice such as the one I experienced in Portugal has been both empowering and enlivening. It contributed to my decision to stay after the attack. Furthermore, returning to these memories, drawing out what gave me strength and processing them by treating them as the subject of my life research is proving to be an aesthetic (self-) healing practice in and of itself. And finally, the sharing of this story becomes a form of social activism, in the sense that '[n]arrative provokes thought, thought provokes conversation, conversation provokes change' (Thomas, 2010 in Bartoş & Langdridge, 2019, p. 242).

On ways of making life worth living

'You are not the way you are supposed to be!' This is the message queer people get from living in a heteronormative reality. It is communicated in many ways: parental disapproval; lack of representation; verbal and physical violence; discrimination; being conceptualized as a sinner in religious contexts; and a lack of education that truly helps one understand one's personal (divergent) experiences of gender and sexuality. Doubting one's identity becomes an internalized oppressive voice that is constantly in the background – even if one finds oneself in a supportive environment. It is the cause of anxiety, trauma and potentially problematic coping mechanisms. Much research has been done to map out the stressors that LGBTQIA+ people deal with on a daily basis. This work is needed to advocate for changes towards a more inclusive, educated society that is appreciative of all its members. Here, however, I focus not so much on the stressors, but on the ways in which queer people make life worth living in this imperfect world – through aesthetics (communal, relational) and enlivening practices. I need to understand what makes them 'keep on keeping on' (West, 2014, p. 171) in order to make sense of and do justice to the subtle, empowering dynamics at work in my own experiences of queer survival. The beauty and strength, what can be seen as 'an aesthetic' of the LGBTQIA+ community, lie in the creative ways we developed to deal with challenges (Bartoș & Langdridge, 2019; Singh & McKleroy, 2011) – ways that could be of inspiration to others.

To some extent, the experiences in the introductory case story may be exemplary of the creative strategies people in the wider LGBTQIA+ community employ to make life worth living. However, it needs saying that this community is diverse in itself. Subgroups such as transgender people deal with different struggles than, for example, cis-gay or intersex people. Even within the 'community', battles are fought over who belongs and who doesn't. Furthermore, geographical and social contexts make for extremely different experiences. Covering all perspectives would be out of the scope of any one study. Therefore, I focus on the strategies of resilience that I know first-hand from my engagement with people who consider themselves 'queer'. Queer can mean many things, but here, it roughly denominates a questioning attitude towards normativity and hegemony of any kind, a 'commitment to a wandering curiosity' (McGlotten, 2012, p. 3), and a non-assimilationist attitude. Most people in 'my community' I met in Berlin or through Berlin-based contacts. They are trans men and women and non-binary people of various sexual orientations, as well as cis gay, and bisexual people. Many are migrants from Latin and North America, the Middle East and various European countries. All speak English and most attended higher education, though plenty dropped out and are self-taught. In terms of occupation, there is a high proportion of artists, drag performers and people working in LGBTQIA+ advocacy and support organizations.

What makes these people strong? The big number one factor is the sense of community (Bartoș & Langdridge, 2019; Singh & McKleroy, 2011): being 'other' is what connects us. Fellow queers become a family of choice, replacing or substituting the family of origin. Encountering humans in a similar position allows for mutual support, validation and empowerment. We learn from each other. Additional factors are queer people's creativity and their ability to think 'outside of the box' – capacities needed to make life work in the margins.

These skills make for vibrant arts practices that are both political and close to life. The Berlin drag scene is another great example of queer aesthetic culture. It commentates on what it means to live in a heteronormative society and draws on the artists' rich imagination to put forward alternative ideals and realities. It functions as an educational and politicizing platform, addressing issues of gender, sexuality, racism, the ecological crisis and more. Drag shows also fulfil a therapeutic and spiritual function, as rituals involving preaching, song, dance, poetry and collective cheering. They provide a sense of belonging and meaning, as well as a space for communal grief and cathartic excitement. Most of all, they give performers and audience a sense of recognition by communicating that it is okay to be who they are. There is a strong aspect of celebration and pride. Derogatory slurs like 'faggot'

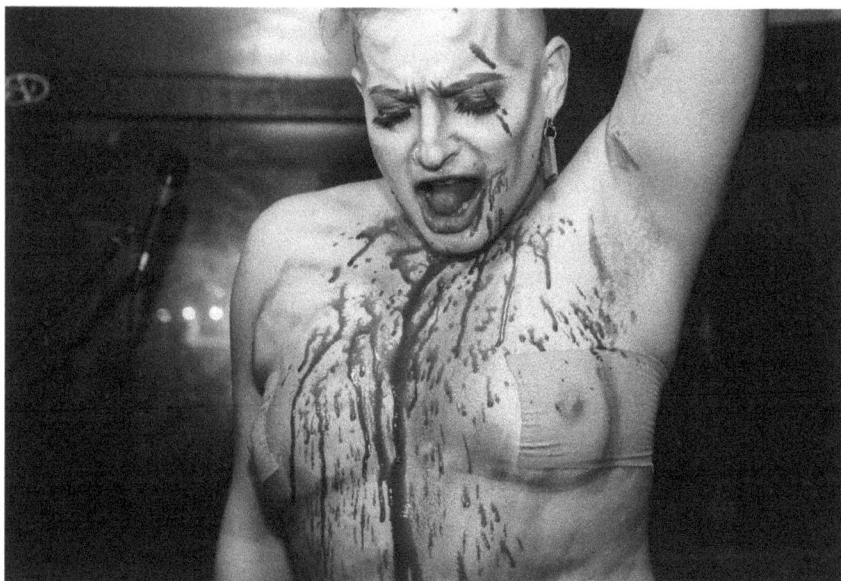

Figure 7.4 *Drag king HP Loveshaft at Morgan's Dragshow for busy people, Berlin.* Photo by Aaron J. Cunningham (2020).

and, historically, 'queer', are turned into badges of honour. Imperfection and contradiction are acknowledged as part of reality and not something to be hidden. Moral imperatives are challenged, boundaries of comfort are pushed. Beauty and fabulousness in their many forms are displayed unapologetically. Everybody can be queen, king, quing or thing – as per their desire. An inclusive and DIY spirit makes it possible for complete newbies to appear side by side with professionally trained artists. People unite in the intention to not go under.

Dark realism

Communal experiences like the Berlin drag events are created for a reason. They are life-giving, necessary to survive in a world that would rather not acknowledge one's queer existence. Not all forms of dealing with oppression and trauma, however, may seem as constructive and wholesome as what I just described. Examples of edgy coping mechanisms are excessive hedonism and drug use, sometimes framed as self-medication. The decision to stay in the Portuguese retreat in spite of the ongoing threat to our lives was arguably questionable, too. In good psychoanalytical fashion, however, I believe that every 'symptom' is the best possible response a system can come up with (Jung, 1953–83, CW 18, par. 389). Therefore, withholding judgement is in place. As it happens, some responses to stressors defy the usual categories of healthy and normal, making them queer in some respect. To echo Burstow (2003), this is not to say that someone cannot benefit from making an effort to change habits that are perhaps not particularly life-giving. But as Burstow argues

> so-called symptoms are best theorized as survival skills. Correspondingly, traumatized people are most adequately conceptualized as competent practitioners of their lives, none of which means that they do not get stuck or that help is inappropriate.
>
> (p. 1305–6)

The picture that emerges from my reflections on creative strategies of queer resilience as exemplified by the Portugal case story, the Berlin drag scene, and the artistic collaboration and love story described in the final part of this text is one of Dark Realism. As Brown (1995) notes, people who have experienced trauma and oppression have lost the 'cloak of invulnerability' (cited in Burstow, 2003, p. 1298). But rather than looking at trauma from a deficiency point of view, assuming that the wounded need to be 'fixed' and returned to a so-called state of normality, one can acknowledge the value of the realism that ensues from their experiences. Burstow goes as far as to say that 'a case could be made that the highly traumatized person actually sees the world more accurately than the less traumatized' (p. 1298). Hence, it appears that something can be learnt from the ways in which queer people handle oppression and create healing practices. Being marginalized, othered and sometimes violated is a dark place to be. But darkness doesn't necessarily equal bad. Light is often associated with clarity and order, whereas darkness comes with images of chaos and being lost. But there are two sides to the coin. Light can blind one to aspects of reality, and order can turn into rigidity and oppressive normativity – harming not only queer people, but *all* people. Darkness as the locus of chaos, on the other hand, can act as a birthing ground of new ideas and 'queer' approaches to life – which, again, could be beneficial to everyone.

In the end, I find that resilience is not a matter of either/or and black/white – beautifully exemplified by the queer attitude of thinking in spectrums rather than binaries. Learning, healing and growth happen in the movement between the poles of darkness and light, chaos and order. Clinging to either end of the spectrum causes anxiety and frustration. In some way, one-sidedness is self-destructive. What is required to let go of either extreme and allow inspiration from 'the other side' is love and trust. Not a blind trust that the world is 'essentially benign and safe' (Burstow, 2003, p. 1298), but a trust that emerges from knowing that there will be someone who will catch you when you fall, and that there is a place where you are seen and where your experiences are validated. This is something my queer community has ample practise with.

Mexico, March 2021: A love story

The love and trust required to be able to live well enough and be able to cope with challenging situations is the same love and trust that allows for creativity to thrive. I am in La Fábrica Puebla, an old metal factory where I am doing an artist residency with my lover and collaborator Allan Laurent Colin. We hadn't seen each other for almost a year when I finally made it to Mexico six weeks ago. Corona. One of the things that connects me with Allan is that we discovered our queerness together, dancing at a party, then in my flat, then in the woods. I felt like a boy dancing with a girl. The feeling was mutual. And so it happened that for each of us, this encounter marked the beginning of our exploration of what it means to be transgender. (Does this mean our souls are connected? Allan says *in lak'ech* – Mayan for 'you are my other me'.) Coincidentally, the living space and studio we find ourselves in now, one and a half years later, is in trans flag colours. Blue, pink, white, pink, blue. We take pleasure in seeing the pattern everywhere we look and make a game out of spotting it. In a church, a child's dress, in someone's hair at a party, on cigarette filters. It even starts making its way into our work.

Arriving in Mexico for me is entering into a context that is different from anything I am used to. I spent all my life in Europe. Allan was concerned about this – after all we'd met in the 'free' city of Berlin, where allegedly anything is possible and there are so many queer people that you can pretend there is nothing outside of this bubble. To arrange for my travel in these strange times, I need an invitation letter. Unfortunately, it has to have my document name on it, but I am so excited by the idea of receiving an official invitation that I ask Allan to write me an *actual* one. It reads:

> Querido Ivan: I feel a lot of excitement for you to come, to see you again, to introduce you to my country, my dynamics, so that you can understand how my performance of gender unfolds here.
>
> I would be lying to you if I told you that I am the same, I have geographic facets that dissolve and reconstruct themselves between frontiers. But that's what excites me, that you come and experience another reality.

Coming here, I am trying to understand this different location and its gender dynamics. What is it like to be queer in Mexico? What is it that makes Allan feel less free here? They (the pronoun Allan uses as a genderfluid person) tell me about the culture of machismo with all its expectations around being 'a real man', and coming with that, the blatant misogyny. They despise it and yet they feel associated with it. Being together again, though, seems to help them reconnect with the sense of possibility they'd experienced with me back in Berlin. They start dressing differently, more feminine, less in boy disguise. What I have seen in them from the first moment begins to show on the outside once more. As for me, I am delighted to discover that everyone here reads me as a man – in spite of being well aware of the problems with toxic masculinity. (Why must I be one of them? Couldn't I be non-binary instead?) We walk outside together, holding hands, most likely being read as a gay couple. Sometimes, people look – but if anything, a little startled, never aggressive. We may just be lucky, because it is not uncommon for visibly gay and trans people to be subject to violence here. It could also be that so far, we have been spared such attacks because we appear white and non-local (Allan is half French and therefore often perceived as a foreigner). Yet, we both can't help but feel some excitement over the unexpected absence of the public homo- and transphobia we experienced even in Berlin.

For both of us, life feels easier since we are back in each other's company. We are adapting to co-existence on this other continent. As we share new experiences, we continue to learn and grow together. I remember a sticker I saw on a bin back in the streets of Berlin. It said: TRANS HAPPINESS IS REAL. I paint a little sign with this text and put it on my desk. A few days later, a law is approved in the state of Puebla that allows trans people to change their name and gender in official documents. Allan and I had been to a trans protest outside a government building, but we were under the impression that we were just making pressure into the void with a handful of others. On our way back, Allan lamented how difficult it can be to organize for change in Mexico. Hence, the actual approval of the law on that very day – after a process of more than ten years – caught us by happy surprise. A rare moment of witnessing how things that appear as static and heavy as a law can actually shift in a positive way. We are in a celebratory mood and more good things are about to happen. Opportunities to share our work and make new connections appear. On some days, inspiration feels effortless. We work and work and enter into the flow of creating images together. I paint our bodies. We let objects and places speak to us as we make films and photographs. I watch over my lover's shoulder as they are handling their camera. I learn to see the play of light, which is also always a play with moments. Nothing is more temporal and site-specific. Light *is* a moment, Allan says. We need to be present with it, not dwelling in the past or the future.

The way we experience our collaboration is as a space for play. Here, we can do those things that we have too many doubts about much of the rest of our time. In a magical way, we seem to be capable of taking away each other's fears and anxious life expectations – for some precious moments. This alchemy of love and trust allows for our creativity to come out and for us to express ourselves more freely. We co-exist without a plan, take time to share experiences in the world and then suddenly feel the urge rising to bring out what we have been gathering, only half-knowing what it is but finding it along the way. Whatever needs to happen will happen, says Allan. Go with the darkness. I add how we are also creative agents in making things happen. Artists of life can also play with the light.

We are working on a new short film. As we are making different shots, all the conversations we've been having about the joys and struggles of queer life feed into the images we create. *El Sueño de la Sirena: Un Cuento de Realismo Trans Mágico* offers an entry point into what is difficult, what is not yet resolved as long as 'otherness' remains a problematic category in many people's minds. But the portal we build is beautiful, and it carries the viewer on a wave of love and a celebration of life. I can't help but feel that there is something in this aesthetic mode that can act as a catalyst for mobilizing the energy needed to shape a better world.

Figure 7.5 *El Sueño de la Sirena.* Poster photo by Ivan Kirchgaesser (2021).

References

Bartoş, S. E., & Langdridge, D. (2019). LGBQ resilience: A thematic meta-synthesis of qualitative research. *Psychology & Sexuality, 10*(3), 234–47.

Brown, L. (1995). Not outside the range. In C. Caruth (Ed.), *Trauma: Explorations in memory* (pp. 100–12). Johns Hopkins University Press.

Burstow, B. (2003). Toward a radical understanding of trauma and trauma work. *Violence Against Women, 9*(11), 1293–317.

Cixous, H., & Calle-Gruber, M. (2003). *Hélène Cixous, rootprints: Memory and life writing.* Routledge.

Clover, D., Sanford, K., & Butterwick, S. (Eds.). (2013). *Aesthetic practice and adult education.* Taylor & Francis.

Formenti, L., & West, L. (2018). *Transforming perspectives in lifelong learning and adult education: A dialogue.* Palgrave Macmillan; WorldCat.org.

Formenti, L., West, L., & Horsdal, M. (Eds.). (2014). *Embodied narratives: Connecting stories, bodies, cultures and ecologies.* University of Southern Denmark Press.

Freedman, D. P. (1992). *An alchemy of genres: Cross-Genre writing by American feminist poet-Critics.* University Press of Virginia.

Hartling, L. (2010). Strengthening resilience in a risky world: It's all about relationships. *Women & Therapy, 31*(2–4), 51–70.

Jackson, N. B. (2003). Critical conditions: Coleridge, 'common Sense', and the literature of self-experiment. *ELH, 70*(1), 117–49.

Jordan, J. V. (1992). Relational resilience. Work in Progress, No. 57. Stone Center Working Paper Series.

Leddy, T. (2016). *Dewey's aesthetics. Stanford encyclopaedia of philosophy.* https://plato.stanford.edu/entries/dewey-aesthetics/

McGlotten, S. (2012). Always toward a Black queer anthropology. *Transforming Anthropology, 20*(1), 3–4.

Merton, R. (1988). Some thoughts on the concept of sociological autobiography. In M. White Riley (Ed.), S*ociological Lives* (pp. 17–21). Sage.

Read, H., Fordham, M., & Adler, G. (Eds.). (1953). *The collected works of C.G. Jung.* Routledge.

Sacks, S. (2018). Sustainability without the I-sense is nonsense: Inner 'technologies' for a viable future and the inner dimension of sustainability. In O. Parodi & K. Tamm (Eds.), *Personal sustainability: Exploring the far side of sustainable development* (pp. 171–88). Routledge.

Singh, A. A., & McKleroy, V. S. (2011). 'Just setting out of bed is a revolutionary act': The resilience of transgender people of color who have survived traumatic life events. *Traumatology, 17*(2), 34–44.

Singh, A. A., Hays, D. G. & Watson, L. S. (2011). Strength in the face of adversity: Resilience strategies of transgender individuals. *Journal of Counselling & Development, 89*, 20–7.

Stanley, L. (1992). *The auto/biographical I: Theory and practice of feminist auto/biography.* Manchester University Press.

Thomas, D. (2010). Queering silence: A narrative look at the parallel stories of LGBT and hard of hearing students in the educational setting (Doctoral dissertation). ProQuest Dissertations and Theses database.

Tompkins, J. (1987). Me and my shadow. *New Literary History, 19*(1), 169–78.

West, L. (2014). Transformative learning and the form that transforms: Toward a psychosocial theory of recognition using auto/biographical narrative research. *Journal of Transformative Education, 12*(4), 164–79.

Chapter 8

Bringing Research into Life: An Experience of Feminist Practice with Artists

Laura Formenti, Silvia Luraschi and Gaia Del Negro

Introduction

We are three Italian researchers and adult educators using auto/biographical and aesthetic research to generate learning (Formenti & West, 2016; Formenti et al., 2019, 2020a), reflexivity (Hunt, 2013) and transformation (Formenti & West, 2018) in our own and others' personal and professional lives. Through our work we (re) connect binaries in our lives, specifically, the personal and the professional, theory and practice, the body and the affect. In this chapter we present a creative process that resulted in a performance during the Triennial Conference of the European Society for Research on the Education of Adults (ESREA) in Belgrade (Serbia), September 2019. Exploring the place of the body, artistic imagination and ecology in society and adult education, we consider in this chapter how feminist methods operate as an important source of experience and knowledge, not least to contrast neoliberal and patriarchal values and discourses.

We began our creative project with a practice of writing as a research practice, specifically creating stories from and after 1968 which were inspired by Italian feminism in the 1970s (Lonzi, 1970). Milan, where we work, has an important history of feminism, as we explain in the next paragraphs. In the 1970s feminism claimed the power of imagination, and we took inspiration ourselves, to ask: What is our imagination as women, researchers and adult educators, now? How can we fuel our imagination to bring new awareness and new ways of working? A final element of our project was to work together with two artists, a pianist and a dancer, in dialogue about the aesthetic imagination. The aesthetic imagination is a form of relational imagination entailing the body and senses (from the Ancient Greek word *aisthesis*) as a fundamental link with the world, oneself and the other – and used this as a means to explore our own paths of learning in relation to feminism's adage, 'the personal is political' (e.g., Hanisch, 1970). Our project therefore starts from ourselves and our lives in order to show how we are part of larger systems of social power but also, social change. Writing our lives as a form of research allowed us to engage in a more feminist, embodied and imaginative pedagogy of possibility.

Feminism in Milan: The roots of our study

The feminist methodology that we used was developed in a very peculiar context. In the 1960s and 1970s, Milan was a place of the cultural avant-garde and the feminist movement was a key part of this. Women participated in large numbers in 1968–9 student protests but soon realized with great disappointment that gender roles often confined them to activities of care and service (Formenti, Luraschi & Del Negro, 2020b). In addition, the problems and challenges they faced as women, what mattered to them, were left unacknowledged by male protesters. These included oppressive hegemonic relationships between sexes, and the belief that giving birth was an obligation or seemingly natural role for women (Hajek, 2018). Many women began to feel the need for both a new language to express their different experiences and ideas, and a space of their own but which could be different from the private traditional space of the household. However, public spaces and discourses were occupied by men and patriarchal institutions such as the Catholic Church and the Communist Party, which were powerful in Italy at that time (Formenti & West, 2018). In addition, in the booming economy of the post-war era, the growth of industrial sites around Milan had begun to attract millions of workers from southern Italy, creating an alienated migrant underclass living in the peripheral suburbs, quickly constructed with no attention to integration or community life. Within this industrializing context, the dominant cultural model for the majority of migrants was based a naturalization of the nuclear family. Working-class migrant women were expected to work in waged jobs, at least until marriage, after which they were expected to stay at home and do the unpaid work as *casalinghe* (housewives) for the remainder of their lives.

However, feminism was bringing a new awareness and ideas for women. Women across the social classes and cultures were beginning personal quests for more meaningful lives through practices of self-realization (sense of identity and subjectivity) that took them away from social gender norms and into acting as 'unexpected subjects' in the public scene (Lonzi, 1970). For the first time in history, it was possible for a new generation of female students, workers, immigrants and housewives to go to the cities to study or work, but equally importantly, to claim women-specific urban spaces where they could practise *autocoscienza* (self-consciousness). Central to this was the practice of exchanging personal stories as a pedagogical strategy to build greater political awareness (e.g., Vacchelli, 2008).

Building on this, the women's movement in Milan was boosted by transnational exchanges with the French movement *Psychanalyse et Politique* (hereafter Psych et Po), a diverse group that developed a feminist reading of psychoanalysis (Zamboni, 2019). Melandri (2000), an Italian feminist writer and adult educator, bore witness to this in 1972 when she participated in an international meeting organized by Psych et Po in Vendee (France). She, alongside twenty other Italian women from Milan, Rome, Turin and Florence, came face to face with the exciting work of feminist intellectuals and researchers, Lia Cigarini, Antonella Nappi, Luisa Passerini and Maria Schiavo. As told by Antonella Nappi in *Nudity* (1977/2010), the meeting placed a strong focus on the connections between the body and the unconscious, discussing freely with no programme or fixed agenda, the physical, intellectual and emotional experiences of women. In particular, participants 'discovered' the female body in this all-female context, which as much as possible in a patriarchal world was free from the male gaze, that which objectifies and stereotypes women's bodies for its own pleasure. The conference provided a space to explore meaning and the feminine unconscious in depth, as a political and embodied act. As Hajek (2018) noted, women eyes were opened 'to the necessity of a women-only space for the development of a more authentic relationship with one's body, one where the latter is no longer considered an aesthetic object of male desire or subject to a distorted relationship' (p. 86). These types of transnational encounters continued through other forms of experimental feminist practices. In addition, there was the editorial success of the book *Our Bodies, Ourselves*, translated into Italian in 1973, which helped to make feminism more visible in the every day of Italy, and also, bring the body even more into the forefront of women's liberation efforts.

Throughout the 1960s and 1970s the feminist movement in Italy mirrored a diversity of interests with several feminist groups emerging and strengthening while others closed down due to internal conflicts. Radical feminists started to write, publish and disseminate in separate spaces (Lonzi, 1970) but across the board, there was a keen interest in women's education. In the larger cities, these often came in the form of feminist consciousness-raising groups. Most particularly, women creatively took up the '150 hours' scheme, a state programme established in 1973 for workers, mainly aimed at obtaining a secondary education diploma (Causarano, 2016). These courses were particularly important for immigrant and working-class women in search of education as a means to improve and expand their lives. Some of the classes operated as spaces for critical learning; radical feminist educators provided opportunities for women to share stories and knowledge, create a sense of agency and identity and to form new types of relationships. While the course gave women students a formal certificate, the real power was as a means to enable women to socialise and to reflect upon the lives in relation to the world beyond home and family.

A creative/imaginative research methodology

The herstory of feminists/ism in Milan outlined above speaks of the possibility of creating a space of one's own, to borrow from Virginia Woolf, to think together with body and mind, and to write from experience. In adult education, auto/biographical enquiry (Merrill & West, 2009) and embodied narratives (Formenti, West & Horsdal, 2014) have become important generative methods that we use in our individual and collective explorations. These methods enable us to build our critical reflection and reflexive capacities and the energies, commitments, imaginations and intimacies we need as women to be/come more aware, intentional, and relational in the world and with each other. Auto/biography with a slash, a practice in British feminism (e.g., Stanley, 1992), is a narrative process between two or more subjects who tell stories of their lives in ways that illuminate different life contexts, constraints, and determinants through juxtaposition and resonance.

Our self-study was inspired by the stories of the late 1960s and early 1970s outlined above, and more particularly the work of Melandri (2014). Melandri taught Italian for many years in the neighbourhood of Affori, metropolitan Milan. When the first '150 hours' course for housewives was launched in 1976 in response to a request by twenty local women, Melandri used with the women a form of 're-compositional writing', a collection of chosen literary texts that could help the students to connect reading materials with their lived experiences. This method was a weaving of words with embodied experience with creativity and the unconscious. For the women students who had not only been locked inside patriarchal norms, but also had deep feelings of being an outsider in elitist literary culture, Melandri's practice of feminist life writing was a liberating feminist experience as well as a practice of cultural democracy. Melandri (2017) believed that because literature often comes from the author's lived experience, it contains illuminating references to the human condition. Literary writing is therefore an 'underlying universe reluctant to be translated and assimilated into words' (p. 17, our translation) and as such, it resists rational analysis and deconstruction and allows us to 'mine' our lives. On this latter, Melandri designed a more contemporary version of the '150 hours' beginning in 2014 in the suburbs of Milan. She engaged her 'students' in a critical and creative method of writing, a story weaving method Melandri refers to as a 'mineralogy of thought' (*mineralogia del pensiero*), a mining of thought (p. 17). It is this work that most inspired our method which we outline shortly.

Melandri's feminist method is different from normative autobiographical approaches to literature because she challenges the notion of memories. Memory practices can be ego-centric, cognitive patriarchal approaches that separate the author from her context, body, emotions, and more importantly, our unconscious messiness. Memory can be colonized by dominant discourses, producing monolithic narratives. Instead of memory, Melandri talks of 'writing from experience' (2017, p. 10, our translation) as a way to encourage hidden zones of consciousness, relying on fragments or splinters of thought, emotions, making their appearance in ways that disrupt linear thinking and meaning making. Melandri's work exposes subjectivity as well as intersubjectivity and the more 'universal' features of women's condition, without essentializing this experience. Her method is to invite women to read literary texts and underline words or phrases that stand out or connect. The underlined sentences and words are transcribed by hand onto a piece of paper to embody the words. In phase three, women use these words to write new texts based on their own lives. The lists made in phase one and the final stories are read aloud to the group. This is a very powerful moment, when the 'mineralogy of thought' in the texts is performed in a deep emotional atmosphere of conscious and unconscious listening. By creating a new awareness out of the shadows of the human condition even their relationship with language is challenged. The patriarchal shaping of common sense which has informed the lives of these women is disrupted by reappropriating words into or as their own experience. We are shaped by language, so naming is never a neutral act (with all due respect to Freire). In Melandri's practice, critical awareness and (re)creative wording are interconnected to create a sense of agency in literature that once was, as noted above, considered to not only be beyond these women, untouchable as an art. But in Melandri's method, we make the words ours; we select what is meaningful for us and we shape them in new forms. Sometimes this means respecting and using the original meaning, but at others, it is about reversing or reframing that meaning. It is not storytelling as there is no coherent story; it is playful, joyous, relational and emotional which we illustrate in the next section.

New research fellows

The three of us have been working together and separately for some years in the areas of multimodality, emotions, sensations and embodiment as key to human flourishing. To bring new perspectives into our work we have called upon artists who we have found have a constant relationship with other ways of knowing, not only cognitive, but creative, sensuous, imaginative and relational. Artists practice their creative language so regularly that it is often simply a part of their identity. As academics, we too wanted to start an imaginative dialogue in a way that could unearth the important matter of experience, often obscured, considered 'other' or an inadequate mode of knowing and thinking in the patriarchal politics of the academy.

When thinking about artists we knew, two people came to mind. The first was Marino Formenti, a pianist and Laura's brother and the second, Cinzia Delorenzi, a dancer and Gaia's teacher. We knew some aspects of their artistic paths and therefore we were pretty sure that listening to their stories would inspire new insights in us.

Gaia's story of her relationship with Cinzia

I met Cinzia for the first time during a dance class in Milan in January 2017. She was indicated to me by a dancer friend as a 'very special person'. Cinzia has more than 20-year practice of research in contemporary dance and somatic movement, with a pedagogical approach oriented towards personal and artistic development. Specialised in sensitive dance*, BMC* and other approaches, she developed her artistic research in nature, e.g. sea, forest, desert (Figure 8.1), alone and in small groups, based on the body as medium of transformation. I had just recently come back from the UK, then. In fact, I felt quite lost and lonely, struggling with my VIVA, missing Canterbury, and a new direction. So, I attended a class.

The dance practice was only apparently simple. There were basic schemes to explore individually and in pairs, in search for inner connection to inhabit movement with perception, function, purpose, drive, need, desire. A joyous yet

Figure 8.1 *Cinzia dances in the Sahara Desert, Morocco*, January 2018. Frame from a video by Semira Belkhir.

difficult search, a nomadic practice of attuning concentrated in a room space. My body felt goofy, and yet new and known. I loved the process. Just after a few sessions, Cinzia communicated that she was going to launch her first independent training in April 2017, called 'RHIZOME, the listening practices', devoted to fostering personal orientation to more sustainable and fulfilling paths in difficult transitional times of our lives through collective experience of touch and artistic creation. I joined in. At the time of the interview, we were in the second year of training, followed by me in bits and pieces, since I had gone back to Canterbury to work at the university. When funding finished, I was back in Milan again. The interview took place in my living room, on a sunny day of February 2019. A key moment: as Cinzia told her story, I recognised a seed beyond words. I think we planted a seed of entrustment in life in my sunny living room.

Silvia's story of meeting Marino

Before interviewing Marino, I had listened to one of his piano performances. Laura, his sister, had sent a message that in Milano he would perform 'Nowhere[1]*', a form of installation where he eats, sleeps and plays the piano for weeks in a space that is open to the public, complete with 24/7 live streaming. Visitors are invited into the space to listen, sleep, read a book, go away, return, make drawings, etc. Impressed by this description, I went there and was invited to come in and listen to the music. The room was scattered with pillows and mattresses, even under the piano and I chose to listen from that unusual spot* (see Figure 8.2). *Marino played Brian Eno's 'By this river' and I found myself deeply immersed in a world of sounds reaching my heart.*

Figure 8.2 *Nowhere*, Milano, May 2018. Photo by Emanuele La Scala.

I cried for the intensity of that unexpected, embodied emotion. Sensibility ... the music taught me!

Marino is a contemporary pianist of international renown who explores the relationship between classical and contemporary music involving the living body and mind of the public. Born in Brianza (Italy), he has been living in Vienna (Austria) for several years. We therefore had to use Skype for the interview. In Figure 8.2, I am laying under the piano played by Marino during his performance of 'Nowhere'.

Our mineralogy of thought

The two interview/stories above became the basis for our mineralogy of thought. As illustrated in Figure 8.3, each of us worked on our own transcribed texts, following the three steps outlined above as Melandri's method to create our own re-compositions. Struck by the connections emerging from them, we decided to go further in our collective composition, bringing in more texts, both popular and academic, as well as images, photos, artefacts and the transcripts of our own conversations with each other about the process, to create a playscript and present it at ESREA's Triennial Conference in Belgrade which we noted in the introduction to this chapter.

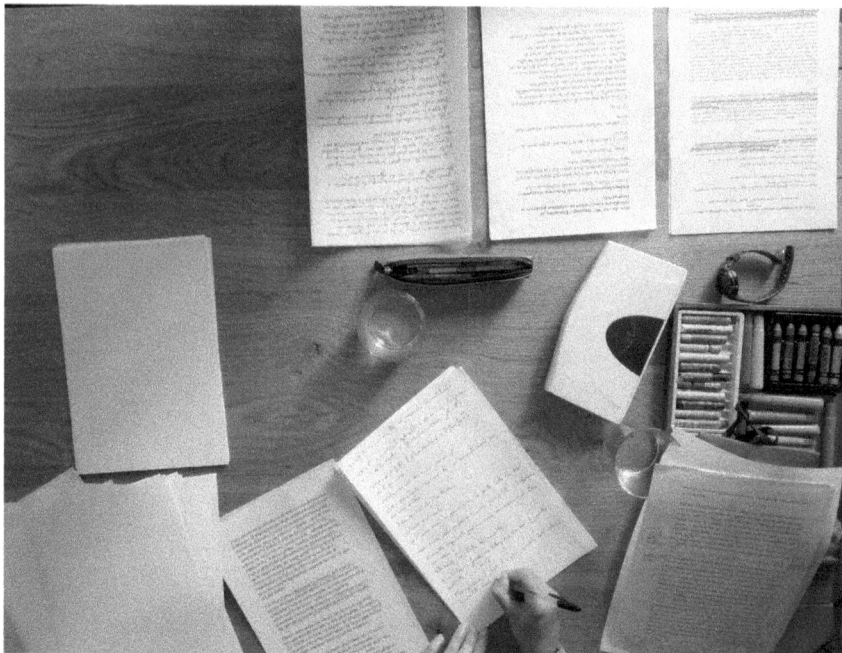

Figure 8.3 *Transcribing our materials by hand*, Verderio, July 2019. Photo by Silvia Luraschi.

Towards the playscript: Expanding circles of knowledge

Various questions guided us in extracting and composing fragments from the artist's stories including which stories are told and which are silenced? What could be learnt about experience, truth and language, in conversation with a musician and a dancer? Our exploration developed through three levels, what Bateson (1972) refers to as intersecting and expanding circles of knowledge.

Level 1: The auto/biographical interviews

Level 1 was our relationship with the artists and the knowledge built from interviewing them. For the interviews, we chose an open-ended approach, based on the question: How would you tell your story as an artist? We were hopeful that understandings about memories, embodied experiences, relationships to knowledge and language, the academy, education, creativity, discipline, improvization, and silenced stories would emerge, and they did. Cinzia and Marino read and commented on the transcripts. We also discussed their impressions of the research experience and the overall project. Both artists were pleased with the quality of the words and stories.

Figure 8.4 *Gaia and Laura at Laura's kitchen table*, Verderio, July 2019. Photo by Silvia Luraschi.

Level 2: A mineralogic creative analysis

Level 2 was the 'mineralogy' analysis of the interviews and then our own performance of these over a weekend at Laura's home. In choosing 'mineralogy' we were able to explore other possibilities of method and analysis. Our aim was creative and generative: reading the interviews through the lenses of our different subjectivities, weaving together the transcripts, living at Laura's home, sitting at the kitchen table with the printed interviews, pens and colours, the same table where we had meals with Laura's family in the evening (see Figure 8.4), reminded us of the spirit of the seventies, when women started to share intimacy to take action and generate new forms of knowledge.

We followed the method, as said above. A long, body engaging activity. Finally, we recomposed our words in a personal poetic text that we read aloud to each other in a performative act in the courtyard. The result was insightful, if strange and poetic. That is when the idea of a 'Playscript in Six Acts' came about!

Level 3: Playscript in Six Acts

Level 3 was the public presentation at an adult education conference with scholars acting as 'listeners' and in some ways, co-researchers. We presented our work at the ESREA Triennial Conference in Belgrade (September 2019) as a way to share the process we had just experimented with. We present our 'conference paper' as a playscript, where all the traditional ingredients of an academic paper (theoretical background, research questions and final discussion) were translated into six acts. Our script was entitled *Relational Aesthetics: Emotion, Perception, and Communication in Adult Education Research.* The script contained several voices: Silvia, Gaia and Laura (respectively the 'sensitive', the 'nomadic', and the 'senior' researchers); the Italian feminist adult educator Lea Melandri, representing feminism and our methodology; the artists – Marino Formenti and Cinzia Delorenzi representing lived experience. We also included in our script, the Chilean biologist Humberto Maturana (1992), and the American scholar Elizabeth Adams St. Pierre. We included Maturana because he maintains that it is the very biological structure of the human being that makes language and emotion the building blocks of our experience, our knowledge and our life. He represents our theoretical roots in constructivism. We included St. Pierre (2011) because she challenges us to find a new language that goes beyond humanism.

The session took place in a traditional lecture room, on Sunday morning. There were about twenty-five participants sitting at desks. Silvia handed out the printed text of the script with roles marked in colours, while Laura explained what we were about to do. We began the presentation by inviting the conference participants to join us in a rehearsal of a theatrical performance and in fact we needed them to play the various characters in the script. There was a moment of quiet when we asked for volunteers but then someone raised their hand, thankfully! We started our PowerPoint with photos of the characters and the script's lines.

Play Script: Selected parts

Act N. 1 The Project

Silvia, Gaia and Laura (together): 'Learning comes from "touching" each other, literally or metaphorically. All languages do this: gesture, music, images, words, even the non-human speech of animals, objects, and nature … And yet, our work as researchers and educators is often alienated from the interacting body and its communicative capacity. This is why we decided to involve professional artists in our quest.'

Humberto Maturana, the biologist: 'We say that words were smooth, caressing, hard, sharp, and so on: all these terms refer to body touching. Indeed, we can kill or relate with words … because, as co-ordinations of actions, they take place through body interactions that trigger in us body changes in the domain of physiology' (1988, p. 48).

Act N. 2 The theory

Elizabeth Adams St. Pierre – the theorist: 'The work of post qualitative inquiry is, indeed, to experiment and create the new … social sciences, like everything else, did not always exist. They are historical, they were invented, and were likely not recognised at their beginning' (St. Pierre, 2018, p. 29).

Act N. 3 The method

Lea Melandri – the feminist adult educator: 'In other words, the point is to salvage the sphere of feelings, emotions, dreams, imaginary, as consciousness, and as "value", and integral part of our judgements, our intellectual formation, our choices … ' (our translation).

Act N. 4 Artists' voices – from their narrative interviews

Marino – the pianist: 'The attempt is to not create a focus on me, as in 'let's go to see the pianist, but to bring the focus back on you … huge stars (like Callas) who play concerts full of exceptions, for example pushing on pitch, colour etc. intentionally doing things "out of the norm", but today if you do that, it is considered as a mistake and your career is sort of finished'.

Cinzia – the dancer: 'Then this thing made its way. I don't know why, I did not come from a family that had ever had this experience […] All this movement of peoples, cells, foreigners to one another and … there is a big orchestration so if you go from macro to micro, the vision changes. How can I dance?'

Act N. 5 Re-compositional analysis

Gaia – the nomadic researcher:

> *We delegated music to an increasingly smaller group*
> *of great starts (like Callas)*
> *who play concerts full of expectation*
> *it is the 1980s and I jump from course to course*
> *who am I,*
> *where do I come from?*
> *who's speaking?*

Laura – the senior researcher:

> *It starts in the egg, in childhood,*
> *you feel a sort of union, being one.*
> *You soon discover that it's impossible to communicate this vision,*
> *[due to] family narrative.*
> *Then it happens.*
> *You meet the soul while crossing a meadow, walking barefoot,*
> *start making space for shared experience. You know*
> *it and you feel it.*

Silvia – The sensitive researcher:

> *All my performances are about participation. I've always felt, and I'm feeling today, this collective dimension: this, my body, is not only this shape that I see, but a house for more germs than cells ... and all are taking part in it. Nobody thinks if they are good enough to do it or what other people think of me.*

Act N. 6 Artists' responses

Marino <marino … @ … > 29 July 2019 16:57
And hello to you all, from here, a torrid Vienna
Speaking of 'errors' (because this also is a perspective, isn't it?), I share with you a little something that I just discovered, Herbie Hancock speaking of Miles Davis:
https://www.youtube.com/watch?v=FL4LxrN-iyw
the whole short narrative is hilarious (I find), with hyper-technologic young Herbie trying to 'stop the moment' by recording old Miles with his brand-new device …
Cinzia <cinzia … @ … > 30 July 2019 14:56
hello everybody
It's been a while since I felt
A physical emotion,
in reading …
the world's resonance received inside us
through others' words
can generate and regenerate
a meaning and thin tie, a conjoint practice …

With these last words' echoing, silence reigned. An active silence, however, as what Silvia called the 'thinking faces' illustrated just how deeply the participants were entangled in our performance. Laura invited everybody to add their own lines to the script starting from the prompt: 'This reminds me of a story'. Someone read aloud what they had written. Some days later, we received a touching email from Linden West, a friend and colleague, and a remarkable voice in the field (West, 1996; 2016), saying:

> This reminds me of a story …
> Of the deepest feelings
> In the desire to know.
> And of her enemies, the demons of abstraction
> And of the cold gaze that would shred our humanity.
> Imagination with a thought
> Beyond fragments
> Souls singing together for every tatter in our mortal dress.
> A glimpse of heaven, of hell too.
> We are touched, in moments, by glimpses of eternity and of seeing anew.
> (Fragments of Linden's e-mail, 23 September 2019 20.37)

Conclusions

In this chapter we presented the practice and process of our auto/biographical method of diverse knowledge making inspired by Milanese feminism. For us, it was an opportunity to challenge normative conventions of language in academy and education. As feminist researchers we have learnt how can ally with artists to bring academic knowledge closer to lived lives, as we discovered over the last few years (e.g., Clover et al., 2013). Marino has also brought our attention to value of embodied participation and improvisation as an antidote to perfectionism, which kills emotion and relational learning. Cinzia challenged us to think about the role of imagination to explore other possible worlds and choices in our lives, starting from perceiving the smallest mysterious components of biology that make us intelligent bodies. Our collaboration with artists, educators, researchers opened possibilities to widen our perception of human complexity and beauty, in a lively yet fragile planet.

Note

1   Nowhere, https://marinoformenti.net/nowhere/

References

Asor Rosa, A. (1985). *L'ultimo paradosso*. Einaudi.

Bateson, G. (1972). *Steps to an ecology of mind*. Ballantine Books.

Causarano, P. (2016). La scuola di noi operai. Formazione, libertà e lavoro nell'esperienza delle 150 ore. *Rivista di Storia dell'Educazione, 1*, 141–59.

Clover, D. E., Sanford, K., & Butterwick, S. (Eds.). (2013). *Aesthetic practices in adult education*. Routledge.

Formenti, L., Luraschi, S., & Del Negro, G. (2019). Relational aesthetics: A duo ethnographic research on feminism. *European Journal for Research on the Education and Learning of Adults, 10*(2), 123–41.

Formenti, L., Luraschi, S., & Del Negro, G. (2020a). Connective cards to interrogate the museum. In D. E. Clover, S. Dzulkifli, H. Gelderman, & K. Sanford (Eds.), *Feminist adult educators' guide. To aesthetic, creative and disruptive strategies in museums and community* (pp. 41–91). University of Victoria Gender Justice, Creative Pedagogies and Arts-Based Research Group. https://onlineacademiccommunity.uvic.ca/comarts/wp-content/uploads/sites/3036/2020/08/Clover-Suriani-D-Gelderman-Sanford-Feminist-Adult-Educators-Guide.pdf

Formenti, L., Luraschi, S., & Del Negro, G. (2020b). Signs images words from 1968: From duoethnographic enquiry to a dialogic pedagogy. In K. Sanford, D. E. Clover, N. Taber, & S. Williamson (Eds.), *Feminist critique and the museum. Educating for a critical consciousness* (pp. 115–34). Brill Sense Publishing. http://dx.doi.org/10.1163/9789004440180_007.

Formenti, L., & West, L. (Eds.). (2016). *Stories that make a difference. Exploring the collective, social and political potential of narratives in adult education research*. Pensa Multimedia.

Formenti, L., & West, L. (2018). *Transforming perspectives in lifelong learning and adult education: A dialogue*. Palgrave Macmillan.

Formenti, L., West, L., & Horsdal, M. (Eds.). (2014). *Embodied narratives. Connecting stories, bodies, cultures and ecologies*. University Press of Southern Denmark.

Hajek, A. (2018). A room of one's own: Feminist intersections between space, women's writing and radical bookselling in Milan (1968–1986). *Italian Studies*, 73(1), 81–97. DOI:10.1080/00751634.2018.1414376.

Hanisch, C. (1970). *The personal is political: The women's liberation movement classic with a new explanatory introduction*. http://www.carolhanisch.org

Hunt, C. (2013). *Transformative learning through creative life writing*. Routledge.

Lonzi, C. (1970/2010). *Let's spit on Hegel*. (Trans. V. Newman). Secunda. http://blogue.nt2.uqam.ca/hit/files/2012/12/Lets-Spit-on-Hegel-CarlaLonzi.pdf

Maturana, H. (1988). Reality: The search for objectivity or the quest for a compelling argument. *Irish Journal of Psychology, Radical Constructivism, Autopoiesis and Psychotherapy*, 9(1), 25–82.

Maturana, H. (1992). *Emociones y Lenguaje en Educación y Política*. Centro de Educación del Desarrollo (CEO) Ediciones Pedagógicas Chilenas S.

Melandri, L. (2000). *Una visceralità indicibile. La pratica dell'inconscio nel movimento delle donne degli anni Settanta*. Franco Angeli.

Melandri, L. (2014). *Il femminismo a Milano, puntata 7: femminismo e 150 ore*. https://memomi.it/il-femminismo-a-milano/il-femminismo-a-milano-puntata-7-femminismo-e-150-ore

Melandri, L. (2017). *Alfabeto d'origine*. Neri Pozza.

Merrill, B., & West, L. (2009). *Using biographical methods in social research*. SAGE.

Nappi, A. (2010, May 4). *Nudity*, 4, 71–2.

Stanley, L. (1992). *The auto/biographical I: The theory and practice of feminist auto/biography*. Manchester University Press.

St. Pierre Adams, E. (2011). Post qualitative research: The critique and the coming after. In N. K. Denzin & Y. S. Lincoln (Eds.). *Sage handbook of qualitative inquiry* (4th ed. pp. 611–35). SAGE.

St. Pierre Adams, E. (2018). Post qualitative inquiry, the critique of method, and the creation of the new. Unpublished Talk, Department of Human Sciences for Education, Università degli Studi di Milano Bicocca, 9 October.

Vacchelli, E. (2008). Milan 1970–1980: Women's place in urban theory. *Research in Urban Sociology*, 9, 29–51.

West, L. (1996). *Beyond fragments: Adults, motivation and higher education; a biographical analysis*. Taylor and Francis.

West, L. (2016). *Distress in the city: Racism, fundamentalism and a democratic education*. UCL Institute of Education Press.

Zamboni, C. (2019). La pratica dell'inconscio: Un ponte tra 'psychanalyse et politique', Antoinette Fouque e il pensiero femminista italiano. *Diotima*, 16, http://www.diotimafilosofe.it/larivista/la-pratica-dellinconscio-un-ponte-tra-psychanalyse-et-politique-antoinette-fouque-e-il-pensiero-femminista-italiano/

Chapter 9

#MeToo and the Feminist Digital Imaginary: Public Pedagogy on Sexual Consent and Violence

Salsabel Almanssori

What do young people learn online about sex and rape? The emergence and evolution of the internet in the past few decades has driven such enquiries amongst sexual violence prevention stakeholders around the world (e.g., Dobson & Ringrose, 2016; Mendes et al., 2018). This chapter offers an alternative vision of the possibilities of feminist public sexual violence pedagogy. It exists at the colourful intersections of the #MeToo movement and digital political activism, public pedagogy, aesthetics and feminist understandings of sexual violence and prevention education. Each of these topics justifies a genealogy of scholarship on its own; however, within their crossing exists a particularly relevant topic for feminist educators.

As young people increasingly turn to media platforms for their sex education needs (i.e., Bragg, 2006; Meaney et al., 2009), it is of interest to adult educators to understand the ways in which young people produce, negotiate and participate in online public pedagogy on sexual ethics and sexual violence, particularly in a post #MeToo world. In my review of the literature, I found that this is an under-researched topic, and in my practice as a feminist sexual violence prevention educator I have found this to be a point of interest, curiosity and struggle. Located within a feminist theoretical framework, this chapter thus draws attention to the complexities, epistemological significances and aesthetics of public sexual violence pedagogies in a post-#MeToo world. It engages with the feminist imagination that exists in digital spaces following the #MeToo movement that engage with the feminist collective roar through story and digital aesthetics, countering the too long taken for granted sexual scripts by centring and honouring truth-telling. Since the movement began in 2017, there have been various changes in our collective social understanding of sexual violence. In keeping with feminist theorizations of sexual violence, this chapter observes sexual violence as gendered and based within patriarchal power and control (Brownmiller, 1975; hooks, 1981), as an insidious phenomenon that is produced and reproduced by systemic structures, discursive representations, and individual behaviours (Gavey, 2005, 2019) and as an occurrence within a continuum that encompasses its various, interrelated forms (Kelly, 1987; McMahon & Banyard, 2012; Stout, 1991).

I have divided my chapter into five sections. Following this introduction, I outline the key concepts involved in understanding feminist sexual violence prevention. Section three shifts focus to #MeToo as a form of public pedagogy on sex and sexual violence. The fourth section is dedicated to the research on discursive representations of sexual violence in digital spheres and brings my own research, a discourse analysis of YouTube vlogs wherein women discuss experiences of sexual violence, in conversation with recent, similar literature. The final section then ties the theoretical ideas in the second and third section to the recent literature in the fourth section and engages with the aesthetic possibilities of feminist public pedagogy.

Feminist approaches to sexual violence prevention

Feminist approaches to sexual violence prevention rely on the concepts that are valuable in understanding how individual behaviours connect to social, cultural and political fabrics in which gendered experiences of sexual violence are insidious, ubiquitous and simultaneously unapparent. These include the continuum (Kelly, 1987), rape culture (Gavey, 2005, 2019) and the situating of consent negotiations within sociopolitical contexts (Butler, 2011; Gilbert, 2018). Over four decades ago, Kelly (1987) theorized the concept of the continuum as a more comprehensive way of understanding incidences of sexual violence. Her research showed that women experienced many unwanted sexual acts within what could be considered to be consensual relationships both legally and culturally, such as within intimate relationships. The concept of a continuum reflects both the difficulties of defining forms of sexual violence and the complexities and ambiguities of women's experiences.

For Kelly (1987), understanding sexual violence as a continuum means that violent acts of various severity are linked to one another. Furthermore, there exists a relationship between the severity of sexually violent behaviours and the legal and social recognition of their levels of appropriateness. At one end of the continuum are behaviours that are generally recognized as sexually violent, such as rape (McMahon et al., 2011); these more overt behaviours are generally legally recognized as crimes and largely acknowledged as inappropriate by most people, although they are also much less prevalent. At the other end are behaviours that are more commonly accepted, such as rape jokes and sexist comments (McMahon et al., 2011); they are less likely to be recognized as harmful and are thus a normalized part of everyday life and the most prevalent. Prevention efforts that focus on this end of the continuum contribute to more sustaining social change because people in societies begin to trouble commonly accepted and highly prevalent sexually violent behaviours (McMahon & Banyard, 2012).

In conjunction with the continuum of sexual violence, feminist pedagogues often turn the concept of rape culture as a key part of effective prevention education. Rape culture refers to a culture in which all forms of sexual violence are common and prevalent attitudes, practices and media normalize, excuse, tolerate and accept sexual violence (Brownmiller, 1975; Buchwald et al., 1993; Gavey, 2019). Buchwald et al. (1993) characterize rape culture as

> a complex set of beliefs that encourages male sexual aggression and supports violence against women. It is a society where violence is seen as sexy and sexuality as violent. In a rape culture, women perceive a continuum of threatened violence that ranges from sexual remarks to sexual touching to rape itself.
>
> (p. vii)

Across the decades, feminist scholars have pointed to the link between the acceptance of rape myths and adherence to traditional sex and gender roles, sexist attitudes and beliefs (e.g., Gavey, 2019; Lonsway & Fitzgerald, 1994). In rape cultures, women who report incidents of sexual violence are likely to be met with scepticism, incredulity and difficult questions.

Feminist scholars often point out that consent education has a key role to play in prevention. In North America, sex education does not adequately engage with the intricacies that inform sexual encounters, often positioning consent as a 'transparent, communicative, and rational experience and mistakes compliance for learning' (Gilbert, 2018, p. 296). Butler (2011) points out that power relations impact the decision-making processes which inform consent and non-consent. In reality the idea of consent 'is laden with the broad social context in which people utter "no" and "yes." A person who refuses sexual activity navigates many cultural, historical, and personal complexities' (Harris, 2018, p. 159). Feminist educators thus contend that in addition to consent, we need to learn about non-consent, coercion and desire, all within a gendered context that considers power relations (Fenner, 2017; Fine & McClelland, 2006).

The feminist concepts of the continuum of sexual violence, rape culture and consent all exist within what bell hooks (2004, 2015) terms the capitalist, white supremacist, imperialist, colonial patriarchy. For example, there is a growing body of research which demonstrates that communities where there are higher levels of patriarchal norms and sexist and misogynistic beliefs tend to have higher rates of sexual violence (e.g., Casey & Lindhorst, 2009; Lonsway & Fitzgerald, 1994). Although patriarchy is the most prominent context in which sexual violence occurs, it is often simultaneously an instrument of other systems of oppression.

Public pedagogy through social media platforms

Feminist educational approaches to sexual violence prevention carry a rich history of engagement with the role of mass media and pop culture in producing rape culture and shaping public understandings of sex, sexual ethics and rape. Feminist researchers have historically investigated the role of television, magazines, music videos and advertisements in shaping dominant discourses of female domination

(Dentith & Brady, 1999; Luke, 1996). In recent years, feminist scholars have shifted their attention to social media as key spaces wherein dominant discourses are produced, reproduced and resisted.

Much of this work is situated within the context of public pedagogy. While there are a number of definitions and framings, public pedagogy encompasses 'educational activity and learning in extrainstitutional spaces and discourses' (Sandlin et al., 2011, p. 338). This field of study emerged when scholars began to emphasize that learning was not limited to the walls of schools nor to prescribed pedagogical processes. However, sophisticated understandings of public pedagogy do not frame it as 'a simple movement of norms from society to individual', but, rather, in a way wherein such 'norms can be examined as they are developed and contested' (Hickey-Moody et al., 2010, p. 229). I argue that this is particularly significant for feminist thinkers, who emphasize the agency of individuals in making sense of, negotiating and resisting problematic pedagogical content.

Sandlin et al. (2011) point to how feminist scholars have pioneered the term public pedagogy, particularly in their enquiries into learners' complex interactions with media, popular culture and various institutions. Dentith et al. (2014) go further, arguing that public pedagogy is a historically feminist project. Even before the term emerged in scholarly journals, feminists were doing work that constituted public pedagogy. This chapter positions feminist and public pedagogy as inextricably linked both materially and theoretically. In recent years, feminist researchers have prioritized the study of how rapidly evolving digital spheres serve as learning platforms and how young people participate in producing, reproducing and negotiating discursive understandings of important issues. My interest lies in the discursive and aesthetic mechanisms that women and girls use to understand, and educate others about, their experiences of sexual violence in a post-#MeToo world.

#MeToo as public pedagogy

In 2006, activist and sexual violence survivor Tarana Burke coined the term 'Me Too' on MySpace following an interaction with her friend in which she found herself unable to respond to her disclosure of an experience of rape. In retrospect, Burke recalled that what she had wished she had said was, *me too*. On 15 October 2017, after the dozens of sexual crimes of American film producer Harvey Weinstein began to permeate the news, American actress Alyssa Milano (2017) posted a picture on Twitter that read, 'Suggested by a friend: If all the women who have ever been sexually harassed or assaulted wrote "Me too" as a status, then we give people a sense of the magnitude of the problem' (n.p.). This was followed by another tweet that read, simply, 'Me Too'. A number of high-profile celebrities responded, including Ashley Judd, Gwyneth Paltrow, Jennifer Lawrence and Uma Thurman. What resulted was a viral, global social media phenomenon, popularly referred to as the #MeToo movement.

Clarke-Vivier and Stearns (2019, p. 55) describe #MeToo as an educational movement, a form of public pedagogy that places 'a premium on truth-telling' in a post-truth era. In the digital space, this means that '#MeToo aggregated personal stories into a networked visibility campaign, illustrating the systemic nature of sexual violence' (Clark-Parsons, 2019, p. 3). For Clark-Parsons, the feminist public performative nature of #MeToo means that survivors' collective voices create a collective global roar that reverberates across various digital platforms, from Twitter, to Facebook, Instagram and YouTube.

Although the #MeToo movement in many ways elicited a network of survivors and facilitated a safe space for collective disclosures (Gallagher et al., 2019), it must be recognized that in some sexual violence supportive cultures, saying #MeToo comes with several vulnerabilities for women. As Clark-Parsons argues, 'publicly performing the identity of a survivor in a cultural context where sexual violence victims are shamed and doubted leaves one vulnerable to personal attacks' (p. 10). Although some scholars have pointed out that the #MeToo movement also relies on intersectionality theory, other activists and scholars troubled its inclusion of marginalized women and pointed out that the movement tends to centre white, able-bodied, heterosexual women (Phipps, 2019). Phipps argues that 'public feminisms in this area, as in many others, have been demographically and politically dominated by white women, who have often ignored or co-opted the experiences and contributions of women of color [*sic*]' (p. 2). Phipps further points out that not all voices that emerge from the #MeToo movement are considered equal and highlights several high-profile instances in which speaking out has become 'speaking over' (p. 9). These observations are critical for understanding public pedagogies within the framework of intersectional feminism (Collins, 2015; Crenshaw, 1989).

The discursive and the counter-discursive: Understandings of sexual violence on YouTube

Mendes et al. (2018) point out that while disclosures have been studied by feminist scholars for several decades, 'the emergence of digital technologies opens new ways of communicating, disclosing, and narrating previously invisible experiences, emotions, and affects' (p. 1292). I present findings from a research project I conducted with a student of mine, in which we used feminist discourse analysis to explore women's discursive methods of understanding and communicating experiences of sexual violence through vlogging on YouTube (Almanssori & Stanley, 2021). We found that the YouTube vloggers simultaneously reproduced dominant rape discourses and simultaneously resisted these which counter-discourses. We were particularly interested in the discourses that were present when women, fuelled by their engagements with #MeToo movement, discussed their experiences of sexual violence. #MeToo and YouTube's nature as a narrative platform allowed the women and girl vloggers in my study to locate their stories of sexual violence within broader contexts and connect them to a continuum of experiences and a complex cultural problem (Almanssori & Stanley, 2021). Situated within a feminist theoretical framework, my discourse analysis yielded six discourses, grouped together as pairs of dominant and counter-discursive themes: the *refusal* (Carmody, 2009) and the contrasting *complicating consent* counter-discourse; the *deviant perpetrator* discourse (Anderson, 2007; Estrich, 1987) and the contrasting *community problem* counter-discourse; and the *not that bad* discourse (Gay, 2018) and *truth telling* counter-discourse (Almanssori & Stanley, 2021). The vloggers troubled dominant discourses by articulating their inherent shortcomings and contradictions, thereby opening up opportunities for alternative discursive understandings. The presence of their counter-discursive ways of understanding and communicating their experiences is supported by other research into networked activism and digital feminist responses to sexual violence (Mendes et al., 2018).

My finding of the *refusal* (i.e., Carmody, 2009) discourse was characterized by a pattern of meaning in which girls are deemed responsible for communicating refusal to engage in sexual acts in an overt and unmistakable way and in which such communication averts sexual violence. This finding affirms previous findings in the feminist scholarship of sexual violence. In particular, the refusal discourse is connected to dominant discourses of girls as gatekeepers of sexual experience (Valenti, 2009), in which women and girls are viewed as responsible for granting permission and defining the parameters of sexual activities (e.g., Hlavka, 2014; Hindes & Fileborn, 2020). Our findings suggested that women and girls used the dominant refusal discourse to make sense of their experience and simultaneously, they disrupted it and communicated an alternative pattern of meaning through the *complicating consent* discourse (Almanssori & Stanley, 2021). This counter-discourse was emblematic of the feminist scholarship on consent (Butler, 2011; Fenner, 2017; Gilbert, 2018; Harris, 2018).

The finding of the *not that bad* discourse, as well as its counter-discursive counterpart, as a way that the vloggers made sense of their experiences of sexual violence is especially significant (Almanssori & Stanley, 2021). With the exception of Gay (2018), there was little evidence of the not that bad discourse in the sexual violence literature. Gay explains that understanding her experience as not that bad was simultaneously a way to 'break down [her] trauma into something more manageable, into something [she] could carry with [her], instead of allowing the magnitude of it to destroy [her]' (p. 1). However, Gay points out that in the long run, diminishing her experience caused her more harm than comfort. In a similar way, the vloggers in our study used the *not that bad* discourse to cope with their experiences of sexual violence. On the other hand, most of them also point out its flaws and reveal their understanding of their experiences as valid, harmful, important to share, and connected to the experiences of other women from across the continuum of sexual violence, as is consistent with the *truth-telling* counter-discourse (Almanssori & Stanley, 2021).

The finding of the *truth-telling* counter-discursive theme evidences women's coming to understand sexual violence at the structural level in a post-#MeToo world. Mendes et al. (2018) call this a transformation from solidarity to a feminist consciousness and write that it is a common experience amongst participants of hashtag feminism. Moreover, 'as feminist hashtag movements weave intimate truths into wider social stories', they set the motions for a world in which 'responsibility for sexual violence can be understood as a social and institutional problem' (Clarke-Vivier & Stearns, 2019, p. 59). This truth-telling movement is present in various public spaces wherein women practice epistemic justice (du Toit, 2009) by telling their stories and listening and responding to others' stories.

Vlogging, creative practice and feminist aesthetics

This section unpacks how the YouTube vlogs we analysed (Almanssori & Stanley, 2021) can constitute an 'aesthetic rupture' that Clover et al. theorize in the introduction of this book. Existing literature, though still in its infancy, has begun to explore the digital sphere as a form of public pedagogy, but is yet to theorize the creative potential of platforms as part of Wildermeesch's (2019) 'aesthetic turn'. As Wildermeesch articulates 'education and arts are aesthetic because they relate to (the questioning of) the order of "what makes sense"', and that 'changes in aesthetic regimes often are signals or symptoms of changes in the way we understand the social, cultural and political order' (p. 117). Meanwhile, Dentith and Brady (1999) state that public pedagogies involve the examination of daily experience and the complex interactions between the self, media and popular culture, and thereby create sites of struggle in which 'images, contradictory discourses, canonical themes and stories, and common-sense versions of reality are disputed' (p. 1). Given these definitions, both of which highlight the piercing of the status quo and the centring alternative ways of knowing, it can be argued that feminist public pedagogy in its various forms can certainly constitute aesthetic regime.

In my review of the literature on media education and digital literacy, I have found that both news media and scholarly conversations often give more focus to the detriments of social media and its perpetuation sexist and sexual violence (e.g., Bragg, 2006; Buckingham, 2007). However, I join other feminist and media studies scholars in conceding that social media platforms can be deeply transformative spaces insofar as users and creators exercise resistance and social change (Caron et al., 2017; Garcia & Vemuri, 2017; Mendes et al., 2018; Raby et al., 2017). The research we conducted (Almanssori & Stanley, 2021) provides evidence that discourses are 'multiple, and they offer competing, potentially contradictory ways of giving meaning to the world' (Gavey, 1989, p. 464) and that individuals can resist dominant discourses and produce counter-discourses (Cahill, 2000).

The vloggers practised resistance by narrating their own embodied experiences, and reflecting on how they previously understood sexual violence, as contrasted to how they have come to see it in a post-#MeToo world (Almanssori & Stanley, 2021). By narrating the counter-discursive of sexual violence using aesthetic medium, the vloggers contribute to digital spaces in which the feminist imaginary can flourish. In my findings, YouTube vlogs were forms of critical self and social reflection and political activism and counter-discursive (Almanssori & Stanley, 2021). YouTube thus extends the collective feminist consciousness of the #MeToo movement that originated on Twitter by allowing for a slower, deep engagement of the virtual storying involved in vlogging.

Undoubtedly, the discussion of feminist public pedagogy as aesthetic practice cannot neglect the imaginative visual production involved in filming a vlog and the creative digital skills involved in editing, uploading and distributing it across platforms. This includes things like engaging with audiences even past production with practices such as responding to comments and reactions. Audience members also practice aesthetic meaning making by engaging with vlogger, narrative, content to answer their questions about a topic, rather than, for example, seeking an article online or 'expert' insight. Although within our research (Almanssori & Stanley, 2021) we discuss the vlogs as forms of public pedagogy, yet to be examined in the literature is how engagement with vlogs as aesthetic content, particularly that which is made by women engaging in the counter-discursive, can be used within traditional classroom settings to augment learning. Certainly, education is not limited to the classroom, but it is still a question worth asking given that much of the literature on feminist praxis is situated in the postsecondary setting (Almanssori, 2020).

The YouTube videos that we studied were youth created and youth accessed; they were a form of sexual violence education that is intended primarily for youth, by youth. The term youth is of course used loosely, to represent young people including those in early adulthood. Feminist understandings of public pedagogy thus are at odds with the myth that youth consume media in a passive and disengaged manner (Raby et al., 2017). Although such platforms often reflect broader political, cultural and systemic inequities that circulate in the social world (Phipps, 2019), users and creators nevertheless have agency to produce, share and make meaning within them (Bragg, 2006). This agentic power is multiplied through the heightened visibility and broader network of the content that is distributed and redistributed throughout social media platforms. Movements such as #MeToo are emblematic of when this agentic power becomes collective social action, and narrative platforms such as YouTube that allow users to engage with the aesthetic feminist imaginary can serve to amplify this power.

Conclusions

In addition to sex educators and sexual violence prevention practitioners, the discussion in this chapter is of importance to media literacy educators and scholars. According to Bragg (2006), media education at its best is not preventative, but rather, 'it is not an inoculation against pernicious media influence, but instead about enabling young people to participate in media cultures and make their own meanings and interpretations' (p. 322). The same can be said about sex education – feminist scholars have been pushing for a more nuanced and comprehensive approach to education that focuses on pleasure, ethics and the complexities of consent (Fine, 1988; Fine & McClelland, 2006) and highlighting that these lessons are critical for sexual violence prevention (Carmody, 2015). Literature has also pointed us to see discursive understandings of sexual violence as crucial to prevention efforts. As Lazar (2007) explains, sexual violence can be an overt form of power but is more often 'a subtle and seemingly innocuous form of power that is substantively discursive in nature' (p. 148). Therein lies the strength of research that examines the discursive components of meaning making in relation to sexual ethics and sexual violence (Almanssori & Stanley, 2021; Durham, 2015; Hindes & Fileborn, 2020). Furthermore, where the counter-discursive and the aesthetic come together to inform the feminist imaginary on digital platforms is an area worthy of further scholarship.

My answer to the question posed at the beginning of this chapter (what do youth online learn about sex and rape?) is complex and unfinished. Youth engage with public pedagogy on sex and sexual violence in active and multifaceted ways, including both those that are regressive and progressive (Gavey, 2019), exemplified through my research on YouTube as a counter-discursive space for sexual violence pedagogy (Almanssori & Stanley, 2021). Scholarship into the feminist pedagogical possibilities of social media platforms in general is still at its infancy. In this chapter, such possibilities were discussed in relation to the aesthetic turn in education. As hashtag feminism, which is a key part of the 'feminist media repertoire' (Clark-Parsons, 2019, p. 1), moved into YouTube and women began vlogging their experiences in a deeply narrative platform, they, along with their audiences, engaged in aesthetic meaning making that troubles taken for granted ways of understanding sexual violence.

References

Almanssori, S. (2020). Feminist pedagogy from pre-access to post-truth: A genealogical literature review. *Canadian Journal for New Scholars in Education/Revue canadienne des jeunes chercheures et chercheurs en éducation, 11*(1), 54–68.

Almanssori, S., & Stanley, M. (2021). Public pedagogy on sexual consent and violence: A feminist discourse analysis of YouTube vlogs after #MeToo. *Journal of Curriculum and Pedagogy*, 1–24. DOI: 10.1080/15505170.2021.1895382

Anderson, I. (2007). What is a typical rape? Effects of victim and participant gender in female and male rape perception. *The British Journal of Social Psychology, 46*(1), 225–45.

Berman, H., McKenna, K., Arnold, C. T., Taylor, G., & MacQuarrie, B. (2000). Sexual harassment: Everyday violence in the lives of girls and women. *Advances in Nursing Science, 22*(4), 32–46.

Bragg, S. (2006). 'Having a real debate': Using media as a resource in sex education. *Sex Education, 6*(4), 317–31.

Brownmiller, S. (1975). *Against our will: Men, women, and rape.* Simon & Schuster.

Buchwald, E., Fletcher, P. R., & Roth, M. (Eds.). (1993). *Transforming a rape culture.* Milkweed Editions.

Buckingham, D. (2007). Digital media literacies: Rethinking media education in the age of the internet. *Research in Comparative and International Education, 2*(1), 43–55.

Butler, J. (2011). Sexual consent: Some thoughts on psychoanalysis and law. *Columbia Journal of Gender and Law, 21*(2), 405–29.

Cahill, A. J. (2000). Foucault, rape, and the construction of the feminine body. *Hypatia, 15*(1), 43–63.

Carmody, M. (2009). Conceptualising the prevention of sexual assault and the role of education. *Australian Institute of Family Studies,* (10), 1–20.

Carmody, M. (2015). *Sex, ethics, and young people*. Springer.

Caron, C., Raby, R., Mitchell, C., Thewissen-leblanc, S., & Prioletta, J. (2017). From concept to data: Sleuthing social change-oriented youth voices on YouTube. *Journal of Youth Studies, 20*(1), 47–62.

Casey, E. A., & Lindhorst, T. P. (2009). Toward a multi-level, ecological approach to the primary prevention of sexual assault. *Trauma, Violence, & Abuse, 10*(2), 91–114.

Clark-Parsons, R. (2019). 'I SEE YOU, I BELIEVE YOU, I STAND WITH YOU': #MeToo and the performance of networked feminist visibility. *Feminist Media Studies, 21*(3), 1–19, 362–80.

Clarke-Vivier, S., & Stearns, C. (2019). MeToo and the problematic valor of truth: Sexual violence, consent, and ambivalence in public pedagogy. *Journal of Curriculum Theorizing, 34*(3), 55–75.

Collins, P. H. (2015). Intersectionality's definitional dilemmas. *Annual Review of Sociology, 41*, 1–20.

Crenshaw, K. (1989). Demarginalizing the intersection of race and sex: A black feminist critique of antidiscrimination doctrine, feminist theory and antiracist politics. *University of Chicago Legal Forum, 1989*, 139–68.

Dentith, A. M., & Brady, J. (1999, October). *Theories of public pedagogies as possibilities for ethical action and community resistance: A curricular notion*. Paper presented at the *AERA: Research on Women and Education SIG Conference*. Hempstead, NY.

Dentith, A. M., O'Malley, M. P., & Brady, J. F. (2014). Public pedagogy as a historically feminist project. In J. Burdick, J. A., Sandlin, & M. P. O'Malley (Eds.), *Problematizing public pedagogy* (pp. 26–39). Routledge.

Dobson, A. S., & Ringrose, J. (2016). Sext education: Pedagogies of sex, gender and shame in the schoolyards of Tagged and Exposed. *Sex Education, 16*(1), 8–21.

Durham, M. G. (2015). Scene of the crime: News discourse of rape in India and the geopolitics of sexual assault. *Feminist Media Studies, 15*(2), 175–91.

Du Toit, L. (2009). Introduction: Meaning/s of rape in war and peace. *Philosophical Papers, 38*(3), 285–305.

Estrich, S. (1987). *Real rape*. Harvard University Press.

Fenner, L. (2017). Sexual consent as a scientific subject: A literature review. *American Journal of Sexuality Education, 12*, 451–71.

Fine, M. (1988). Sexuality, schooling, and adolescent females: The missing discourse of desire. *Harvard Educational Review, 58*(1), 29–54.

Fine, M., & McClelland, S. (2006). Sexuality education and desire: Still missing after all these years. *Harvard Educational Review, 76*(3), 297–338.

Gallagher, R. J., Stowell, E., Parker, A. G., & Foucault Welles, B. (2019). Reclaiming stigmatized narratives: The networked disclosure landscape of #MeToo. *Proceedings of the ACM on Human-Computer Interaction, 3* (CSCW), 1–30.

Garcia, C. K., & Vemuri, A. (2017a). Girls and young women resisting rape culture through YouTube videos. *Girlhood Studies, 10*(2), 26–44.

Gavey, N. (1989). Feminist poststructuralism and discourse analysis: Contributions to feminist psychology. *Psychology of Women Quarterly, 13*(4), 459–75.

Gavey, N. (2005). *Just sex? The cultural scaffolding of rape*. Routledge.

Gavey, N. (2015). *Just sex? the cultural scaffolding of rape*. Routledge.

Gavey, N. (2019). *Just sex? the cultural scaffolding of rape* (2nd ed.). Routledge.

Gay, R. (2018). *Not that bad: Dispatches from rape culture*. Harper Perennial.

Gilbert, J. (2018). Contesting consent in sex education. *Sex Education, 18*(3), 268–79.

Halley, J. (2016). The move to affirmative consent. *Signs: Journal of Women in Culture and Society, 42*(1), 257–79.

Harris, K. (2018). Yes means yes and no means no, but both mantras need to go: Communication myth in consent education and anti-rape activism. *Journal of Applied Communication Research, 46*(2), 155–78.

Hickey-Moody, A., Savage, G. C., & Windle, J. (2010). Pedagogy writ large: Public, popular and cultural pedagogies in motion. *Critical Studies in Education, 51*(3), 227–36.

Hindes, S., & Fileborn, B. (2020). 'Girl power gone wrong': #MeToo, Aziz Ansari, and media reporting of (grey area) sexual violence. *Feminist Media Studies, 20*(5), 639–56.

Hlavka, H. R. (2014). Normalizing sexual violence: Young women account for harassment and abuse. *Gender & Society, 28*(3), 337–58.

hooks, b. (1981). *Ain't I a woman: Black women and feminism*. South End Press.

hooks, b. (2004). *Understanding patriarchy: The will to change: Men, masculinity, and love*. Washington Square Press.

hooks, b. (2015). Feminism is fun! *The Bell Hooks Institute*. http://www.bellhooksinstitute.com/blog/2015/12/12/feminism-is-fun-by-bell-hooks

Kelly, L. (1987). The continuum of sexual violence. In J. Hanmar & M. Maynard (Eds.), *Women, violence and social control* (pp. 46–60). Palgrave Macmillan.

Lazar, M. M. (2007). Feminist critical discourse analysis: Articulating a feminist discourse praxis. *Critical Discourse Studies, 4*(2), 141–64.

Lonsway, K. A., & Fitzgerald, L. F. (1994). Rape myths: In review. *Psychology of Women Quarterly, 18*(2), 133–64.

Luke, C. (Ed.). (1996). *Feminisms and pedagogies of everyday life*. SUNY Press.

McMahon, S., & Banyard, V. L. (2012). When can I help? A conceptual framework for the prevention of sexual violence through bystander intervention. *Trauma, Violence, & Abuse, 13*(1), 3–14.

McMahon, S., Postmus, J. L., & Koenick, R. A. (2011). Conceptualizing the engaging bystander approach to sexual violence prevention on college campuses. *Journal of College Student Development, 52*(1), 115–30.

Meaney, G. J., Rye, B. J., Wood, E., & Solovieva, E. (2009). Satisfaction with school-based sexual health education in a sample of university students recently graduated from Ontario high schools. *Canadian Journal of Human Sexuality, 18*(3), 107–25.

Mendes, K., Ringrose, J., & Keller, J. (2018). #MeToo and the promise and pitfalls of challenging rape culture through digital feminist activism. *European Journal of Women's Studies, 25*(2), 236–46.

Milano, A. (2017, October 15). If you've been sexually harassed or assaulted, write 'me too' as a reply to this tweet. [Twitter Post]. https://twitter.com/alyssa_milano/status/919659438700670976?lang=en

Phipps, A. (2019). "Every woman knows a Weinstein": Political whiteness and white woundedness in #MeToo and public feminisms around sexual violence. *Feminist Formations, 31*(2), 1–25.

Raby, R., Caron, C., Théwissen-leblanc, S., Prioletta, J., & Mitchell, C. (2017). Vlogging on YouTube: The online, political engagement of young Canadians advocating for social change. *Journal of Youth Studies, 21*(4), 495–511.

Sandlin, J. A., O'Malley, M. P., & Burdick, J. (2011). Mapping the complexity of public pedagogy scholarship: 1894–2010. *Review of Educational Research, 81*(3), 338–75.

Stout, K. D. (1991). A continuum of male controls and violence against women: A teaching model. *Journal of Social Work Education, 27*(3), 305–19.

Valenti, J. (2009). *The Purity myth: How America's obsession with virginity is hurting young women.* Seal Press.

Wildermeesch, D. (2019). Adult education and aesthetic experience. *European Journal for Research on the Education and Learning of Adults, 10*(2), 11–17.

Chapter 10

We Are Here and We Are Not a 'Minority': Co-creating a Decolonizing Feminist Space and Narrative for Non-white Women through Photography

Suriani Dzulkifli

Introduction

'I have everyone's phone number saved in my phone except for yours. Because I didn't know how to spell your last name.' These were the words uttered to me by a former co-worker few summers ago in 2019. Everyone on our team was female. But I was the only person who is not white, and a non-Canadian, coming from Malaysia. When she uttered those words, we were all having breakfast on the ferry to Vancouver to attend a conference in a town an hour away from Vancouver. I expected a follow-up from her, but there was none. There was an awkward silence on my part. I wondered, what was the point of saying those sentiments to me? I was too shocked and perplexed at the time to say anything constructive, too flabbergasted by her audacity to insinuate that my surname was too difficult to spell and not worthy of her time to learn. We had been working together for over a year. How could she so nonchalantly speak like this to me and in the presence of our team? Did I feel singled out? Absolutely. Did I feel discriminated against? Absolutely. Did I feel she was being subtly racist? Absolutely. I was not new to facing covert racism or racism in general but this incident clearly stayed with me. I was disappointed that none of my team members had seen anything wrong with her prejudiced words. They were eating silently. In their defence, they might have been too hungry from travelling or not heard her clearly. That, and also *maybe* how society, has come to normalize racism, especially the hard-to-recognize implied or covert racism. This normalization, which I elaborate further in this chapter, has an impact. I have remembered Every. Single. Detail. About it.

My former colleague might not call herself a feminist, but she is female and this event contributed to my scepticism of feminism. I was unfamiliar as I had grown up in a household where all of us, my brothers included, were expected to do the same chores irrespective of our gender. I only become cognizant of the term feminism when I began my undergraduate education in Canada. It was a politics course taught by a white male professor who exposed me to feminism and feminist movements. What he was teaching us was the normative problematic 'waves of feminism' conceptualized in and about the United States. Supposedly, these waves were meant to represent all women globally, and how their lives had progressed. However, listening to his lectures, and reading the required materials, I did not feel represented in this narrative. At all. I did not feel like I was part of this so-called movement to 'liberate' women and fight for women's rights. In fact, I began to believe it was a purely American/Western construct. Moreover, why had he not at least invited a woman guest speaker? What experiences could he possibly have had that would enable him to understand the struggles of women around the world? This unrelatable and narrow positioning of the lives of women and their struggles turned me away from what he called 'feminism'. This did not mean I disagreed or was unaware of women's rights and other gender justice issues, but I did not see this particular discourse of universalising 'feminism', positioned through a male perspective, as related to me. There were layers of my identity and my struggles that were being ignored in the discourse or at least not central to this framing of a 'global' movement, including my cultural and spiritual backgrounds and beliefs. These layers of my identity were significant in informing the kinds of experiences – negative or positive – I endured as a woman, as well as for other women I knew. I have come to realize just how 'standard' and normative these American/Western waves are to our historical understandings of feminism and a lot has been left out or lost.

But of course, all is not lost or forgotten. Non-white feminists worldwide who do not see themselves or their societies in the constricting 'waves' have expanded the discourse of feminism, drawing on their own experiences to articulate and practise it differently (e.g., Hamad, 2019; hooks, 2014). I use the terms 'white' and 'non-white' throughout this chapter as political, rather than physically descriptive.

Yet it remains imperative to continue to have discussions surrounding the dynamics of feminisms and race in order to expand the discourse of feminism and challenge systemic patriarchy. In this chapter, I discuss how I used photography to facilitate these conversations with non-white women students at my university. I begin with a discussion of 'feminism' through the decolonizing lens, focusing most specifically on white privilege and the impact its denial has had on non-white women. Following this, I discuss photography as a feminist tool focussing most specifically on images made by two non-white international student participants, Layla and Rae (pseudonyms), who took part in a photography-based study with me as part of my doctoral thesis.

Feminism and white privilege: Is there a place for non-white women in feminism?

As someone who is not white and a visitor living, studying and working in Canada, I have noticed there has always been this lingering notion – implied or not – that if you are deemed as 'different' by society, you will automatically be labelled as 'unliberated'. My experience, therefore, is that you are then seen as 'oppressed'. I find this an irony, especially when Canada prides itself for its multiracial and diverse population. Despite Canada being multiracial, I couldn't help but question *whose* society we are referring to? I have observed there can only be one standard – or societal norm – in this Canadian society, and that dominating standard is the Western white standard, also known as the Western gaze (Chao-Ju Chen, 2007). This Western gaze underlines white privilege and contributes to the normalization of racism I previously mentioned. This white standard and privilege bring an unfair advantage to people who are hereditary white, established by Western patriarchal power through colonialism. In understanding white privilege, we must recognize that its existence was due to the violent acts of 'divide and conquer' imperialism, of the physical and psychological colonialism of lands, peoples and resources by Western patriarchies, including Canada. Colonialism solidified both a patriarchal system and, in parts of the world like Canada and the 'common wealth', white supremacy. As time passed, remnants of colonialism have been erased from (some) history books but it is well and alive today, albeit in different guises such as systemic racism and sexism. In other words, many parts of the world are still grappling with the violence of colonialism, manifest in the wars of several Middle Eastern countries, concentration camps to torture and murder the Uyghurs in China, caging and separation of 'illegal' immigrant families in the United States, genocide of the Rohingyas in Myanmar and the case of hundreds of missing and murdered Indigenous women and girls in Canada.

A major challenge is that many white people, including white women, are unwilling to acknowledge the privilege of their race. As hooks (2014, p. 55) argues, 'all white women … know that whiteness is a privileged category. The fact that white females may choose to repress or deny this knowledge does not mean they are ignorant: it means that they are in denial'. This denial is dangerous and problematic to the advancement of feminism as it perpetuates the very patriarchal system we have been trying as feminists to dismantle. White privilege is worn, as McIntosh (1989) noted, as an 'invisible package of unearned assets which I can count on cashing in each day, but about which I was "meant" to remain oblivious' (p. 10). Her description of white privilege supports the notion that whether one was willing to recognize it or not, white women have been heavily indoctrinated into this mindset with major implications, as Hamad (2019, p. 22) states so eloquently: 'It is how white society regards you. It is how white society treats you. Because you, as a woman of colour, do not measure up to their image of what a woman is and should be in order to be believed, supported and defended.' Hamad's words affirm my concerns with a universalism of feminism taught to me as 'white' womanhood. This white standard in feminism silences other women facing different kinds of struggles because they are not white. This alone is very problematic and promotes exclusivity that non-white women have no place in feminism. Going back to the incident with my former colleague, I now recognize the presence of her white privilege gave her the ammunition to be able to say things that would make me feel excluded and stood out in a negative way, without flinching and fearing of dealing with consequences. It did not matter we were both women. I was 'different', because my last name did not fit her white standard. There was neither womanhood nor spirits of feminism there.

Further reflections on the incident had me thinking, what I could have done differently in the situation? This reflection was both sad and empowering. It is sad for the fact I have to think there will be a next time, but empowering in that the next time it happens, I would be more prepared to use my voice and stand up for myself. However, one thing I could not shake off from my mind was this unspoken fear. The fear that regardless of how excluded or diminished I feel, my feelings would not be taken seriously or be seen as valid, instead I would be seen as the one who could not take a 'joke', or who makes a big deal out of 'nothing', or worse, an 'aggressor'. All in the name of preserving this white societal norm. If this preservation was not a possibility, society would not stereotypically view women in the Black community as 'the Angry Black Woman', or women in the Latin community as 'the Fiery (meaning hot-tempered) Latin Woman' or women in the Asian community as 'the Dragon Lady', referring to all of these non-white women's temperaments, marginalizing them further whenever they tend to speak up for themselves or respond in a way that is not a portrayal of their timid and docile selves as expected and believed by the mainstream Western norm. Hamad (2019, p. 24) explains, 'This culture of fear has stayed with us. This weaponisation of [w]hite [w]omanhood continues to be the centrepiece of an arsenal used to maintain the status quo and punish anyone who dares challenge it.' Speaking up for non-white women, whether in general or against white women who had harmed us subtly with their words to fit us into their societal standard would mean we must be one of those stereotyped characters based on our heritage. It is unthinkable that non-white women could ever speak up because we feel discriminated based on our race, ethnicity, skin colour and/or other attributes over which we have no control. This fear was perhaps why I refrained from having a conversation with my former co-worker afterwards. Unfortunately, at an early age, we have been conditioned by society to think subtle racism is not detrimental to our beings. It is viewed as something 'trivial'. Most would label it as just a 'harmless' statement. After all, she did not physically assault me, so I should be fine. But the depth of the internal scarring I felt has stayed with me until today. I still think about it every now and then. It was a prejudice against me based on my name, a huge part of my identity, my cultural heritage and who I am.

Bigger picture: White privilege denial produces the 'visible minority'

As Song (2002) emphasizes, 'many well-intentioned people who do not see themselves as racist can end up reinforcing racially discriminatory structures and institutions' (n/p). Being in denial of their white privilege 'excuses' them from taking responsibility to challenge their understanding of how their privilege contributes to the widening racial gap. Embracing this white privilege denial brings repercussions at the expense of others on the margins as it has an impact on the kinds of policies that are written and produced since racism is a systemic issue. This includes the kinds of words and languages used to categorize people, including non-white women. As I have highlighted, words can be harmful and leave lasting negative impacts on people.

One example of this is the term 'visible minority' used in Canada to describe anyone who is not white. It was created as a part of the Employment Equity Act, which defined visible minority as 'persons, other than Aboriginal peoples, who are non-Caucasian in race or non-white in colour' (Statistics Canada, 2015, n/p). While the intention of creating such terms was to promote hiring equity among non-white people including women, the generalization of non-white ethnicities into one 'minority' group risks the homogenization of experiences of each unique ethnic group. This homogenization is very contrary to the intention and purpose of creating a term to provide 'visibility' for non-white people. Song (2020) highlights, 'Visibility (signifying non-White) has been central to our understandings of a stigmatized ethnic minority status. But exactly who is considered visible in constantly changing and diversifying multi-ethnic societies, is less than clear' (n.p.).

Non-white women as 'visible minorities' are often discriminated against as a 'double minority'. Henry (2015), a Black woman professor and head of department at a Canadian university, experienced this first-hand, stating,

> I found myself working in an environment in which certain white colleagues did not seem to care what they said in my presence, or perhaps I should say, that they seemed unaware of the messages of undesirability and inferiority that they were communicating regarding people of colour … one of my staff found no shame in sharing racist comments about students who were not white.
>
> (p. 598)

Her experience was somewhat similar to mine; we often find ourselves to be in uncongenial situations having to deal with racism despite having the Employment Equity Act to 'protect' us against discrimination. Evidently, the given term of 'visible minority' to non-white people, especially women, does the opposite of protecting us from discrimination. It diminishes us to our identity as a 'double minority' and is a constant reminder of our lesser racial and gender (systemic) power. It invites the opportunity for white people to marginalize us further, as Henry recounted. Moreover, the United Nations asked Canada to reconsider using the term 'visible minorities' as the phrase itself is discriminatory (Term, 2007). Thus, it is better to spell out each racial and/or ethnic group as a way to amplify their identity and experiences appropriately.

Photography and feminism

In centring the voices and experiences of other non-white women as part of my doctoral study, I adopted the use of photography. It is important to state at the outset that photography has not always been viewed in a positive light. Predominantly, the use of photography in research was introduced in anthropology as a passive instrument of collecting data by capturing photos of artefacts, nature, cultural practices in an attempt to understand a particular community without the active engagement of the community. Strack (2004) has since found that researchers then hold power in narrating and interpreting the stories and meanings behind the photographs and 'may therefore fail to capture the insider's (emic) perspective' (p. 49).

While photography has its own challenges, feminist researchers have used it as a creative and critical tool of empowerment for silenced individuals and communities, including non-white women (e.g., Yang, 2014). Photography permits marginalized individuals and communities to speak of their difficult experiences. Additionally, feminist scholars argue that using 'the principles of feminist theory ... no one is in a better position to study and understand the issues of a group than are the people within that group, and that discovery is best promoted through shared experience' (Strack et al., 2004, p. 49). Photography research methods invite participants to take series of photos based on a theme/topic. Participatory photography like photovoice allows individuals to be actively involved in narrating their unique experiences through visual representations, symbols, metaphors and juxtapositions they take in a series of snapshots based on their own viewpoints of a chosen theme. Photographers hold the power of delineating their own stories and making meaning of their own experiences in their own voices through visual images. Since photography produces visual images, it aids participants to express themselves without the worry of using a common spoken language perfectly, as was the case of my study, since English is not the first language for most of the participants. Photography research allows participants the space to reflect on their personal experiences and expand their awareness of social issues as women are experts of their own knowledge based on their everyday experiences. With the expanded consciousness of how their personal experiences are impacted by political situations in this patriarchal society, they will then have the potential capacity to act and improve their reality and/or the reality of society. Photography allows participants to be both reflective and reflexive.

Co-creating a decolonizing feminist space for non-white women through photography

My experience of facing covert racism that I previously shared is not an isolated example. It is a small sliver of what many other non-white women have experienced. For my doctoral research, I organized a three-day workshop and recruited other international student participants from various countries in Asia, South America, the Middle East and the Caribbean. The participants were non-white, and five out of the six were women. They were a mix of international undergraduate and graduate students. The overall objective of my doctoral research is to inquire about international students' awareness regarding social justice issues, including gender justice, through their formal and non-formal education and informal learning on campus. These issues could either be new issues they learnt from living and studying in Canada, or issues they faced since arriving in Canada. I was also interested in finding out the kinds of action they might have taken to improve the unjust situations in their home countries or later in life. However, in this chapter I only focus on the discussions specific to some of the problematic issues pertaining to their journey in Canada that informed their experiences as non-white, international student women.

Photovoice

For my research, I used a practice of participatory photography called photovoice and the theme of social justice. I had set this very broad theme to enable participants the greatest creativity in terms of expressing and exploring their experiences, both positive and negative. The participants wandered around the university grounds separately taking four to five abstract photographs that represented the idea of social (in)justice. I chose photovoice as a more specific photography research method for several reasons. The first is because photovoice is used a lot in communities as visualizing/storytelling tool for empowerment, especially when working with marginalized groups, such as non-white women. Methods like photovoice create spaces for women who have been under-represented and silenced, in my case non-white international student women, to speak both visually and orally to issues they may have endured on their everyday lives in a foreign country and university. Photovoice allows them to acknowledge, narrate and explore their experiences in their own voices through the lens of a camera or other photographic devices. This exploration through the meaning-making of creative representation, symbols and metaphors using photography enables them to act as agents of change, having the capacity to identify and reflect on their personal experiences and challenges.

Secondly, photovoice images have the ability to raise critical consciousness in individuals. Leavy (2015) explains that visual images such as photovoice 'can evoke particular kinds of emotional and visceral responses from people; they are typically filed in the subconscious without the same conscious interpretive process people engage in when confronted with a written text' (p. 225). The powerful impact visual images have on our emotions provides us with a different kind of consciousness that encourages us to become reflexive upon our reflected thoughts. When individuals become agents of change through their learning, it is indeed more meaningful as they carry out informed actions and bring about change in their lives through the different positions they hold in their personal and professional capacities.

Thirdly, Yang (2014) found that in using photovoice her participants developed 'a sense of the agency of intentions, meaning seeking actively to bring about change in one's life in a positive way, through self-reflection, social interaction, therapeutic experience or gained knowledge of photography (the method itself)' (p. 247). She wrote, 'attending to their intentions to bring about change in their lives is as important as attending to how they actually act. This intention is what I think of as a critical, but often underrated, component that constitutes agency' (Yang,

2014, p. 247). This was the case for my participants. The photovoice activity we did and the collective discussions we had surrounding each photo inspired and shifted our conversation to a higher level of consciousness. We were actively thinking of attainable ways to bring about change in our lives and towards the amelioration of our most vulnerable members of society, particularly Indigenous women (and girls), and the unhoused community. The raised consciousness developed through this activity also helped us to recognize that some of us were already agents of change through our different engagements outside of the classrooms such as volunteering through clubs.

That really happened: Amplifying non-white women experiences of racism and Islamophobia

During the photovoice activity, several different subthemes under the umbrella theme of social justice emerged. Interestingly, no participants chose the same themes. This confirmed my purpose of having the broad theme to allow the participants to stay true to their experiences and awareness of social justice. Two of the chosen themes had direct correlations with the women's racial and spiritual backgrounds and beliefs, and how the continued discriminations they face informed their awareness and experiences as non-white, non-Canadian women. Coincidentally, both of these participants, Layla and Rae, were Black Muslim women but from different countries and parts of the world. Both wore the hijab, so it was apparent by their appearances they were Muslims. They took a series of photos that they used to story their experiences of racism and Islamophobia as non-white women in Canada. Although both Layla and Rae focused on one main theme (one had chosen racism, the other Islamophobia), when sharing their experiences and narratives behind representations of their photos, they had touched on the overlapping experiences of facing both racism and Islamophobia in Canada.

Experiencing racism: Two stories

Layla, who chose the theme of racism, shared her budding realizations that she was viewed differently by people around her while taking the morning bus to the university which was part of her daily routine. She shared this by taking a photograph of the bus route number located at the stop at the main bus loop on campus (see Figure 10.1). Layla had frequently taken this particular bus route from her house to the university and vice versa. In explaining the meaning of her photo, she described that she was living in a very white area. Around the time she would ride the bus, she was possibly the only Black woman who also a visible Muslim was given her appearance. She shared that while on the bus, she noticed she would get weird looks from other passengers including non-white women; some would purposely make it obvious they were glaring at her. Layla recognized

Figure 10.1 *The bus stop*. Photo by Layla.

several faces by the frequency of taking the same bus. She spoke to how it was a 'normal' occurrence that when someone would first sit next to her, they would immediately move and sit elsewhere once they had taken a look at her. In sharing her experience of people's avoidance to sit beside her, Layla noted how at times when the bus was very packed, people would still actively avoid sitting beside her even when it was the only empty seat. Occasionally, people would make racist comments about her appearance.

Through the metaphoric representation of her photo, Layla told a story of overt and covert forms of racism. She noted how taking the photo had given her a means to tell her story and to reflect differently on her personal experiences. In fact, she had not really given the experiences much thought. The photo is simple, a bus stop but her stories is not just a simple bus journey. It speaks to Layla's expanded consciousness, to her bravery to admit how these spiteful racist acts and incidents affected her. The photovoice project had given her a platform to acknowledge the unkind words and stares, to recognize that although these 'normal' occurrences should not be 'normal'. Layla had challenged herself to unlearn the normalization of subtle racism. It was more heartbreaking when she told us that prior moving to Canada, she had looked forward to 'gett[ing] on the bus, hav[ing] a good time, go[ing] to campus and to class'. Layla had not let these incidences, nor her recognition of them, break her spirits. She attended anti-racism workshops on campus and was a volunteer with the Human Rights club.

The experience of Islamophobia

Rae chose Islamophobia as her theme but share very similar racist encounters that she experienced on the bus. However, the photos she had taken to depict her experience were different. One of the photos was of a yellow tape with the words 'CAUTION DO NOT ENTER' (see Figure 10.2). This tape was continuously wrapped around several trees creating barriers to access the enclosed area skirted by the tape. Rae's story was that although she had experienced several instances of Islamophobia on campus, the worst of these happened to her was on a bus.

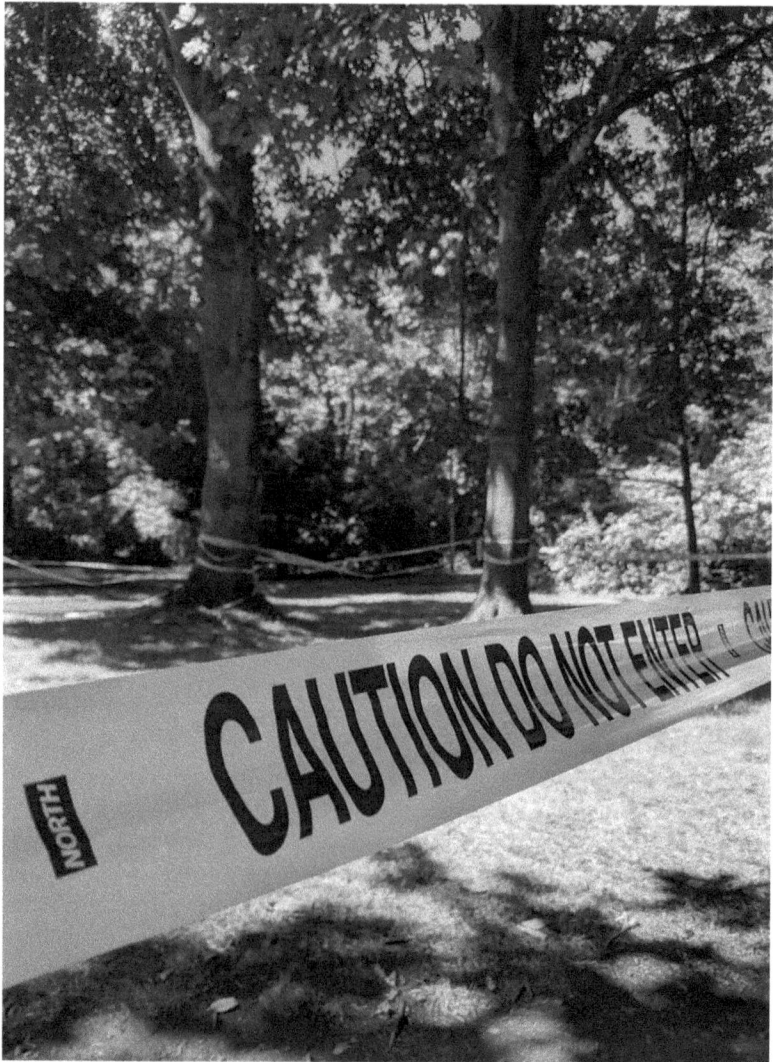

Figure 10.2 *Caution do not enter.* Photo by Rae.

Rae told stories of keeping her eyes downcast to avoid eye contact. In sharing the depiction of her photo, she recalled a man coming up to her out of nowhere and cursing at her, using racial slurs in a packed bus. He yelled that she did not belong in Canada and to go back to her country. While she endured his verbal assault silently, no one stood up for her to stop him, including white women passengers. Passive attitudes make people complicit. By not intervening, the people around her, including white women, enabled the damaging effects to happen right in front of them.

Through the photovoice activity, Rae told us of others in buses staring down at her in ways that she felt questioned her rights and identity. Although she prides herself as someone who is outspoken and proud of who she is, the stares never failed to intimidate and silence her.

For Rae, the photo captured her sense of aloneness and apartness from the others travelling on the bus, as though she was closed off by the tape. Like Layla, the photovoice project really encouraged Rae to think about these encounters. But the tape in the photo also symbolized something else. Rae defined this as 'something' that was prohibiting others from feeling any kind of empathy for her. Although this incident had happened a few years before she still remembered every detail, including the exact words said to her – testament of how words can have lasting, negative impacts, especially when someone is being attacked due to their identity. After the incident, Rae said that she was ready to leave Canada, disappointed that she had been so naïve in believing Canada was welcoming country. But she found herself reaching out to people she trusted and has created her own community of support. Rae has also become an advocate for others experiencing diverse forms of discrimination, especially Islamophobia and racism.

Where do we go from here?

The experiences of racism and Islamophobia shared by Layla and Rae tell us that while a regular activity like taking the bus for white women and men may not be a problem, it is for non-white women when skin colour and/or clothing are different. Non-white women deal with constant uninvited stares for looking 'different', and hear too often the slurs. These women do not know which individual will curse them next, change seats or scream at them to get out of the country because of their appearances. These racist occurrences happen in public and private spaces. This is a deeply entrenched systemic problem which at the extreme can be fatal.

Non-white feminists have expanded feminism to include various forms of discriminations like racism and Islamophobia. The use of photography, of photovoice gave two non-white women a space to speak and to tell their stories that are different from their white counterparts. But for feminism to be fully inclusive, white women with inherited privilege must take responsibility by unpacking their own privilege to make space for multilayered identities of race, culture and spirituality, and find ways to speak out against racism and Islamophobia.

Author's note

As a Malaysian, I do not have a family name. To cite this chapter, please use my full name: Suriani Dzulkifli. This is another way to create visibility for non-white women like myself.

References

Chen, C.-J. (2007). The difference that differences make: Asian feminism and the politics of difference. *Asian Journal of Women's Studies, 13*(3), 7–36. https://doi.org/10.1080/12 259276.2007.11666028

hooks, b. (2014). *Feminism is for everybody*. Routledge.

Hamad, R. (2019). *White tears brown scars: How white feminism betrays women of colour.* Melbourne: Melbourne University Publishing Limited.

Henry, A. (2015). 'We especially welcome applications from members of visible minority groups': Reflections on race, gender and life at three universities. *Race Ethnicity and Education, 18*(5), 589–610. https://doi.org./10.1080/13613324.2015.1023787

Leavy, P. (2015). *Method meets art: Arts-based research practice* (2nd ed.). New York: The Guilford Press.

McIntosh, P. (1989). White privilege: Unpacking the invisible knapsack, *Peace and Freedom Magazine, July–August*, 10–12, Women's International League for Peace and Freedom, Philadelphia, PA. https://psychology.umbc.edu/files/2016/10/White-Privilege_McIntosh-1989.pdf

Song, M. (2002). Rethinking minority status and 'visibility'. *Comparative Migration Studies, 8*(5). https://doi.org/10.1186/s40878-019-0162-2

Statistics Canada. (2015). Visible minority of person. https://www23.statcan.gc.ca/imdb/p3Var.pl?Function=DEC&Id=45152

Strack, R. W., Magill, C., & McDonagh, K. (2004). Engaging youth through photovoice. *Health Promotion Practice, 5*(1), 49–58. https://doi.org/10.1177/1524839903258015

Term 'visible minorities' may be discriminatory, UN body warns Canada. (2007, March 8). *CBC News.* https://www.cbc.ca/news/canada/term-visible-minorities-may-be-discriminatory-un-body-warns-canada-1.690247

Yang, K.-H. (2014). Participatory photography: Can it help adult learners develop agency? *International Journal of Lifelong Education, 33*(2), 233–49. https://doi.org/10.1080/0260 1370.2013.852143

Part III

DECOLONIZING AND THE FEMINIST IMAGINARY

Chapter 11

Indigenous Feminist Aesthetic Work as Cultural Revitalization: Facilitating Uy'Skwuluwun

Dorothea Harris

Uy' skweyul (Good day). My name is Dorothea Harris. My parents are Sandra and William Good from Snuneymuxw First Nation. I was raised and taught in Snuneymuxw territory, and it is my responsibility to honour my Elders and their teachings, and to pass those teachings to the next generation. I am currently a guest living and working on Lekwungen, W̱SÁNEĆ and Sc'ianew territory, in Victoria, BC, Canada. Following the protocol that has been taught by my Elders, I give thanks to these Nations for allowing me on their territory. I also give thanks to the Elders and Knowledge Keepers who have given me permission to share their teachings.

Introduction

I was raised in an art studio on Nicol Street, on the south side of Nanaimo, BC. Our home was a community hub, a safe space for the locals to learn and create art. My Mum, Sandra Good, was a contemporary artist, competent in several mediums. She taught drawing, painting, pottery and eventually, silk screening and fashion design. Her traditional name, Thul Te Lada, translates to 'maker of beautiful things' in Hul'q'umi'num. It was given to her by my Grandmother (Dad's Mother), Tsum Quat (Hazel Good). My Dad, Tseskinakhen (William Good), was a carver who spent many years reviving the Coast Salish[1] art form by researching the archives of the local museums, using his art form to create plaques, totem poles, jewellery and prints. Together my parents collaborated, combining their non-Indigenous and Indigenous art styles into wearable Indigenous fashion. My parents continue to create art, as does my brother, a master carver, and my two sisters, who have a Coast Salish fashion design house called *Ay Lelum*, the *Good House of Design*.

I share this personal history because it embodies the teaching that is often spoken of by Elders in Coast Salish territory – we must know who we are and where we come from. 'We have been told many times, in many different ways that we can only speak about what we have experienced' (Brown, 2016, p. 4). Mithlo

(2009) also emphasizes asserting 'the primacy of self-narratives and self-naming ... of experiential knowledge while diminishing disembodied, cognitive theorising' (pp. 12–13). It is my experience of growing up in a culturally safe Indigenous feminist aesthetic workspace that has enabled me to recreate those spaces in the community work that I have done, and to now theorize on the principles, or what some may call 'best' practices, that support that work.

Discussing feminism

Theorizing Indigenous feminist aesthetic work as cultural revitalization requires a brief discussion of feminism. I grew up with my Grandma, Mum and Aunties, having leadership roles in my family. My Dad's Indigenous worldview was informed by teachings from his Grandfather and namesake William Good, and he sees himself as a feminist, often reminding me, 'we are matriarchal, you know'. Robina Thomas (2018), in her book *Protecting the Sacred Cycle: Indigenous Women and Leadership,* documents the leadership roles that women historically held, and continue to hold, in Coast Salish communities. She states, 'Our culture and traditions have teachings that embrace very similar perspectives to Indigenous feminists ... however, they are rooted in our snuw'uy'ulh (Indigenous ways of knowing and being)' (p. 33). Coast Salish Elder, Sarah Modeste explains that 'in our culture the women, from the beginning right from the time they are born are trained to be a leader' (as cited in Thomas, 2018, p. 42). My understanding of feminism comes from this perspective; it is rooted in the roles and responsibilities inherent in matriarchal leadership that exists in Indigenous communities and it is egalitarian in nature. As Thomas states, 'If we are to embrace our teachings, we must do this together – Indigenous women and men' (p. 34).

I also acknowledge that Indigenous feminism in Canada is a response to the detrimental impacts of colonization. 'Settler colonialism is a persistent social and political formation in which newcomers/colonizers/settlers come to a place, claim it is as their own, and do whatever it takes to disappear the Indigenous peoples that are there' (Arvin et al., 2013, p. 12). The impacts have often been disproportionately borne by women who were previously 'held in high regard because of their roles as givers of life, carriers of culture and tradition, caretakers of the land, healers, and carriers of language' (Thomas, 2018, p. 20) but 'whom settlers, colonial police, and officials considered sexually available and expendable' (Razack, 2015, p. 22). Indigenous women 'have paid psychologically, economically, socially, culturally, and politically because of state sex discrimination' (McIvor, 1999, p. 175). Several generations of Canadian Indigenous women endured the loss of their 'Indian status'[2] due to sex discrimination in Canada's Indian Act and subsequent removal from their communities as a result; having their children forcibly removed to attend residential schools, or through apprehension by the child welfare system; high rates of sexual abuse and suicide; and being six times more likely to be murdered than non-Indigenous women (Beattie et al., 2018; Kirmayer et al., 2003; Sherlock, 2017; Thomas, 2018).

Because 'Native communities became gendered communities as a result of colonialism' (Mithlo, 2009, p. 23), Indigenous resurgence has required taking up both feminism and returning to more traditional understandings of matriarchal leadership.

My journey with Indigenous aesthetic work

I have worked for twenty years in various areas of social work with many Indigenous women whose lives have been impacted by the multi-generational and multi-faceted impacts of colonization that 'has resulted … in the marginalisation and clientization of these groups in contemporary society' (Poonwassie & Charter, 2001, p. 64). One of my most vivid memories, when I was doing front-line work in an urban drop-in centre that served the homeless community, was a young woman who sat down in a Talking Circle and announced that she had been sexually abused by twenty-seven men in her life. She had also had her children apprehended by child welfare and lost her housing because she no longer qualified for low-income family housing without her children. This was not an isolated incident. Taking up Indigenous feminist aesthetic work in this environment evolved out of the needs of the women that I was working with.

I was the Programme Coordinator in the drop-in centre, and many of those who were homeless were also struggling with poor mental health and addictions. I discovered that aesthetic work grounded people who were suffering from post-traumatic stress disorder (PTSD) or substance withdrawals as it calmed their central nervous system, and I understood from my training that somatic work, or body work, could help move trauma out of the body (Rothschild, 2000). Doing something physical with the hands while participating in wellness programmes, for example, was extremely beneficial. One reason, as Clover (2012) notes, is because the arts 'provide a platform for individual voices to be heard' (p. 94). Beading, painting, cedar weaving, knitting and making medicine bags, dream catchers and button blankets, all became central to the programme offerings.

The women that I worked with were often not well supported culturally by programmes that used Western medical models of PTSD or addiction treatment, so I invited local Elders and Knowledge Keepers, 'someone who has knowledge and understanding of the traditional ways of his or her people, both the physical culture of the people and their spiritual tradition' (Malloch, 1989, p. 107), to facilitate the work. Indigenous communities have had ways of maintaining the physical, mental, emotional and spiritual health of their communities for thousands of years, and 'collective healing is an important step to maintaining and preserving our spiritual growth' (Brown, 2016, p. 45). The aesthetic work that the women engaged in also became a source of pride in themselves and their abilities, challenging the myth of their invisibility and disposability. As Atleo (2016) explains, 'the cultural revitalisation work of Indigenous women is a form of critical adult education that interrogates the socio-cultural myths that reduce the horizon of social consciousness and enables social justice and equities to promote societal change and transformation' (p. 36). Providing access to cultural programmes, finding funding, creating space to do the work and educating co-workers, administrators and funders about the work, was a social justice issue for me, and became a focus of my professional work.

Later in my career, I worked as the Manager of Education and Programmes for a small First Nations' community. The context was somewhat different, but there were also similarities. In Canada, Western knowledge has been engaged in what Hall and Tandon (2017) call 'epistemicide, or the killing of other knowledge systems' (p. 6) for hundreds of years, which is evidenced in urban and community settings, on and off reserves. The women in community had more access to participate in culture and ceremony than the women in the urban setting, but a loss of their Indigenous languages, traditional parenting practices and knowledge of women's aesthetic work, is a consistent impact of colonization. Furthermore, racism and discrimination within the child welfare system had severely impacted the families I was working with.

My work in this community focused on keeping children in school and monitoring their success, which required that they remained in their homes (not being removed by child welfare), and that parents or caregivers were resourced adequately. One of my strategies became offering parenting groups to mitigate child welfare involvement and strengthen the community. I connected with the local Native Friendship Centre, who provided the community with a cultural parenting specialist, Maria Sampson, a well-respected local First Nations woman who was taught weaving practices, and the accompanying traditional teachings, by her Elders.

Maria uses the revitalization of Coast Salish women's aesthetic practices, such as cedar and wool weaving, to teach traditional parenting practices in their embodied form. Atleo (2016) describes survivance as 'a unique cultural response by Indigenous peoples wherein critical consciousness counters genocidal contexts by activating traditions, affirming presences, and embracing rights and responsibilities' (p. 37). The traditional teachings embodied in the weaving practices affirmed the identity of the women and their rights and responsibilities as parents and community members. Mililani Trask (as cited in Mihesuah, 2003) emphasizes the importance of revitalizing Indigenous women's traditional practices as part of community life: 'As Indigenous women, we have rich traditions upon which we can rely and from which we can and should draw our sustenance ... incorporating them to the greatest extent possible in our daily lives are keys to self-empowerment and self-determination for indigenous peoples' (p. 170). I witnessed the self-empowerment and self-determination that emerged as the community came together to weave cedar hats, spin wool and weave Coast Salish blankets.

Uy'skwuluwun: Cultural safety

Facilitating Indigenous feminist aesthetic work as cultural revitalization, particularly in response to the impacts of colonization, necessitates an understanding of cultural safety. The concept of cultural safety requires that community workers 'engage in a process of reflection on their own cultural identity and recognise how cultural and social positions impact their relationships with clients from different backgrounds' (Greenwood et al., 2017, p. 182). Creating cultural safety involves decolonizing one's own beliefs and practice while honouring and respecting the practices, beliefs, teachings and protocols of those we work with.

Vicki Boldo (as cited in Richardson, 2017) gives a personalised description, 'I look at cultural safety as a positive outcome from an exchange with any individual where I have remained aware of the importance of providing a space of non-judgement, non-interference, dignity, respect, honesty and love' (p. 193). I liken this definition of cultural safety to one of the most important teachings that I have received from Elders in my community: we must have 'a good mind and a good heart or, to use the Hul'q'umi'num word, uy'skwuluwun' (Thomas, 2005, p. 249). Facilitating culturally safe Indigenous feminist aesthetic work requires approaching the work we do in community with a good mind and a good heart.

Uy'skwuluwun, as a framework for cultural safety, has several principles that I believe constitute some practical teachings that are necessary to embody this work with a good mind and heart. They are all principles that I have received as traditional teachings that became part of my praxis in my community work, and they align with Coast Salish guiding values – 'relationships, respect, reciprocity, and responsibility' (Thomas, 2018, p. 49). At times, they were teachings that I received in my family or educational life, and then I realized the significance of them as I strove to create cultural safety in my professional practice. Other times, they were teachings that I received directly from Elders who were teaching me, or correcting my work.

Tthihwum Hwiyuneem: Please listen

Several years ago Bill White, a Snuneymuxw knowledge keeper and guest lecturer, was sharing cultural teachings in one of my undergraduate classes. At the end of the class I rushed up to him to ask questions. I was firing questions at him, one after the other, a practice that I had learnt in school as my instructors would often rush off at the end of the lecture. He said, 'If you want to learn, you have to listen.' I was embarrassed, as I knew immediately what he was saying. The way that I was talking, in such a fast and abrupt manner, was very culturally inappropriate, and he was correcting me. While Western settings often reward people for speaking up, in Coast Salish and many Indigenous communities, deep listening is a preferred value that is taught through sitting in ceremony and listening to speakers or teachers, storytellers and singers (Tanaka, 2016; Tepper et al., 2017).

Deep listening is a reflexive practice that requires both listening and reflecting on the meaning(s) of what you are witnessing or learning. It also means 'reading between the lines'. Communication is often indirect and direct communication may seem aggressive or demanding. It lacks the subtlety of allowing the listener to think and decide for themselves what knowledge that they need and internalize it. When Elders are speaking they will often say, 'Take what is good for you and leave the rest behind' (Chief Janice George as cited in Tepper et al., 2017, p. 145). In Coast Salish communities 'this is how teachings work; you must sit with them for three or four months. Then, you make sense of the teachings and what they mean to you. Then, they become your teachings' (Ellen White as cited in Thomas, 2018, p. 56).

Thuythut Tseep Kwus Syaays Tse: Be prepared for the work to come

Another principle that is very important when working in Indigenous communities is honouring the traditional teachings and protocols of the community that you are working in. 'In every community we enter and with every person we work with, we must follow and respect their cultural protocols … In fact, by being positioned in our work and following protocol, we will always produce ethical work because it is done with a good mind and spirit' (Thomas, 2018, p. 51). This requires cultural humility and decolonizing one's own thinking. 'Decolonisation is the process of deconstructing colonial ideologies of the superiority and privilege of Western thought and approaches … [it] is the process of examining your beliefs about Indigenous Peoples and culture by learning about yourself in relationship to the communities where you live' (Cull et al., 2018, p. 7). For myself, that means that I come with teachings from my own community that may not be appropriate for the community that I am working in, as teachings differ from Nation to Nation and from family to family. It also means that my Western education may bias me towards ways of thinking that contradict Indigenous ways of knowing and being.

Robina Thomas (2018) shares the teaching: 'thuythut tseep kwus syaays tse – be prepared for the work to come' (p. 72). Learning about whose traditional territory that you are working on, consulting with Elders and community members about what work they would like done in their community and how they would like it to be done – respecting their teachings, protocols and self-determination, is being prepared for the work to come. This is a process that often takes a substantial amount of time and energy, so you must commit yourself to it. One example of this was when I was working for the inner-city agency the Director dreamt that we were supposed to host a potlatch. In my community we do this as a family, not an agency, as there are many sacred and logistical aspects to the ceremony which require years of preparation. I expressed my concerns, but he was convinced that we were meant to do it, so I brought together Elders and local First Nations' community members for months of weekly consultation meetings. They guided me as I sought to host this ceremony in the most respectful way possible. It required an incredible amount of preparation, both in relation to cultural protocol and physical resources, as we honoured all of the people who had passed on the streets through a memorial ceremony and served over 2400 plates of food that day. Despite my initial concerns, community members came from near and far to attend, and many thanked us for the good work that we had done and the healing that the ceremony brought to the community.

Ts'ewut: Help

Ts'ewut translates to 'help'. I received this principle, this teaching rather abruptly from an Elder when I was working in community. The Nation was hosting a community event and there was a lot of work to do. I was relatively new to my position and not that comfortable with taking charge in the community's longhouse (ceremonial hall), so I was standing around acting a little helpless, and asking what I should do to help. MaryAnn Thomas, the Chief's wife, answered, 'Just do it!' Confused, I asked again, 'Do what?' and she responded, 'Just do it!' In that moment, I started helping with whatever needed to be done – serving food, bringing tea to the Elders, cleaning up. Afterward, I realized asking someone to stop what they are doing to explain what needs to be done is a way of centring oneself, and it doesn't fit with an Indigenous pedagogy that is more oriented towards learning by observing and doing (Tanaka, 2016). My Western education which often requires that things be taught, extrapolated and even theorized, before being enacted, was getting in the way of meaningful community engagement.

The principle of helping in whatever capacity is necessary became even more apparent as I began programme development in the community. The Chief was very concerned about the loss of language and cultural teachings in the community and made it clear to me that he wanted the children to 'learn what it means to be an Indian' (Chief Andy Thomas, personal communication, 2014). As a result, culture and ceremony were prioritized and I was frequently expected to participate, contribute to and even host large cultural events, at times being thrown in with little training or explanation. To decline would have been very disrespectful, so I learnt as I participated. Eventually, my programmes took on a life of their own. The community presented a need; I consulted the Elders and knowledge keepers, and then responded to the need. The parenting/weaving programme developed in this context.

Lhuw'unuq: Heal

The parenting/weaving classes exposed many Coast Salish teachings. 'Weaving is part of the Salish tree of life; from the roots of this tree grow the teachings that form the Coast Salish worldview' (George as cited in Tepper et al., 2017, p. 31). Because one of the principles is learning by doing, making mistakes and correcting those mistakes is also part of the learning: 'If they are not allowed to make mistakes, they will be afraid to learn' (Sarah Modeste as cited in Thomas, 2018, p. 74). The weaving classes would often start with Maria helping someone once and then leaving them to work on their own until they made a mistake, and then she would ask them what was happening for them. If their work was becoming twisted, knotted, too tight or loose, she would talk about their feelings. If they were upset, preoccupied or not aligned with the work, she would teach them to take a break or undo part of their work, as a way to attend to the mistake, or offer cultural advice, such as suggesting that participation in a ceremonial practice was necessary to bring them back into alignment.

Mistakes that are made that are harmful to someone can also be healed, or 'made right' culturally – lhuw'unuq. For example, one of the most important principles for Coast Salish people is reciprocity, and this is an area that can often be overlooked when doing community work. If you ask someone do to work – cultural work, physical work, sharing their words or time (territorial welcomes, wisdom, prayers), it is appropriate to give them a handshake, which is remuneration in the form of money, honoraria or a gift, based on what you can afford. Using someone's teachings, songs or art, requires their permission as well. As Tepper et al. (2008) explain, 'traditional knowledge among the First Nations living on Canada's Northwest Coast, belongs to certain families or to particular members of those families' (p. 193). This principle constitutes a traditional law, and as such, if it is breached then restitution must be made. It is a mistake that must be corrected, which can involve giving someone money or a gift and wrapping them in a blanket to heal their spirit. I have experienced this, sometimes not acknowledging or compensating someone for their work, as an oversight, and I have had to make it right. Both the giving of a handshake and restitution are typically done in front of witnesses, because 'the process of witnessing was an integral part of our governance' (Thomas, 2018, p. 73).

Lal'um'uthut: Be careful

Harming someone is taken so seriously in Coast Salish communities that one of the most common phrases is lal'um'uthut, which means 'to watch, to be careful, to take care of oneself'. It is about walking in a good way so as not to bring harm to yourself or others, being careful with your thoughts, words and actions. This is taken so seriously that according to Marcella Baker (as cited in Tepper et al., 2017), even 'while we were weaving, we were to think good thoughts and we were to put good energy into those pieces because you don't know who is going to be wearing them or where they're going to be shown' (p. 53). Janice George (cited in Tepper et al., 2017) further explains:

> Because the weavings are alive, they radiate the feelings of the Weaver. Some people teach that you should not weave when you are angry or sad. The Weaver should feel confident she is doing the right thing on all levels, that she is following the teachings. Then the weaving will contain good feelings, love, prayers, and protection.
>
> (p. 106)

These teachings aptly illustrate a Coast Salish worldview, that we are not to even think a harmful thought. If harm is done we must forgive; we must heal ourselves and restore the good feelings (MaryAnn Thomas, personal communication, 31 January 2021). Coast Salish Elders often teach that as we enter a ceremonial space, or do cultural work, we must leave our bad feelings outside.

Nuts'a'maat: We are all one

Another important teaching that is frequently taught by the Elders in Coast Salish territory speaks to both relationality and responsibility. Nuts'a'maat 'teaches us that we are all one … Nuts'a'maat reminds us – because we were all one – that we all matter equally and collectively we make the whole' (Thomas, 2018, p. 26). This is a teaching that encompasses all living things. A tree, for example, 'is treated with the respect given to a human and thanked for the use of its wood, bark, and roots' (Tepper et al., 2017, p. 2). The understanding that all things are connected and thus interact with one another, and even have spiritual significance or consequences, is central to Salish cosmology which 'maintains that the realm of human experience exists alongside spiritual or supernatural worlds' (Tepper et al., 2017, p. 2).

Relationality is a serious responsibility. It means that we are accountable to the communities that we work in and with, and the people, creatures, land and spiritual entities of the territories that we are on. Thomas (2018) provides salient instructions:

> We must begin all of our work by building relationships ... If our [work] brings us into an Indigenous community, relationships become even more significant. We cannot exploit folks by wanting their knowledge, but not being willing to spend the time necessary to build relationships ... Relationship building is the beginning of what makes our work rooted in traditional ways of knowing and being.
>
> (p. 49)

'Exwe't: Sharing

In my work, embracing nuts'a'maat has meant spending time being present and getting to know community members before I start any project, doing community consultation by deeply listening to community needs and concerns, and maintaining relationships with community members after my work there is done. There are many ways that this can be done, but one of the most pertinent in my practice has been by eating together. In Coast Salish teachings we must cook our food with love, so as to ingest good feelings, and while we are eating together with good feelings, we can readily absorb the teachings of the Elders. "Exwe't, or sharing, is an essential aspect of nuts'a'maat ... As we are taught to never send a guest home hungry, with each visitor, you must offer food, coffee and tea' (Thomas, 2018, p. 80). For this reason, I have always provided food during community consultations and programmes and eaten with the participants, as well as accepting invitations to participate in community feasts and ceremonies.

> Of all the teachings we receive
> This one is the most important:
> Nothing belongs to you
> Of what there is,
> Of what you take,
> You must share.
> (Chief Dan George, 1974, as cited in Thomas, 2018, p. 52)

Conclusion

My Dad shared with me one day that when you get up early in the morning to do your work, particularly your artwork, everything is either uy' (good) or qul (bad) and you have to set your mind, your intention for the day, on what is good, letting go of bad thoughts and feelings (William Good, personal communication, 2019). Indigenous feminist aesthetic work must be approached this way, as it is central to cultural revitalization, healing and wellness in community. With uy'skwuluwun as a framework for cultural safety, grounded in the values of relationships, respect, reciprocity and responsibility, I have provided some principles that I believe help to actualize how to work with a good mind and heart in a community setting. These principles are: tthihwum hwiyuneem, please listen; thuythut tseep kwus syaays tse, be prepared for the work to come; ts'ewut, help; lhuw'unuq, heal; lal'um'uthut, be careful; nuts'a'maat, we are all one; and 'exwe't, sharing. These are teachings that I have received that have guided me in my community work.

In closing, I am reminded of the words of Songhees Elder Dr Skip Dick, who said, 'We are not a programme we are human beings' (Skip Dick, personal communication, 1 April 2019). Facilitating Indigenous feminist aesthetic work is not just about creating a healing and wellness programme, engaging in social justice or even in cultural revitalization; it is about Uy' skwuluwun – a good mind and heart.

Notes

1   Coast Salish, which is an anthropological term, includes several First Nations on Southern Vancouver Island, BC, Canada. 'Though each Salish community has its own traditions, many of the teachings are commonly held among them, and personal experiences, such as learning to weave or bringing out a new blanket, are similar' (Tepper et al., 2017, p. xx).
2   The term Indian is an outdated term. The term Indigenous is the more inclusive term, which includes First Nations, Inuit and Métis peoples in Canada.

References

Arvin, M., Tuck, E., & Morrill, A. (2013). Decolonimeing feminism: Challenging connections between settler colonialism and heteropatriarchy. *Feminist Formations, 25*(1), 8–34. http://doi.org/10.1353/ff.2013.0006

Atleo, M. (2016). All my relations: Networks of First Nations/Metis/Inuit women sharing and learning. In D. Clover, S. Butterwick, & L. Collins (Eds.), *Women, adult education, and leadership in Canada* (pp. 33–44). Thompson Press.

Beattie, S., David, J.-D., & Roy, J. (2018, November 21). Homicide in Canada, 2017. Retrieved from https://www150.statcan.gc.ca/n1/pub/85-002-x/2018001/article/54980-eng.htm.

Brown, J. (2016). Culture is lived; language gives is life Unpublished Master's Thesis. University of Victoria, Victoria, BC, Canada.

Clover, D. E. (2012). Aesthetics, society and social movement learning. In B. L. Hall, D. E. Clover, J. Crowther, & E. Scandetti (Eds.), *Learning and education for a better world: The role of social movements* (pp. 87–100). Sense Publishing.

Cull, I., Hancock, R., McKeown, S., Pidgeon, M., & Vedan, A. (2018). *Pulling together: A guide for indigenization of post-secondary institutions. Front-line staff, student services, and advisors: BC Campus.*

Greenwood, M., Lindsay, N., King, J., & Loewen, D. (2017). Ethical spaces and places: Indigenous cultural safety in British Columbia health care. *AlterNative: An International Journal of Indigenous Peoples, 13*(3), 179–89. Retrieved from https://doi.org/10.1177/1177180117714411

Hall, B. L., & Tandon, R. (2017). Decolonization of knowledge, epistemicide, participatory research and higher education. *Research for All, 1*(1), 6–19. doi:10.18546/rfa.01.1.02

Kirmayer, L., Simpson, C., & Cargo, M. (2003). Healing traditions: Culture, community and mental health promotion with Canadian aboriginal peoples. *Australasian Psychiatry, 11*(s1), S15–S23. https//doi:10.1046/j.1038-5282.2003.02010.x

Malloch, L. (1989). Indian medicine, Indian health: Study between red and white medicine. *Canadian Women Studies, 10*(2–3), 105–13. Retrieved from https://cws.journals.yorku.ca/index.php/cws/article/view/11187

McIvor, S. D. (1999). Self-government and Aboriginal women. In E. Dua & A. Robertson (Eds.), *Scratching the surface: Canadian anti-racist feminist thought* (pp. 167–86). Women's Press.

Mihesuah, D. A. (2003). *Indigenous American women: Decolonization, empowerment, activism.* University of Nebraska Press.

Mithlo, N. (2009). 'A real feminine journey': Locating indigenous feminisms in the arts. *Meridians, 9*(2), 1–30. Retrieved from www.jstor.org/stable/40338781

Poonwassie, A., & Charter, A. (2001). An aboriginal worldview of helping: Empowering approaches. *Canadian Journal of Counselling, 35*(1), 63–73. Retrieved from https://journalhosting.ucalgary.ca/index.php/rcc/article/view/58663

Razack, S. (2015). *Dying from improvement: Inquests and inquiries into indigenous deaths in custody.* University of Toronto Press. Retrieved from https://utorontopress.com/ca/dying-from-improvement-4

Richardson, C., Carriere, J., & Boldo, V. (2017). Invitations to dignity and well-being: Cultural safety through indigenous pedagogy, witnessing and giving back. *AlterNative: An International Journal of Indigenous Peoples, 13*(3), 190–5. https//doi:10.1177/1177180117714413

Rothschild, B. (2000). *The Body remembers: The psychophysiology of trauma and trauma treatment.* Norton & Company.

Sherlock, T. (2017, November 22). Disproportionate number of Aboriginal children in foster care: Care system criticized as 'the new residential school'. *Vancouver Courier.* Retrieved from https://www.vancourier.com/opinion/disproportionate-number-of-aboriginal-children-in-foster-care-1.23101923

Tanaka, M. T. (2016). *Learning and teaching together: Weaving Indigenous ways of knowing into education.* UBC Press.

Tepper, L. (2008). Coast Salish weaving–Preserving traditional knowledge with new technology. *Indian Journal of Traditional Knowledge, 7*(1), 188–96. Retrieved from https://www.researchgate.net/publication/267792318_Coast_Salish_weaving-Preserving_traditional_knowledge_with_new_technology

Tepper, L. H., George, J., & Joseph, W. (2017). *Salish blankets: Robes of protection and transformation, symbols of wealth.* University of Nebraska Press.

Thomas, R. (2005). Honoring the oral traditions of my ancestors through storytelling. In L. Brown & S. Strega (Eds.), *Research as resistance: Critical, indigenous and anti-oppressive approaches* (pp. 237–54). Canadian Scholars Press.

Thomas, R. (2018). *Protecting the sacred cycle: Indigenous women and leadership*. J. Charlton Publishing Ltd.

Chapter 12

Decolonizing Aesthetics of the *Witness Blanket*

Catherine Etmanski and H̲aya̲łk̲an̲ga̲me'– Carey Newman

This chapter explores the intersection of feminist aesthetics and decolonization in the context of Artist and master carver Carey Newman's acclaimed work, the *Witness Blanket*. The *Witness Blanket* is a national monument of the Indian Residential School Era. It is made of items collected from residential schools, churches, government buildings and other traditional structures across Canada. Through a mixture of tangible objects, documents and photographs, the *Witness Blanket* weaves together a comprehensive narrative of Survivor experience and history of residential schools in Canada.

There are 886 contributions in the *Witness Blanket*, collected during a year-long cross-Canada, in-person engagement process and represented in the form of physical objects and images integrated into the installation. The full installation is 40ft long, with a height of 10.5ft. Readers can learn more about the *Witness Blanket* online at http://witnessblanket.ca/, by visiting it in person at the Canadian Museum for Human Rights (CMHR) in Winnipeg, by viewing the documentary (Newman & Graham, 2015), or by reading earlier works (Newman & Etmanski, in press/2019; Newman & Hudson, 2019). Carey not only conceived of and designed the 40-foot installation, he was also the project manager. He attained the commission through a national call for proposals by the Truth and Reconciliation Commission (TRC) of Canada.

In this chapter, we look at the decolonized approaches embedded within Carey's process of making the *Witness Blanket* and consider these in relation to feminist aesthetics. Since each of the 886 contributions has a multitude of stories attached to it (Newman & Etmanski, 2019), this chapter focuses on two braids of hair that Ellen and Marion Newman, Carey's sisters, grew and cut as their contributions to the *Witness Blanket* (Newman & Hudson, 2019). We examine the intersecting stories, Kwakwaka'wakw[1] epistemology, traditional ceremony and artistic treatment behind their inclusion. We suggest that, taken together, these beliefs, processes and artistry constitute Carey's decolonized approach that led to what we call in this chapter the decolonizing aesthetic of the *Witness Blanket*. In support of this we reference lessons learnt from Kwakwaka'wakw cultural

Figure 12.1 The *Witness Blanket* on display at the Canadian Museum for Human Rights (CMHR). Courtesy of Jessica Sigurdson, CMHR.

teachings; a child's shoe and a family mask that resides in the Ethnologisches Museum in Berlin. Finally, we discuss Carey's experience of being raised in the environment of homeschooling. The decisions he made in pursuit of working in *a good way* as he was leading the process of collecting the pieces and creating the *Witness Blanket* and the factors that influenced his thinking were largely decolonized. We see decolonization and decolonizing as pertaining to dismantling something that is inherently colonial. They are ongoing actions against and in response to colonialism. We think of decolonized as a way of being that is inherently emancipated from colonial ways.

In making the *Witness Blanket*, Carey was determined that the process must reflect the goal of reconciliation and he has tried to embody that ethos in all subsequent projects (Newman & Etmanski, in press). Coming from a matrilineal society on his father's side, where gender roles existed but were valued equally and Two-Spirit people were recognized and respected for having strength within a spectrum of gender roles, Carey is aware that colonial patriarchy has in some ways infiltrated and influenced what is now considered traditional. As such, undertaking a project with the scope of the *Witness Blanket* in a way that honours the precolonial intention of his cultural traditions involved acknowledging his male privilege, listening to women and uprooting internalized colonialism. It also meant rejecting an extractionist approach towards engaging with community, where researchers publish Indigenous knowledges as their own, and instead initiating an ongoing consent practice that placed him and those working within the sphere of the *Witness Blanket* in relationship with, and therefore continually accountable to, the people and communities they engage, the objects given and the multiple intersecting stories they represent.

Curiously, people who do not know Carey often presume he is a woman. Not only is his name gender-neutral, in Eurocentric cultures blankets are often associated with quilts and quilting is often perceived as women's work. This innocuous assumption is a reminder that the male/female binary is so deeply embedded within colonial societies (see, e.g., Hunt, 2018; Wilson, 2008; 2015) that when people extrapolate gender, in Carey's case they often guess female. In our work together, we focus on identifying and unbraiding these kinds of hierarchical gender assumptions and uprooting and transforming underlying misogynistic and colonial beliefs. We attempt to transcend a hierarchy of grievances – where one person's oppression is pitted against another's – by aligning around the deeper intention and common purpose for our work.

This chapter draws upon four years of collaboration between the two authors who share a vision for a decolonized world where 'fully self-actualized [humans of all identities are] able to create beloved community, to live together, realizing our dreams of freedom and justice' (hooks, 2000, p. x). Our working relationship is encapsulated in the following adage by Indigenous Australian activist groups: 'If you have come here to help me, you are wasting your time. But if you have come because your liberation is bound up with mine, then let us work together.'[2] It is this idea of working collaboratively towards a new world and in solidarity for mutual liberation, freedom and justice that draws us, Catherine and Carey, together.

Self-location

In Carey's Kwakwaka'wakw culture, taking the time to introduce and locate oneself in relation to the context is an essential part of personal accountability. Carey introduces himself like this:

'Yo! 'Nugwa'ạm Carey Newman, He'mạn bak̲wạmx̱tła'yi' H̲ạyałk̲ạngạme'. Through my father I am Kwakwak̲ạ'wakw from the Kukwak̲ạm, Gix̱sạm, and Wawałaba'yi clans of northern Vancouver Island, and Coast Salish from Cheam of the Sto:lo Nation along the upper Fraser Valley. Through my mother my ancestors are Settlers of English, Irish, and Scottish heritage.

Catherine introduces herself like this:

My name is Catherine Etmanski and I am a descendant of immigrants. My first known family members arrived in the lands now understood as Canada in 1772. They were Scottish settlers on Prince Edward Island. My mother's ancestors were Irish-American, Dutch, and British. My father's ancestors were Kashubian from Poland and Scottish from Clan MacDonald of Clanranald. I have a deep curiosity for learning and research through the arts and a commitment to the ongoing unlearning and relearning processes of decolonisation and reconciliation, within myself and in my identity as an educator.

Decolonizing aesthetic of the Witness Blanket

Feminist aesthetic theorists have critiqued the legacy of Kantian aesthetics and the long-standing classed, gendered, ableist, homophobic and racialized hierarchies in the art world that determine what counts as high, good, beautiful or simply *art* (see, e.g., Bovenschen, 1985; Lippard, 1984; Nochlin, 1988). The *Stanford Encyclopedia of Philosophy* (2017) suggested:

> To refer to feminist aesthetics is to identify a set of perspectives that pursue certain questions about philosophical theories and assumptions regarding art and aesthetic categories. … Those who work in aesthetics inquire into the ways that gender influences the formation of ideas about art, artists, and aesthetic value. Feminist perspectives in aesthetics are also attuned to the cultural influences that exert power over subjectivity: the ways that art both reflects and perpetuates the social formation of gender, sexuality, and identity, and the extent to which all of those features are framed by factors such as race, national origin, social position, and historical situation.
>
> (para 1)

In this chapter, the decolonizing aesthetic of the *Witness Blanket* sits in conversation with feminist aesthetics. The decolonizing aesthetic includes a Kwakwaka'wakw worldview and aligned way of working that honours people, respects stories and acknowledges the spirit of the artefacts contained therein, through the ceremonies, epistemology and processes discussed below. Since the very concept of aesthetics comes from a long lineage of Western thinkers (Jackson, 2016), it is helpful to understand that Carey did not set out to critique Western artistic practices; as such, he did not initiate this project purposefully to decolonize aesthetics. Rather, he began with a question about how to record Canada's residential school history and Survivors' stories through art and how to work in a good way. By its very nature, this inquiry dismantled the interlocking beliefs brought into Indigenous cultures through colonialism, including the commodification of art inherent in colonial aesthetic practice.

In 2008, Alex Wilson, a two-spirit member of the Opaskwayak Cree Nation, wrote:

> Rather than dividing the world into female and male, or making linguistic distinctions based on sexual characteristics or anatomy, we distinguish between what is animate and what is inanimate. Living creatures, animate objects, and actions are understood to have a spiritual purpose (Ahenakew). Our language and culture are rooted in this fundamental truth: that every living creature and everything that acts in and on this world is spiritually meaningful.
>
> (p. 193)

Early in the process of creating the *Witness Blanket*, Carey came to recognize the individual significance and spirit of each artefact collected. His interaction with a child's shoe, in particular, taught him that he 'needed to respect the objects, stories, and people equally' (Newman & Etmanski, 2019, p. 240; see also, Newman & Hudson, 2019).

Reflecting on the process, Carey wrote:

As a carver I have always been taught to respect the materials I use, a concept embedded within the Kwakwaka'wakw ways of a̱wi'nakola – being one with the land, air, waters, heaven and everything within them. The experience with this shoe brought all of those teachings into focus and together, they have since helped me to better articulate and understand the purpose of my artwork and my personal responsibilities within my artistic practice and in pursuit of reconciliation. By changing my medium from raw material to gathered objects, and my process from solitary carving to community engaged assemblage, I had taken on a different level of responsibility. Each object had a unique history that carried many meanings and relationships. I was no longer responsible only to the tree or mineral I carved, or to the animal whose fur or shell I incorporated into my work, I was responsible to each of the multiple stories held within every piece gathered, to the people who entrusted them to me, and also to the collective truth that together they would represent.

Carey and his sisters were raised by their mother, an unapologetic feminist who instilled in them her values of gender equality, and their father, who (when not attending residential school) was raised by a fierce and cultural Stó:lō matriarch. Together their parents agreed that family roles and responsibilities should be assigned based on fair distribution of labour and interests and abilities over gender roles. They each cooked one meal per week, had to do the washing up and house cleaning as well as chores in the yard.

In response to witnessing systemic racism towards Indigenous children while teaching in the school system, their mother decided to homeschool her children. Partly due to his own experiences at residential schools, their father supported this approach and so the Newman children were home, or free schooled until moving on to post-secondary education. Their daily routines looked nothing like a typical classroom. Their education was guided by their natural curiosities with each parent working to support the individual interests of their children. The fluidity of this model made everything into a possible learning experience. Each of the siblings now recognizes that between modelling from their parents and how they were educated, their individual decolonization began at home. Another of the benefits of being taught at home was that they were able to travel to attend potlatches. It was through witnessing and taking part in these ceremonies that Carey's understanding of Kwakwaka'wakw culture and traditions was formed.

Working from a Kwakwaka'wakw cultural context, throughout the process of creating the *Witness Blanket*, Carey and his team took up both ceremony and archival practices to honour the spirit and animate nature of all artefacts included in the installation. This will be demonstrated through the ceremony and meaning behind his sisters cutting their hair for inclusion in the *Witness Blanket* in the story that follows (see also Newman & Hudson, 2019). We express our gratitude to Carey's sisters, Marion and Ellen, who met with us as we were preparing this manuscript.

Figure 12.2 Photo of panel on the *Witness Blanket* with Ellen and Marion Newman's braids. Courtesy of Jessica Sigurdson, CMHR.

Honouring the gift of my sisters' braids

Carey's father doesn't often talk about his time at residential school, but when he decided to record his statement for the TRC, having his head shaved was the first story he told. Seventy years had passed since his head was shorn on his first day at Sechelt residential school, yet decades later, his hands still trembled at the memory, and as he recounted the experience, he wiped tears from his eyes.

Carey wrote the following words for a film called *Picking up the Pieces: The Making of the Witness Blanket* (Newman & Graham, 2015), made from scenes recorded during the process of collecting pieces and building the *Witness Blanket*:

> A common method of extinguishing cultural identity was to cut the children's hair when they first arrived at residential school. Survivors from across the country, including my father, shared stories of this difficult and traumatic experience. In many Indigenous cultures, hair is identified with strength and is only cut during times of mourning.

Kwakwaka'wakw scholar Sarah Hunt (2018) explained how hair cutting was also a mechanism used to enforce Western gender binaries. We quote her work at length as it provides context for the symbolism behind Marion and Ellen's decision to cut their hair:

> Indian residential schools were also integral to processes of imposing racialized gender hierarchies among diverse Indigenous communities. … At the same moment as Native children became 'Indians' through their institutionalization at residential schools, they were simultaneously gendered as Indian boys and girls as systems of race and gender were mutually articulated, enforcing and creating one another. 'Individual accounts of residential school students clearly show the gender uniforms as one colonizing tool – boys had their hair cut short, girls wore bobs and bangs, and they were physically separated from one another in the schools, kept in different dorms in order to ingrain distinct gender roles into them' (Hunt, 2007, p. 43). Residential schools divided sisters and brothers from one another, imposing racialised gender norms onto the young bodies of Native children while denying their traditional gender roles, which differed cross-culturally. After many generations of Native children being indoctrinated in these gendered educational spaces, along with the imposition of Indian Act governance and many other ways of replacing Indigenous cultural practices with colonial ones, the racialized gender binary has become difficult to question.
>
> (p. 24)

Carey's sisters wanted to do something that would honour their father and other residential school Survivors. Early in the planning stages for the project, they agreed to grow their hair as long as possible and, when the time came, cut their hair in ceremony and contribute their shorn braids to the *Witness Blanket*.

Figure 12.3 Close-up image of one braid on the *Witness Blanket*. Courtesy of Jessica Sigurdson, CMHR.

The two braids are now in a shadow box on the blanket, accompanied by several other items related to the Newman family. The hair is braided tightly, but because of the ceremony they went through, the braids are slightly frayed. If you look very closely, you can see a residue of red powder; it is a traditional medicine called ochre and that was applied during the cutting ceremony. Looking at them can be unsettling, because although braids and haircuts are commonplace as a function of personal style and identity, they are not often seen in this context.

Marion described the hair-cutting ceremony like this:

> My sister and I bathed in the clear river waters from melting glaciers for four sunrises in a row, while offering our prayers. On the fifth sunrise, sitting next to the fire our father built, facing the ocean and the hills at our family home, we had our braids cut off as we cried our sorrows away. We cried for our father's loss of his childhood. We cried for our grandparents, our aunts, our uncles, and our cousins who were all torn apart by their experiences at residential schools. We cried for the culture and the sense of self and well-being that was removed from all of those beings at such a young age. We cried in relief that we were brought up in a time and place where we could avoid such persecution. We cried in frustration at having to learn our culture in bits and pieces, rather than having been immersed in our customs since birth, as we should have been. We cried until our tears ran to happy tears. Happy that we are able to walk free and live as we wish to, surrounded by a loving and healthy family and our beautiful culture that managed to survive a near obliteration. On the sixth and seventh days we rose to pray at sunrise over our hair, which lay outside on cedar boughs, sprinkled with ochre. On day eight our brother took our hair and wrapped it in red cloth. My sister and I brought the cedar bough our hair had rested on to the river and let it wash away, taking our grief and worries with it.

The moment of cutting Ellen and Marion's braids was powerful and emotional for everyone involved. Carey writes of how the smoke swirled around, embracing and connecting everyone, recalling details like the crackle and hiss of the fire. But clearest of all, he remembers hearing the rasp of the scissors as Shirley Alphonse, the Elder who performed the ceremony, began to cut the first braid.

Ellen described that moment like this:

> It felt like a part of me, my body, my spirit, was being cut and removed. And I immediately thought of all those children, scared and torn from their families, who had their identities stripped from them.

When Ellen reflected on the experience, she said she learnt 'how important ceremony is. How important allowing time and creating space to purposefully heal is. How important it is to tell people's truths, to hear them – really hear them.' She also spoke about needing to 'just sit silently with those truths. That until we sit in the spaces which are uncomfortable, until we honour those experiences, we cannot have true reconciliation. And that this is a lifelong journey.'

Discussion: Decolonizing aesthetics through process

Ferrari (2020) reminded us that 'the deployment of deep silences is key to a decolonizing aesthetics; it bears witness to experiences of coloniality by upholding, rather than eliding, opacity, thus inaugurating decolonizing sensibilities attuned to silences rather than speech and transparency' (p. 8). As mentioned at the outset of this chapter, there are over 886 contributions in the *Witness Blanket,* each with their own histories, and each treated with reverence by Carey and his team. The story of Marion and Ellen's braids is but one of many stories embedded within the *Witness Blanket,* most of which remain opaque as viewers engage with the installation. As the example above suggests, the *Witness Blanket* in its entirety and each individual contribution are not inanimate commodities. Their particular spirit and the histories they carry were welcomed into the whole with care and through ceremony. In the process of making, to the extent of his artistic ability, Carey honoured and respected the objects and the people who gave them.

This process sits in sharp contrast to the ways in which Indigenous cultural artefacts have been stolen and put on display in museums. For example, a mask that once belonged to Carey's family now sits in the Ethnologisches Museum in Berlin. The name of this mask is Nu'lis, which was Carey's family name before it was Anglicized to Newman. As Carey described:

> The mask depicts our family origin story. There are three versions of that mask in existence, the one in Berlin is the oldest (1882), the second oldest (C.1900-20?) is at the UBC Museum of Anthropology and the third is sleeping in our family box of treasures. I say sleeping, because we think of these masks as ancestors, and when they are not in use, we wrap them in blankets and sing them to sleep. In March of 2012 I went to the Ethnologisches Museum, then in Dahlem, to visit my ancestor. They were in a glass box with museum standard lighting and climate control. It was incredibly beautiful, but also heartbreaking because it was displayed open, frozen in time, eternally awake. For a brief time, I was alone with it, close enough to touch, but separated by glass, like visiting someone in prison. It was emotional. I asked about arranging a loan to bring it home and reunite it with the other versions of itself and perhaps dance them together. I was told that even if it was possible to arrange the loan, which was already very unlikely, it would never be possible to dance it again, or even to touch it with bare hands, because the chemicals they used to 'preserve' it were poisonous. In our ways, nothing is meant to last forever. Poles are carved to carry stories, but there is humility in how they are made to return to the earth, making way for stories of the future. What is lost in making something last forever? What does poison do to the spirit of a mask? I wish I could sing it to sleep.

This story demonstrates that preserving and exhibiting *this* mask in *this* way disregards its inherent spirit and reason for being, and in doing so takes away the heart of what makes it beautiful and important. It is not meant to be on permanent

Figure 12.4 Nu'lis on display at Ethnologisches Museum Transformation mask, 'Nulis', Kwakwaka'wakw, Before 1881, INV No. IV A 1243, © State Museums in Berlin, Ethnological Museum. Photo: Claudia Obrocki.

display; it is meant to sleep, to wake up and to dance. The archival preservation of Carey's ancestor mask places importance on the structure of the object and its value as a commodity above cultural beliefs and the significance of its purpose and function.

As the *Stanford Encyclopaedia of Philosophy* (2017) identified, 'feminist perspectives in aesthetics are also attuned to the cultural influences that exert power over subjectivity' (para 1). This feminist critique reveals that the Western world has made assumptions about what art is and the standards and qualities by which it is appreciated, judged and consumed. The example above brings this critique to life by demonstrating how the museum sees this mask as something that needs to be preserved and thereby exerts its power according to the normative, consumer-oriented patriarchal paradigm; for Carey and his family, its purpose is suspended and agency violated when it cannot dance anymore, or when they can no longer be in relationship with it: 'We cannot hold it without gloves or put it to our face, because it has been conserved with literal poison and placed behind glass so that the wood and paint don't deteriorate. We would need to clean the poison from it for it to be used as it is meant to be used.' This example represents the tragic irony of conflicting worldviews: conserving the mask has extended its material existence, while destroying its spirit. It also illustrates why representation and specific cultural knowledge are vital to decolonizing aesthetics, introducing the opportunity to ask ourselves, what spirit do all objects have?

Conversely, when it came time for Carey's sisters to offer the gift of their braids, they began with four days of ceremony to prepare themselves spiritually. Then their hair was cut in ceremony, followed by four more days of separating their spirits from the braids. After spending eight days thinking about and preparing themselves, they gifted their braids to the *Witness Blanket* with clear intention and purpose. This process demonstrates a level of care towards the spirit of their braids and the act of cutting them that stands in sharp contrast to the way residential schools approached haircutting. How callous the act of shaving children's hair was when understood from an Indigenous epistemology.

Situating this work in broader colonial systems

Catherine remembers visiting the region of Poland where her Etmanski ancestors are believed to once have lived. While there, she witnessed rocks carved in a pagan tradition, hinting at a pre-Christian worldview long forgotten in her family's history. In 1967, historian Lynn White, Jr. published an article in *Science* that acknowledged a historical moment when Indigenous and European worldviews may have been closer than they are today:

> In Antiquity every tree, every spring, every stream, every hill had its own genius loci, its guardian spirit. These spirits were accessible to men, [sic] but were very unlike men; centaurs, fauns, and mermaids show their ambivalence. Before one cut a tree, mined a mountain, or dammed a brook, it was important to placate the spirit in charge of that particular situation, and to keep it placated. By destroying pagan animism, Christianity made it possible to exploit nature in a mood of indifference to the feelings of natural objects.
>
> (White, 1967, p. 1205)

This quotation suggests that people of European descent were not always so prone to extractive capitalism. Colonization is a worldwide, multi-generational phenomenon and many immigrants to the land now known as Canada were themselves descendants of victims of colonization under the Roman Empire (as suggested by Dakota and Anishinabe cultural educator, H. Eagle, personal communication, 21 October 2020). These settlers reproduced the trauma their families, too, had experienced, internalized and normalized and went on to create the colonial institutions in which we continue to live and work today.

The ongoing process of colonization brings with it the intersecting systems of what bell hooks (1994a/1994b) has called white supremacist capitalist patriarchy. This phrase speaks to the complexity of the colonizing forces we are working to overcome. The ongoing process of decolonization therefore requires continually working to disentangle these internalized systems of oppression, no matter one's culture, biological sex or gender.

In our conversations throughout the course of writing this chapter, we (Carey and Catherine) endeavoured to come together in a way that acknowledged our different backgrounds and respected one another's perspectives and gifts. We acknowledge the imperfect and incomplete ways that Kwakwaka'wakw culture and worldview can be described and animated through the written text of this chapter. Nevertheless, through bringing Carey's decolonized process of making the *Witness Blanket* into relationship[3] with feminist aesthetics, we gained new insights into how the decolonizing aesthetic of the *Witness Blanket* can support our collaborative work towards mutual liberation, freedom and justice. In this small way, we are endeavouring to live reconciliation through this writing, in pursuit of dismantling the underlying causes of our shared oppressions.

In closing

As we suggest in the beginning, Carey did not conceive of the decolonizing aesthetic of the *Witness Blanket* as a response against colonialism or Western aesthetics; being homeschooled and having access to culture created in Carey a largely decolonized way of being that shows up in the work as a matter of his method of making.

The processes described in this chapter, and enacted by Ellen, Marion, Elder Shirley Alphonse, Carey and other members of the *Witness Blanket* team can serve as an example of what is possible when we take the time to work with deep intention, honour people, respect stories and acknowledge the spirit of the objects and artefacts with which we enter into relationship. There is deep wisdom in the Kwakwaka'wakw worldview of *gwi'nakola* and aligned way of working through ceremony.

Colonialism perpetuates a destructive relationship with the planet and continues to harm the majority of us. We therefore conclude this chapter by suggesting that transforming the relationship between one another and the world around us into more decolonized ways of being, thinking and working, as demonstrated through Carey's process of making the *Witness Blanket*, can move us towards the collective socio-cultural, ecological and economic healing needed to counterbalance the trauma reproduced through colonial institutions.

Notes

1   In Carey's work editing work that centres Indigenous Knowledges, he has noticed that there is often an expectation that words denoting specific cultural references are explained to readers, while complex academic concepts often go undefined with an expectation that readers will look them up for themselves. This means that space taken to explain foundational knowledge leaves less space to produce new Indigenous Knowledges. Aligned with the decolonizing approach we are taking in this chapter, we encourage readers who are not familiar with Kwakwaka'wakw culture, including potlaches, to look these terms up.

2   This adage is often attributed to Dr. Lilla Watson, Australian Indigenous visual artist, activist and academic from Gangulu country in Central Queensland. The

following source suggests that she prefers that the attribution for this quote go to the collective of Indigenous Australian activist groups: http://unnecessaryevils.blogspot.com/2008/11/attributing-words.html

3   Catherine would like to thank and acknowledge Russ Johntson's influence in how he describes bringing ideas into relationship with one another.

References

Bovenschen, S. (1985). Is there a feminine aesthetic? (B. Weckmueller Trans.). In G. Ecker (Ed.), *Feminist aesthetics* (H. Anderson Trans.) (pp. 23–50). The Women's Press.

Ferrari, M. (2020). Gloria Anzaldúa's decolonizing aesthetics: On silence and bearing witness. *The Journal of Speculative Philosophy, 34*(3), 323–38.

hooks, b. (1994a). *Outlaw culture: Resisting representations.* Routledge.

hooks, b. (1994b). *Teaching to transgress: Education as the practice of freedom.* Routledge.

hooks, b. (2000). *Feminism is for everybody: Passionate politics.* Pluto.

Hunt, S. (2018). Embodying self-determination: Beyond the gender binary. In M. Greenwood, S. de Leeuw, & N. M. Lindsay (Eds.), *Determinants of Indigenous peoples' health: Beyond the social* (2nd ed., pp. 22–39). Canadian Scholars' Press.

Hunt, S. (2007). *Trans/formative identities: Narration of decolonization in mixed-race and transgender lives* [Master's Thesis, University of Victoria]. UVicSpace. https://dspace.library.uvic.ca/handle/1828/2374

Jackson, M. (2016). Aesthetics, politics, and attunement: On some questions brought by alterity and ontology. *GeoHumanities, 2*(1), 8–23, doi: 10.1080/2373566X.2016.1165076

Lippard, L. R. (1984). *Get the message? A decade of art for social change.* E. P. Dutton.

Newman, H. C., & Etmanski, C. (in press). The witness blanket: Responsibility through an ongoing journey of transformation. In A. Nicolaides, S. Eschenbacher, P. Buergelt, Y. Gilpin-Jackson, M. Welch, M. Misawa, & A. Lim (Eds.), *The Palgrave handbook on learning for transformation.* Palgrave MacMillan.

Newman, H. C., & Etmanski, C. (2019). Truthful engagement: Making the witness blanket, an ongoing process of reconciliation. *Engaged Scholar Journal, 5*(2), 235–43.

Newman, C., & Graham, C. (Directors). (2015). *Picking up the pieces: The making of the witness blanket.* [Documentary Film]. Produced by C. Newman & Media One. Presented by Canadian Museum for Human Rights. Available from https://humanrights.ca/story/picking-up-the-pieces-the-making-of-the-witness-blanket

Newman, C., & Hudson, C. (2019). *Picking up the pieces: Residential school memories and the making of the witness blanket.* Orca.

Nochlin, L. (1988). *Women, art, and power and other essays.* Harper & Row.

Stanford Encyclopedia of Philosophy. (2017, January 12). *Feminist aesthetics* (Rev. Ed.). Retrieved from https://plato.stanford.edu/entries/feminism-aesthetics/

White, L. Jr. (1967). The historical roots of our ecologic crisis. *Science, 155*(3767), 1203–7.

Wilson, A. (2008). N'tacimowin inna nah': Our coming in stories. *Canadian Woman Studies, 26*(3/4), 193–9.

Wilson, A. (2015). Our coming in stories: Cree identity, body sovereignty and gender self-determination. *Journal of Global Indigeneity, 1*(1), 1–5. Retrieved from http://ro.uow.edu.au/jgi/vol1/iss1/4

Chapter 13

Murals as Storied Spaces:
An Indigenous Feminist Practice of
Hope and Healing

Tracey Murphy and Edna Ellsworth

you cannot cherry pick what you like
about Indigenous women by only desiring
the ancestral knowledge and beauty that is woven into our dna and spirit
while turning a blind eye on the injustice that
we've faced and endured to even exist today.

Pepakiye Ashley Cooper, *do not disturb us*, 2020

In the above verse from the poem, *do not disturb us* (2020), Pepakiye Ashley Cooper, W̱SÁNEĆ and Nuu Chah Nulth First Nations poet, calls out how the consumption of Indigenous women, rendered through exploitive notions of desire,

Figure 13.1 *Blessing ceremony*. Photo by John Mackenzie.

mimics centuries of violent attempts by the Canadian state and society to disappear Indigenous women. In her poetry, Pepakiye reclaims Indigenous womanhood through converging metaphors of fragility and strength in her vivid descriptions of land, life and beauty. This chapter describes another reclamation of Indigenous feminist womanhood as a storied artistic representation of hope and healing in the form of a powerful participatory mural. This mural was dreamed into being by a group of young Indigenous women in a secondary school on the unceded W̱SÁNEĆ territories, near Victoria, British Columbia and welcome by community through a blessing ceremony (see Figure 13.1). As students in an Indigenous leadership class, these women wanted to bring awareness to the alarming rates of missing or murdered Indigenous women and girls (MMIWG). The sensationalism of violence in media stories of MMIWG, ongoing institutionalized racism and the loss of family and friends made a daily impact on their sense of safety. The final mural image, of an Indigenous woman surrounded by traditional medicinal plants, illustrates how land and cultural teachings can restory colonial space.

The story of the mural is told by two authors. Edna, a current post-secondary science student who comes from the W̱SÁNEĆ territories, was one of the young women who led this project. Tracey, a doctoral student and educator, facilitated the Indigenous leadership class and coordinated the artistic and community contributions of this project. As we will describe, this process reflects the aims of Indigenous resurgence, defined by Simpson (2016) as 'a collective movement that is nonhierarchical, nonexploitative, nonextractivist, nonauthoritarian' (p. 23). According to Simpson, the types of relationships she describes open up the possibilities for imaginative constellations of co-resistance against colonialism.

In keeping with Indigenous protocols of self-locating our origins and intentions, we begin with introductions. Then, in Part 1, Tracey outlines the historical and political context of the attempted erasure of Indigenous women, a hidden story of Canadian history, and how artists have countered this story to disrupt and protest the epidemic of MMIWG. In Part 2, Edna describes the process of creating the mural, along with reflections from Sarah Jim, the mural's lead artist. In this chapter, we highlight how Indigenous feminist art making creates generative possibilities to contest colonial patriarchal oppression and makes important contributions to feminist education and art activism.

We ask you, the reader, to be aware of your lens as you navigate this story. Bring an open mind and heart. Focus your attention and energy on the systematic challenges of colonialism. As you will read, the ongoing violence towards Indigenous women is a national shame. State inertia must be disrupted by prioritizing Indigenous knowledges (Saramo, 2016), and centring the emotionally felt narratives of Indigenous women's experiences over a singular meta-narrative of Canadian history. While it is clear that Indigenous women have been victimized for centuries, de Finney (2014) urges us to notice their bravery and creativity in navigating the traumas of colonization. We ask that as you read, be mindful that this story is about courage, reclamation and beauty.

Edna

TŦE NE SNÁ, ĆSE LÁ,E SEN EṮ W̱JOȽEȽP. My name is Edna Ellsworth. I was born and raised on the W̱SÁNEĆ (Saanich) territory. I am from the W̱JOȽEȽP (Tsartlip) First Nation Community. In my lifetime, I have been fortunate to be surrounded by parents, siblings, family and friends who uplift and enable me to be a strong Indigenous woman. They are the ones who teach the morals and necessities to be part of the W̱SÁNEĆ community, which is to be respectful, kind, honest and caring. It is from these teachings that I draw my strength as a person, as I aspire to fulfil them every day. Throughout my life, my culture and community have helped me to discover and decide on the kind of person I want to be. These teachings have taught me how to walk through life with an open mind to new encounters. I know that I can achieve my goals and still be true to my identity as an Indigenous woman. In my W̱SÁNEĆ cultural teachings, the role of women is vital. Women are the pillars of the community and are respected because they hold great strength as leaders and life givers in our community.

In the W̱SÁNEĆ (Saanich) culture, stories are vital. It is how our history is carried. Stories allow us to learn from our ancestors and bring forward their knowledge. The Flood Story, revived by the recent oral telling of W̱SÁNEĆ Elders Earl Claxton and John Elliott, gives us ideas on how to counter the epidemic of MMIWG. A long time ago XÁLS (the Creator) gave our people instructions to live by and how to care for the land, winds, water and all creatures. In the flood story, the people stopped listening to our creator and consequently, a great flood came. Those who had stayed closed to the original teachings survived in canoes until they could see a mountain rising up out of the water. One of the men said, 'NI QENNET TŦE W̱SÁNEĆ' (Look at what is emerging) as he pointed to the mountain emerging in the distance. This is the name of my community, the emerging peoples and as we reclaim our teachings, once again we are remerging through our teachings. As a student, it was important to have Elders visit us in school settings. They taught us to be proud of ourselves and to carry the values of honesty and kindness. The mountain that the W̱SÁNEĆ' people found was called ȽÁU, WEL₋NE₋W̱ (place of refuge, escape, healing). As an Indigenous student, I have sought out places of refuge and safety in schools and found healing within my community. The moral of this story is that from the teachings of our ancestors, we will rise up and create new beginnings. In the same sense, we are rising up and creating change for our Indigenous women and girls, so that they are safe and able.

Tracey, educator as learner

As a child, land was a place of solace and safety. I grew up on a farm that was composed of square acres of fields surrounded by forests of sweet-smelling cedar trees. I spent my childhood creating imaginative stories with my horses, dogs and a plethora of other pets. I spoke with all of these more-than-human beings and as an adult, have deeply regretted this loss of communication. This space, my home, was located on the territory of the Mohawk peoples. My ancestors are Irish and French; they arrived in Montreal on ships, fleeing wars and poverty. I felt most connected to my heritage through the stories of my grandmothers, most often while waiting for warm meals in the safety of their kitchens. As an adult, I felt a jarring rupture away from the earth, my identity, and my sense of belonging as I learnt the implications of being a settler on stolen territories. When my daughter was born on the W̱SÁNEĆ territory, I struggled to find roots. I felt drawn to landscapes, to the lush west coast rainforests, and to stories in my deepening friendships with women activists and artists. As a feminist, I define feminism as a praxis of becoming, an ongoing process of reflection and action. I appreciate hooks's (1999) suggestion that being a feminist is a constant process of ontological disruption. Regan (2010) emphasizes that settler women must seek to restory dominant colonial narratives as a way to begin deconstructing settler identities. The patriarchal positioning of Canadian white settler women as benevolent, pure and enlightened must also be disrupted to better understand how this racial binary has contributed to the ongoing violence against women in general and Indigenous women in particular (Dowling, 2019). My journey of self-location within this context is a deeply personal investigation of my history, ambitions and yearnings.

Barker and Pickerill (2020) suggest that 'non-Indigenous scholars … work to support resurgent Indigeneity through active, embodied participation in locally situated, Indigenous-directed "co-becoming" through struggle' (p. 63). As an educator, I seek out Indigenous mentors to support my students and through these collaborations I have been generously gifted with new teachings and friendships. I have come to understand my place as bound by relationships, and I am grateful for the teachings and guidance of these young women and the mentors. They have taught me to show up, stand up, stand back, speak out and most importantly, to listen.

Part 1: Disrupting narratives

Deliberate erasure of Indigenous women: Disrupting the historical story

Historically, the imposition of colonial power has sought to disappear Indigenous peoples, and particularly women, and their rich ontological and epistemological understandings and relations with the land as a human-embodied experience. McGurk and Caquard (2020) note how European male explorers viewed Indigenous peoples as non-human and used the concept of *Terra nullius* to appropriate their territories in Australia. Hargreaves (2017) points to colonial policies like the Indian Act in 1876 in Canada and how it displaced all Indigenous people but particularly, Indigenous women onto federal reserves. Women were disenfranchised through legal channels (loss of Indigenous status if they married a white man) and the destruction of their social and cultural practices including disrupting matrilineal lines of leadership and replacing them with patriarchal structures of governance. This violence to Indigenous women is, however, an ongoing process; they have been pillaged, penetrated, raped, and murdered and are still viewed as disposable (Million, 2014; Murphy, 2018; Smith, 2015).

In northern British Columbia, Indigenous women continue to be missing along what is known as the Highway of Tears (Hunt, 2011). Statistically, Indigenous women are five times more likely than non-Indigenous women to die from violence (Saramo, 2016; Suzack, 2010). The Native Women's Association of Canada (NWAC) has criticized government responses such as the National Inquiry into Missing and Murdered Indigenous Women and Girls (MMIWG) for failing women and communities (Galloway, 2017). Simpson (2016) questions the limits of state actions, and complicity of policing in violence against women. Lucchesi (2019) argues that the government fails to keep comprehensive data on the causes of women's deaths as the media continue to perpetuate victim blaming, negative stereotypes and ignore their names. Lucchesi uses maps to identify places where women have perished and to trace how colonial geographies shape the paths of women's lives that put them at risk.

Activist art as resurgence

Indigenous activist art has pushed back hard against statistics of women lost that represent not just the loss of one life, but webs of relationships that maintain the wellness of Indigenous communities. Garneau (2015) captures how art can challenge the narratives that frame our experience and open up opportunities for action because 'it changes our individual and collective imaginaries by particles, and these new pictures of the world can influence behaviour' (p. 9).

Collective community art projects revive the imaginative ability of traditional Indigenous collective decision making and in turn can educate the public (e.g., Bellrichard, 2020). One example is the *Walking with Our Sisters* exhibition, a collective commemoration made up of beaded moccasin tops to represent women lost to MMIWG which toured across Canada (see Simpson, 2016). Indigenous communities beaded the moccasin tops while telling stories of women in their lives. Simpson illustrates how this project worked as a form of community healing by centring Indigenous storytelling into visual practices and to avoid state interference, rejected all government funding. Likewise, the REDress Project, started in 2011 by Métis artist Jaime Black (2020), was created entirely by community contributions. Black asks supporters to hang red dresses outdoors to memorialize MMIWG. Communities choose when and where to support the campaign. The blood red dresses hang in trees, windows or anywhere else that will disrupt the stereotypes of serene Canadian landscapes. During the campaign, organizers offer workshops on Indigenous activism to help communities articulate their voices and goals. This movement inspired the work of Agnes Woodward, who began sewing and gifting brightly coloured ribbon skirts at events for women as a way to honour her missing auntie. Woodward's work has been taken up in community sewing groups, who continue to give away skirts as acts of compassion and sisterhood (Bellrichard, 2020).

Poetic storytelling, like the W̱SÁNEĆ flood story recounted by Edna, repositions Indigenous women as central knowledge keepers (Lucchesi, 2019). Indigenous women have used poetry to challenge the nation-state, recorded as far back as Pauline Johnson, a prolific Mohawk poet and performer of the nineteenth century (Deerchild, 2016, para. 3). In her poem, Harjo (2002) articulates this loss: 'We no longer know the names of the birds here, how to speak to them by their personal names [yet] Once we knew everything in this lush promise.' Lucchesi (2019) and Goeman (2013) point out how reclamation of knowledge begins with the stories of aunties and grandmas in their kitchens, through ceremonies, on car rides, in casinos, or while brewing pots of tea. Edna described how women in her community often begin with endearing stories of humour and gossip that lead into deeper cultural teachings, sharing of experiences and opinions, always within a circle of safety and love.

Our mural began with the stories of young women whose courage named injustice, and whose poetry, filled with metaphors of their strength and wisdom, contributed to Sarah Jim's conception of the mural. As Edna describes in Part 2, the finished mural tells a story but viewers must bring patience and imagination as they reflect on the imagery. For Edna, Sarah Jim and I, the collaborative process and potential of the final image as a tool for storytelling captures the spirit of Indigenous feminism in action.

Part 2: The mural: Process as hope and healing

Inspiring resurgence through collaboration

In this section, I (Edna) describe the mural creation process through my lens as a young W̱SÁNEĆ woman, and then describe key elements of the mural: the place of women, beings and roots. I will finish by describing the impact of our mural through the blessing ceremony. The impetus for this mural came out of educational collaborations with W̱SÁNEĆ educator Beangka Elliott and Project Reclaim, an organization that aims to empower Indigenous youth through restorative land activism. As a young woman in an Indigenous leadership class, I participated in a number of projects with Beangka and found safe spaces to talk about the parallels of violence done to Indigenous bodies and land. These opportunities created a momentum to imagine and bring to life an activist art project on missing and murdered Indigenous women. We invited other students to join us and decided that a mural would be best for the bold impact of its size rather than smaller posters or class presentations. Sarah Jim, an emerging artist and land-based educator with roots in Tseycum on the W̱SÁNEĆ territory, agreed to lead students as her first large-scale community mural project. As Sarah stated, 'facilitating this project was inspired by the youth of the Indigenous leadership class. These young people wanted to express awareness for MMIWG. I found this to be a real draw to the project. The youth had something to say and I wanted to hear what that was.' I would add that the students' passion was not only for meaningful projects, but to imagine our futures and ensure that students who came after us felt a sense of belonging. In our initial meetings, Sarah proposed that the mural centre the resilience of Indigenous women through uplifting themes of hope and healing:

> I wanted the youth to reflect on what made them feel empowered. How do they heal in times of grief? It's important to open up discussion about healthy ways of healing in Indigenous communities because there is so much past and present trauma that affects us.

In our leadership class, we felt safe to discuss issues, especially difficult emotional topics like the MMIWG. We called our class a family and made it a place of healing from supporting and trusting each other. For the mural, Indigenous and non-Indigenous students participated in a number of discussions and presentations about the mural that ranged from colonial history and genocide to qualities of colour, light and space. Small groups sketched out ideas on practice murals as they journalled their reflections. This process of talking with all the students was a beautiful way to get diverse interpretations of hope and healing, which became the central themes of our mural. At the end of our time in discussion and art making, Sarah gathered together images, reflections, sketches and poetry. From these pieces, she began creating the mural. Sarah believes that 'art is a great way to start dialogue about things that are not easy to talk about. Having an open and safe place to talk about MMIWG was important so everyone could feel heard and contribute to the design in their own way. The process was part of the healing.'

Over the summer, we met once a week and painted in a process of energetic co-creation, as you can see in the image of Edna painting (see Figure 13.2). We had a day-long visit from Indigenous Elders Doug and Kathy LaFortune, who shared their wisdom and insight on the issue of gendered violence, along with guidance to incorporate the traditional design techniques as a way to respect the art systems of Coast Salish peoples. Like Sarah, I believe that we learn so much from our Elders. By spending time with different generations, different perspectives are shared, which leads to a broadening view of the impact that the mural holds. Intergenerational trauma is often discussed, but spending wholesome, quality time with Elders can lead to intergenerational healing. Our finished mural is not just a collaborative artwork. It is a beautiful weaving of insight and compassion from students from diverse cultural backgrounds and community members who brought their lived experiences, humility and wisdom. By collaborating with people who had different lived experiences, the mural became a project that illuminated every contributor's passion and commitment.

Figure 13.2 *Edna painting.* Photo by Tracey Murphy.

Women as healers

As the summer passed, we outlined the woman and filled her dress with a deep red colour, symbolic of the REDress movement and wrapped copper bands around her arms. Sun rays illuminate her body and creatures support her journey. In my initial sketches, the woman is crossing over to the other side of life, the spiritual realm. In the finished image, the woman is illuminated by sun rays, to represent positivity and how the light of the rays show that healing is within her grasp. Elder Doug LaFortune is a distinguished Coast Salish artist who helped a young woman sketch out an

Figure 13.3 *Finished mural.* Photo by Tracey Murphy.

eagle in the sun for strength. The intention of the mural is to spark conversations around the themes of hope and healing, while encouraging students and teachers to research the hard statistics and facts about MMIWG. For instance, the woman holds up her fist with an eagle feather in her hand. This image defies the narratives that Indigenous women choose to be victims and put themselves in dangerous situations. Additionally, I believe that how we have placed the woman in the centre of the mural affirms that Indigenous women have places to find love and support.

This artistic decision may help viewers respect the factors that support our well-being and in turn Indigenous women who see this mural at the school may change their self-perception. We want to increase understanding of how Indigenous women are viewed in their communities. In the W̱SÁNEĆ community, women are to be loved and respected, represented in the mural by the Coast Salish hands under the woman's feet, to show how she is always held up by her community. It is a strong Coast Salish belief that women not only give life but are cherished knowledge keepers of the land. A final powerful contribution that symbolized the status of women in Kwakiutl culture, located in the north of what is now known as Vancouver Island, came from Mariah. She envisioned adding copper in the mural, to show the wealth and power of women in her culture. In the mural, copper weaves around the woman's arms and the eagle feather, bringing power to her resurgence and strength. As you can see in the final image (see Figure 13.3), these details show the strength of Indigenous women while energizing our themes of hope and healing.

In the W̱SÁNEĆ territory, Indigenous women like Sarah and Beangka are teaching traditional plant healing and practising the hard work of land restoration.

These women, along with many others, are, as Sarah stated, 'upholding the tradition of women carrying plant knowledge and tending to the land'. From the inspiration of their teachings, many of the mural makers incorporated our key themes of hope and healing through suggestions for land and plants. One of the international students, Sophia from Brazil, came up with the image of healing plants coming out of the woman's head to reach the sky. As one of the last additions, Sarah transformed Sophia's original image and added three medicinal plants of the W̱SÁNEĆ people: salal, ḴEXMIN (consumption plant), and sword fern. This detail mirrors Sarah's suggestion that 'healing the land is beneficial to healing oneself'. I agree but concur with Indigenous feminist Goeman (2013) that healing others is what uplifts a community, and this idea of collective healing is a central theme in the artwork and poetry of Indigenous artists and poets. Sophia suggested that a ball of yarn run off the woman's dress. She felt that the most powerful aspect of our project was how a group of diverse students came together and created a community of care. This unintended outcome, the mutual care and connection between students as we worked together, symbolizes the heart of our project. I believe that making art brings people together, helps us learn with knowledge keepers and strengthens our commitment to create change.

Beings

In the beginning, when the mural was being imagined, many of the students at the school submitted sketches that represented MMIWG in a meaningful way. I was fortunate to have one of my ideas represented in the mural: for the woman in red to be surrounded by the many creatures that represent the ancestors. The ancestors lead and protect the woman on her journey and keep her bridged to the spiritual world. While we painted, participants continued to add beings to hold the woman's place and surround her with safety. I added in a hummingbird, to remind me of my mother who has always had hummingbird feeders and loves their speed and beauty. We added dragonflies too. As a child, my grandmother teased my sister in fun, telling her that dragonflies would bite her hand. Having the ancestors represented as beings in the mural is vital to the central themes of hope and healing, and central to our worldviews as Indigenous peoples. We require the guidance and strength from those who came before. Throughout the mural, the woman is helped along her way through nourishment found in the land and the courage that radiates from the creatures that surround her.

Roots

The roots represent that the woman is connected to her culture and land, and so she is able to gain a deep sense of peace. In Sarah's words, 'The roots represent grounding oneself in place. When we are grounded, we tend to make better decisions.' Natalya, one of the Indigenous leadership students, envisioned the mural to be a picture of strength; she believed herself to be always rooted and connected to ancestors and so protected by their life knowledges. Another student, Hilda, who was of European ancestry and grew up in the rainforests of the Haida Gwaii territory, described how trees had to root down first so they could reach up into rays of light and possibility. Roots anchor a tree and allow it to reach up to the sky. Images of roots in the mural are metaphors of rootedness to our cultures where we find the strength to heal from the traumas of colonialism. As the summer passed, guests from another project going on in the community, the Reef Net Project, joined us to paint and offer ideas. The Reef Net Project brought together young W̱SÁNEĆ leaders to learn about traditional values of land conservation by reviving the reef net, a traditional way to fish and harvest the ocean that was formerly banned by colonizers. The ideals of the Reef Net project and, by extension, the W̱SÁNEĆ people, reiterate the importance of life and the need to sustain life and land.

Blessing ceremony

At the end of the summer, students, their families and invited guests had a small ceremony for the mural. It was important to recognize our hard work and bless the mural for safety, and continued healing. Sarah affirmed how W̱SÁNEĆ traditional ceremony teaches the value of care, and by caring for ourselves first, we can ensure that others are safe and loved. The quality of light that day mirrored the colours of the mural's background, and the wind blew with a soft warmth. I would like the mural to spark conversation about the realities of MMIWG and prompt non-Indigenous students to deepen their personal awareness and encourage activism alongside Indigenous communities. More importantly, as a knowledge keeper pointed out, having Indigenous artwork in the school will invite Indigenous students to feel welcome and have a sense of belonging in the school. I believe that the mural creates a space of safety for Indigenous girls as they discover their identities as women. To end our day, we asked a women's drum group called All Nations Strong Women Education and Reconciliation (ANSWER) to sing and dance. ANSWER is composed of Indigenous women of all ages; for our ceremony, they included a few young women, in affirmation of their strength. They sang the Women's Warrior song last, and our small gathering held our arms up with closed fists. The Sta'timc First Nation of coastal British Columbia created this song and gave permission to sing it, to those who will honour murdered and missing women. The song seemed fitting as our mural was cloaked in summer light, covering the woman's raised hand holding an eagle feather, the symbol for bravery and strength.

The future stories of our mural

We, Tracey and Edna, affirm how this story is one of hope and healing. We know that our mural, the process and final image, offers much to the current discourses of feminist activism. Our mural weaves together a tapestry of experiences to counter how Western culture has taken, benefitted from and silenced the stories of others, to favour a single narrative that seeks to justify colonialism. Hemmings (2010) contends that rather than telling different stories, we can learn to tell stories differently. To borrow from Styres (2011), the stories that became images in the mural bring forward how place is storied, relational and soulful, that 'we are in place as much as it is in us, every experience and expression of place is replete with multiple layers of memories' (p. 16). Telling stories differently happens when we can reflect on our points of view, our locations and as characters with agency to make change. Likewise, Arvin, Tuck, and Morrill (2013) assert that Indigenous feminist theories 'can imagine and realize different modes of nationalism and alliances in the future' (p. 11). Feminist education is unique as a way of learning that responds and evolves by taking on difficult issues of justice, while creating safe spaces and building alliances against systemic racism, privilege and precarity (e.g., Clover, 2020).

The mural was purposefully installed beside the main door of the school. This location is important because it speaks of courage and hope as it reminds us of the work still to be done. From conception to installation our project illuminates how Indigenous feminist arts can work as a form of activism to challenge the violence we feel that is so deeply embedded in all our institutions, including our schools. Our mural is the beginning of a story that offers a glimpse into the future of Indigenous women's resurgence; it is a reawakening of the timeless Indigenous feminist imagination and its knowing of and in place.

Finally, we return to the poem '*do not disturb us*', and its call to 'hear us, value us, acknowledge the courage'. Like the story of rising from the flood, it is an affirmation of Indigenous women's resilience against colonial adversity and equally, a reminder of the Indigenous feminist imagination and its knowing 'place'.

References

Arvin, M., Tuck, E., & Morrill, A. (2013). Decolonizing feminism: Challenging connections between settler colonialism and heteropatriarchy. *Feminist Formations*, *25*(1), 8–34.

Barker, A., & Pickerill, J. (2020). Doings with the land and sea: Decolonizing geographies, Indigeneity, and enacting place-agency. *Progress in Human Geography*, *44*(4), 640–62.

Bellrichard, C. (2020, February 3).Vancouver women sewing 100 ribbon skirts for MMIWG families. https://www.cbc.ca/news/indigenous/vancouver-mmiwg-ribbon-skirts-1.5450095

Black, J. (2020). The REDress project. https://www.jaimeblackartist.com/exhibitions/

Clover, D. E. (2020). Introduction. In D. E. Clover, S. Dzulki, H. Gelderman, & K. Sanford (Eds.), *Feminist adult educators' guide to aesthetic, creative and disruptive strategies in Museums and community* (pp. viii–xvi). University of Victoria.

de Finney, S. (2014). Under the shadow of empire: Indigenous girls' presencing as decolonizing force. *Girlhood Studies*, *7*(1), 8–26.

Deerchild, R. (2016). *Mohawk poet Pauline Johnson's historic home tells a story of duality*. https://www.cbc.ca/radio/unreserved/unreserved-heads-to-six-nations-of-the-grand-river-1.3459885/mohawk-poet-pauline-johnson-s-historic-home-tells-a-story-of-duality-1.3466631

Dowling, P. (2019) Elimination, in the feminine. *Interventions, 21*(6), 787–802.

Gallagher, S. (Ed.). (2007). *Postcolonial literature and the Biblical call for justice.* University Press of Mississippi.

Galloway, G. (2017, May 16). Inquiry into missing and murdered women a failure: Indigenous group. *The Globe and Mail.* Retrieved from: https://www.theglobeandmail. com/news/politics/inquiry-into-missing-and-murdered-women-a-failure-indigenous- group-says/article35003027/

Garneau, D. (2015). Forword. In G. L'Hirondelle Hill, & S. McCall (Eds.), *The land we are* (pp.1–15). ARB Books.

Goeman, M. (2013). *Mark my words: Native women mapping our nations.* University of Minnesota Press.

Hargreaves, A. (2017). *Violence against Indigenous women: Literature, activism, resistance.* Wilfred Laurier University Press.

Harjo, J. (2002). *A map to the next world.* Poetry Foundation. https://www. poetryfoundation.org/poems/49621/a-map-to-the-next-world

Hemmings, C. (2010). *Why stories matter.* Duke University Press.

hooks, b. (1999). *All about love: New visions.* William Murrow.

Hunt, S. (2011). *Restoring the honouring circle: Taking a stand against youth sexual exploitation.* Justice Institute of British Columbia.

Lucchesi, A. (2019). Mapping geographies of Canadian colonial occupation: Pathway analysis of murdered Indigenous women and girls. *Gender, Place & Culture, 26*(6), 868–87.

McGurk, T., & Caquard, S. (2020). To what extent can online mapping be decolonial? A journey throughout Indigenous cartography in Canada. *The Canadian Geographer, 64*(1), 49–64.

Million, D. (2014). There is a river in me. In A. Smith (Ed.), *Theorizing Native studies* (pp. 31–42). Duke University Press.

Murphy, T. (2018). Indigenous womanhood, precarity and the nation state: An arts-based performance that offers a new pathway to reconciliation. *Liminalities: A Journal of Performance Studies, 14*(3), 89–108.

Rajan, B., Jeberi, C., & Mojab, B. (2019). Confronting sexual violence through dance and theatre pedagogy. *Engaged Scholar Journal, 5*(2), 255–62.

Regan, P. (2010). *Unsettling the settler within: Indian residential schools, truth telling, and reconciliation in Canada.* UBC Press.

Saramo, S. (2016). Unsettling spaces: Grassroots responses to Canada's missing and murdered Indigenous women during the Harper government years. *Comparative American Studies: An International Journal, 143*(3–4), 204–20.

Savarese, J. (2017). Challenging colonial norms and attending to presencing in stories of missing and murdered Indigenous women. *Canadian Journal of Women and Law, 29*(1), 157–81.

Simpson, A. (2014). *Mohawk interruptus: Political life across the borders of settler States.* Duke University Press.

Simpson, L. (2016). Indigenous resurgence and co-resistance. *Critical Ethnic Studies, 2*(2), 19–34.

Smith, A. (2015). *Conquest: Sexual violence and American Indian genocide.* Duke University Press.

Styres, S. (2011). Land as first teacher: A philosophical journeying. *Reflective Practice, 12*(6), 717–31.

Suzack, C. (Ed.). (2010). *Indigenous women and feminism: Politics, activism, culture.* UBC Press.

Part IV

CARING AND THE FEMINIST IMAGINARY

Chapter 14

Practising a Feminist Aesthetic Imaginary: Creating Moments of Equality When Researching Sensory Ways of Knowing Homecare

Kerry Harman

We live in a world 'in which carelessness reigns' (Chatzidakis et al., 2020, p. 1). From Black deaths in custody to the ongoing environmental carnage created by deforestation and industrial agriculture, it is all too easy to find examples of carelessness. The list is long and includes the daily fatalities as refugees flee war zones and deprivation, increasing femicide rates in Latin America, and the rise in domestic violence during 'lockdown' in the UK. But what would happen, ask Chatzidakis et al. (2020, p. 5), if 'we were to begin instead to put care at the very centre of life'? And following from this, what if we adult education researchers were to centre attending to, presence, paying attention, closeness, taking care and connection rather than understanding these ways of knowing as aberrations and flaws when conducting research? It is this speculative what if and the creative possibilities enabled by reimagining the world that are understood as the feminist imaginary in this chapter.

I have been working with a group of paid homecare workers in London, UK, since 2018 on a feminist political intervention to reconfigure care. In the UK, homecare work and homecare workers are, for the most part, invisible. Paid homecare work is done mainly by women, often migrant women in cities like London, and takes place in people's homes. It is concerned with the care of the frail and elderly, a group of citizens who, during the Covid-19 pandemic, appeared to be expendable as the government in the UK adopted 'open for business' policy. So how to make the often invisible embodied and sensory knowledges gained in and through paid homecare work seen, heard and felt so that the work and the people doing the work can begin to be counted and taken into account when developing policy in the adult social care sector? In other words, how might care be reimagined?

The *New imaginaries of care* project introduced in this chapter is a feminist aesthetic response to that question. I use the term *aesthetic* as the aim of the project is to reconfigure what Rancière (2004, p. 9) refers to as the 'distribution of the sensible' in terms of *who* and *what* can be attended to (or perceived) in the domain of care, and whose knowledge and what knowledges are able to count. In other words, the project aims to create an 'aesthetic rupture' whereby those who are currently not able to sense (those that cannot be seen and heard) are able to 'appear'. The democratic possibilities of reconfiguring the 'distribution of the sensible' in adult social care and the academy inspire my practices as a researcher of learning in and through everyday practices at work, and hopefully the project will contribute to a currently marginalized group of paid homecare workers being seen, heard and taken seriously as knowledge producers on care.

The research project is designed as a series of political and pedagogical interventions for producing equality for homecare workers, and this chapter describes both completed and planned interventions. In the first section, the current 'crisis in care' is introduced as it directs attention to the urgency of this work. Next, an overview of initial research with homecare workers in the *Invisible work, invisible knowledges?*[1] project is provided. This was the first intervention in reimagining care and the project culminated in a community engagement event where homecare workers spoke about the current challenges associated with providing good care. This work led to the development of the *New imaginaries of care* project, an ongoing collaboration with homecare workers, which is documenting the relationship between care and sensory ways of knowing. In the last section of the chapter the emancipatory possibilities of research *as* a form of aesthetic rupture are explored.

The crisis in care

Large numbers of predominantly women workers are employed in many countries across the globe in the provision of care for the aged. For example, in 2019/20, an estimated 1.52 million people were employed in the adult social care sector in England (Fenton et al., 2020). The same report indicates that the most common job role was 'care worker', with 865,000 working in that role; there were 715,000 domiciliary care (homecare) workers and 84 per cent of those were women and 520,000 new jobs in the sector are predicted by 2035. Care work is a major industry yet homecare workers in the UK are often paid on zero-hour contracts, which means there is no guarantee of work, and when they do work, they receive very low hourly rates of pay, often below the minimum wage (Hayes, 2017). While the Covid-19 pandemic has accelerated the current crisis in care, a long trail of reports reveals the care sector was in crisis well before the start of the pandemic (e.g. BBC Panorama, 2019; Gardiner, 2015; UNISON, 2016). So why has this situation remained acceptable to governments and the general public for so long?

Feminization of care

Low wages are integrally linked with a common perception that homecare work is 'low skilled' work, and this perception is underpinned by a societal taken-for-granted understanding that care is a 'feminine' job that women are naturally able to do without requiring education or training. This view was most recently made explicit in the UK with the call by the current government for care work to be officially categorized as 'low skilled' in immigration policy (Goodfellow, 2020). While this led to a public outcry during the pandemic, it continues to remain acceptable for many homecare workers to be paid below the National Minimum Wage. In an effort to counter the ongoing crisis in care there have been ongoing calls from trade unions and politicians for the professionalization of the care sector in the UK, underpinned by the hope that training and development will improve the quality of care provided as well as contribute to better paid jobs (e.g., Hayes, Johnson, & Tarrant, 2019).

However, the assumption of a skills deficit in the sector, which a training solution implies, is open to question. For example, Cuban (2013) found that a large number of highly skilled migrants, often with nursing qualifications, were specifically recruited to poorly paid homecare jobs in the UK with no career prospects. While these workers used their skills and knowledge in their daily work, this knowledge was not recognized nor remunerated. Similarly, Datta et al., (2010) identified that not only is a significant proportion of care in the Global North undertaken by migrant workers from the Global South, but these workers bring 'distinct values, systems and ethics of care' to this work and often provide a level of care that is 'over and above' (p.94) what is required.

The above examples point to the politics of care and the ongoing undervaluing of care in neoliberal healthcare and adult social care systems (Chatzidakis et al., 2020; Mol, 2008; Tronto, 1995). Indeed, the taken-for-granted notion of care work as necessarily low skilled has been challenged in various strands of feminist research for decades. For example, literature on 'bodywork' and 'intimate labour' highlights the workplace practices and institutional structures that work to reproduce the seemingly natural notion of homecare work as low skilled (e.g., Boris & Parreñas, 2010; Lanoix, 2013; Twigg et al., 2011). An overlapping strand of literature is emerging work on the 'materialities of care' (Buse, Martin, & Nettleton, 2018), which attends to the ways the material practices of care are often made 'mundane', 'immaterial' and 'inconsequential' and thus remain invisible. The hidden elements of care include the importance of touch (Buse & Twigg, 2018; Pink, Morgan, & Dainty, 2014) as well as other senses such as sight and smell. As will be discussed in more detail below, these 'base' senses are frequently aligned with the 'feminine' and have been ignored as legitimate ways of producing knowledge in the academy. As Latimer (2018) asks, is there a need for 'different imaginaries of care' (p.379) to those that currently dominate healthcare policy and the organization of care?

Feminist aesthetics and the imaginary of care

The *New imaginaries of care* project contributes to foregrounding the politics of care by attending to the often-overlooked sensory and embodied dimensions of good care. Rather than focusing on the ongoing oppression of paid homecare workers, which has been demonstrated empirically albeit with little change in terms of recognition, value, support or better pay, a political approach underpinned by feminist aesthetics guides the project. This approach links closely with feminist adult education literature that directs attention to embodied and sensory dimensions of knowing and learning (Lawrence, 2012). From this view, ways of knowing (and learning) can be understood as encompassing more than a cognitive dimension, which is a very different understanding of knowing and knowledge production to that privileged in the Western philosophical tradition. In the Western tradition knowing is understood as a hierarchical ordering of making sense of sense and the white, male gaze (=objective, rational knowledge producer) has been the taken-for-granted standpoint for creating theoretical concepts and what gets to count as knowledge. However, the ongoing privileging of the white, male gaze contributes to dividing the world into two separate levels of intelligence where there are those that know (=active academic subject) and those that are known (=passive, observed, object) (Chanter, 2018).

Feminist aesthetics, however, directs attention to the gendered orderings of the senses and how this has constrained what has been attended to in much critical research emanating from the academy. For example, Classen, Howes and Synnott (1994) and Classen (1998, 2005) have illustrated how in Western culture the senses of smell, touch and taste have traditionally been associated with women/'primitive' cultures, and it is this association which has led to these being understood as the 'lower' senses. Classen argues that it has been taken for granted in Western philosophy that sight and then hearing are the most rational ways of knowing the world, with sight often equated with transparency. It is then only a small step from transparency to Enlightenment notions of objectivity and truth. She proposes that rather than understanding the current dominance of visual culture in modern Western culture as neutral, it is integrally related to a gendered and racist privileging of particular senses when producing knowledge in the academy. Feminist aesthetics provides a fundamental challenge to the privileging of the white, male gaze and the ways of ordering the world arising from this view (e.g. Hein, 1998; Korsmeyer, 2004).

Disrupting the privileging of the white, male gaze, feminist lifelong learning scholars point to the home as an important yet largely invisible site of work and learning. For example, Eichler et al. (2010) provide an insightful analysis of the assumptions and exclusions in much sociological literature on work, which generally tends to ignore household work, whilst Gouthro (2009, p. 163) maintains that a 'patriarchal notion of learning' has led to excluding the homeplace as a sight of learning in literature on lifelong learning. The focus of both these scholars is the unpaid, everyday learning that takes place in the home. My focus takes a new trajectory into women's paid (homecare) work to provide an entry point into an exploration of the multisensory dimensions of care. The aim of the project is to attend to embodied and sensory ways of knowing care in a homecare context and ways in which care can be understood in terms of the typically ignored senses of touch, smell and taste. Through a feminist re-ordering of the privileging of the white, male gaze, the research process and outcomes aim to produce an 'aesthetic rupture' in how care can be imagined.

There has been a long tradition in feminist political struggle to use theory as a strategy (or intervention) for reconfiguring gendered and racist knowledge hierarchies and challenging the politics of knowledge production in the academy (e.g. hooks, 1989; Moraga & Anzaldua, 1983; Sedgwick, 2003). I propose that Rancière's notion of an 'equality of intelligence' (1991, p. 38) is a useful concept and principle in that struggle. This equality of intelligence both presupposes and verifies that *all* have the capacity to speak, to tell stories and make meanings (Rancière, 2017), and this has significant implications for who can be understood as knowledge producers and how knowledge is produced in the academy (2009b). In other words, we theorists of embodied learning at work need to practise equality in the ways we produce knowledge rather than continuing to divide the world into two separate levels of intelligence where there are those that know and those that are known (Harman, 2019). The *New imaginaries of care* project aims to produce ongoing moments of equality rather than reproducing an active academic knower (subject) – passive participant known (object) divide and it is in that sense that the method *is* a political intervention. The strategy is to work with homecare workers to produce new ways of imagining care rather than producing knowledge on homecare workers. While this is not a new political strategy, indeed the presupposition and verification of equality could be said to underpin much feminist adult education research (English & Irving, 2015); this project is yet another piece in an ever-expanding feminist anthology which takes equality as the starting point for disrupting prevailing knowledge hierarchies.

Intervention 1 – Invisible work, invisible knowledges? *project*

The focus of the initial *Invisible work, invisible knowledges?* project, which was completed during 2018 and 2019, was to contact paid homecare workers to explore whether a collaborative project directing attention to their knowledges gained in and through their everyday work practices would be of interest to them. The presupposition of an equality of intelligence underpinned this ambition. For example, if there was no interest from homecare workers in getting involved as paid co-researchers then me studying their often invisible ways of knowing care would be pointless as this would be yet another ethnographic study by an academic on the embodied knowing of homecare workers. An aesthetic rupture required working with paid homecare workers rather than making them the object of academic knowledge.

However, paid homecare workers are not an easy group of workers to make contact with as they work very long hours and, as noted above, are often on zero-hour contracts. This means that any time they take off from work, for example, to meet with a researcher, is time they are not getting paid. Keeping this in mind, and in an effort to presuppose an equality of intelligence, the homecare workers were all paid to attend meetings. This was made possible by securing a small public engagement research grant from my university. The pre-supposition was that these people had experience and knowledge in and of this domain of work and should be recognized as consultants.

I was introduced to most of the homecare workers I spoke with by UNISON, which is the main union for homecare workers in the UK. The meetings with homecare workers were conducted either in small groups or individually, whichever those I was speaking with preferred, and were usually audio-recorded. However, a few workers requested that their meetings not be recorded as they felt it was too risky. Homecare work is precarious, and it is an all too frequent experience amongst homecare workers to have lost hours or to be dropped completely from weekly rotas as a result of what might be considered innocuous requests (Whittome, 2020). One homecare worker recounted:

> The lady – she's disabled – she's stuck in a chair and when you go back and report it you're classed as a whistle blower and what they do [the agency] is take your hours from you because you say 'we've got a lady, she's stuck in bed, she needs a wheelchair, can you please, please, please get onto social services?' and they don't do it.

After introducing myself and the *Invisible knowledges* project, I usually commenced the discussion by asking the homecare workers to describe a 'typical' day at work, if indeed they felt there was such a thing, and what they do during the day. This enabled me to collect accounts of their daily work routines as well as many of the issues they experienced in providing homecare. There was a lot of talk about 'good care' and the importance of taking time and not rushing. Charlotte described it in this way:

> They [the agency managers] don't realise how sensitive it is working with a service user with dementia. It is such a sensitive thing ... You have to be so careful and really, really take your time. Completely take your time.

For the homecare workers, good care takes time and often incorporates sensory elements such as touch. As Doreen pointed out: 'Is it better to act like a robot or to take the time and put your arm around a person and let them know you care?' However, these caring aspects of their job are often organized out of their work by the Care Plans[2] they are required to adhere to. All the workers I spoke with expressed that they did not have enough time to do their work properly as the Care Plans prevent them from spending adequate time with care recipients. Amir found this extremely frustrating:

> [When clients have deteriorated] they expect you to do the same thing you've been doing in the same time they've allocated to you. They aren't going to come around here and say we're going to put another half hour on your rota. No, no, no.

The homecare workers usually have little or no input in the development of these documents and the duration of visits is usually 15, 30 or 45 minutes, depending on the Plan. Maureen pointed out:

I don't think whoever is doing these care packages actually realises what it entails to look after somebody … You're trying to befriend them [the care recipient] as well. Make them feel comfortable, feel safe. So you're trying to build a steady relationship with them.

Many also spoke of the need to work extra unpaid hours to provide a basic level of care for their clients/service users/friends/family – the names used for those receiving care varied but many of the homecare workers had established long-term relationships with care recipients and often considered them family, as Abebi commented:

Most of the time we go out of our way to do things that we're not supposed to do because in 45 minutes you can't do a lot … The work becomes as if I do it the way my client is my relative.

All the workers powerfully described the current undervaluing of care during the meetings, for example: 'We are not valued'; 'We are looked upon as we do the shit work'; 'Nobody appreciates us'; 'People don't value that kind of thing – if it's valued, they'd give you more time to do it and give you more pay'. The audio-recorded homecare workers' accounts were used to produce a short documentary called *Homecare Worker Stories*.[3] As will be discussed below, the documentary proved a particularly effective technique for making this group of workers and the work that they do visible.

The *Invisible knowledges* project concluded with a community engagement event[4] in a public venue in Haringey, the borough in London where most of the meetings with homecare workers had been conducted. This was a vital part of the project as it provided a forum for the homecare workers to speak with other stakeholders in the sector about the challenges they face in their work. Those attending included union organizers, local politicians, agency managers and grassroots activist organizations. The documentary, which provides a compelling account of the everyday challenges these workers face in providing good care, was shown at the start of the event and framed the ongoing discussion.

Roy (2016) has written on the power of documentaries as educational tools and the documentary has been an effective tool in not only representing the voices of the care workers but in having their voices heard. People pay attention to the documentary, and it has been useful in highlighting the challenges faced by homecare workers including the ongoing issue of not having enough time to provide adequate care. The documentary enables the homecare workers and the work that they do to become tangible and thus what was previously invisible, unheard and unknown is able to exist. It also exemplifies that homecare workers have the capacity to speak, to tell stories and make meanings (Rancière, 2017) and that theorizing care is not just the domain of academic 'knowers'. The documentary has been shown at academic conferences as well as more public facing events and audiences engage with concerns and values raised by homecare workers and are able to reimagine what constitutes 'good care', more so than if I was reinterpreting the homecare workers' accounts.[5]

The community engagement event also provided an opportunity to gauge support for a collaboratively developed *New imaginaries of care* project. The homecare workers are hoping that their knowledges and contribution to the sector will start to be recognized and the *New imaginaries of care* project aims to make their often-invisible ways of knowing and doing care more visible. This is work in progress and currently homecare workers are writing blogs and producing podcasts on their experiences of providing care during Covid (e.g. Weimar & Harman, 2020). The homecare workers and I have been invited to present papers we have co-written at various academic conferences on care during 2021 and 2022.

Towards an aesthetics of care?

Through staging the research with homecare workers as interventions with ongoing moments of democratic action, I propose that the existing ordering of what makes sense, both in the hierarchical model of care that currently prevails in the healthcare system in the UK and in the hierarchical model of knowledge production that prevails in the academy, might be reconfigured. In other words, the projects provide an opportunity for aesthetic rupture whereby the homecare workers ignore a certain body of experience, that is as 'low skilled', and this enables new ways of seeing, saying, feeling, thinking and doing care (new ways of sensing) to appear. For some, reconfiguring the existing distribution of the sensible is the very definition of politics (Rancière, 2009a).

There will be opportunities throughout the *New imaginaries of care* project whereby moments of equality can be experienced. I see this as a feminist aesthetic education. In other words, the pedagogic possibility is to learn to be equal. Rather than attempting to 'establish stable relations between states of the body and modes of perception and signification which correspond to them' (Rancière, 2009a, p. 9), whereby the homecare workers (and me) are kept in our 'proper place'; the 'co-production of knowledge', a much-touted phrase in the academy, will be taken seriously. We will no longer be necessarily tied to particular social positions as the 'active academic knower subject' and 'passive object of academic knowledge'. This reconfiguring work includes ignoring traditional academic hierarchies and paying homecare workers as researchers on the project. Of course, simply paying the homecare workers does not guarantee the experience of equality but an unequal financial relationship, whereby the academic is paid to conduct the research but the homecare workers are not, reaffirms an inequality of intelligence rather than equality.

A planned output from the *New imaginaries of care* project is to present a 'compendium of neglected things' at a meeting of key stakeholders in the provision of homecare services. The compendium will document sensory ways of knowing care and will work to verify the marginalized knowledges of homecare workers.

This act will enable the homecare workers, who have largely been ignored in discussions on the provision of good care, and their sensory and embodied ways of knowing to become visible. Of course, we can only speculate as to whether the knowledges produced by the homecare workers (the compendium) will actually be taken up and used by policymakers in homecare. Regardless, continuing to document the previously ignored experiences of homecare workers through film, blogs, podcasts and academic publications, will be an important contribution to re-imagining care and how it might be known and understood.

Moreover, the project will provide the opportunity to ignore disciplinary boundaries as it will enable flows of knowledge between the disciplinary domains of social science, the humanities and adult education in the exploration and conceptualization of 'care'. I have written elsewhere on the importance of 'taking care' in our research methods (Harman, 2016, 2021) but who better to work with than homecare workers if adult educators and, more generally, social scientists, are genuinely interested in better understanding how they might be more caring in their research approaches?

It is the political possibility of reconfiguring the distribution of the sensible, both in terms of how care is conceived but also in the ways that embodied experience and everyday learning might be theorized, that inspires this project. However, rather than being complacent about the proposed research as a pedagogic intervention for presupposing and verifying equality, the effects of the research practices will continue to be examined throughout the project. For example, might the ethnographic exploration of sensory ways of knowing in homecare still be too close to the sociological desire by academics to put everything in its 'proper place'? Is it simply inversing the old cognitive (mind)– sensory (body) binary by drawing attention to the sensory ways that knowledges are made in and through the everyday practices of homecare workers? Rather than working in an aesthetic dimension, where the distribution of the sensible is reconfigured, will focusing on their sensory ways of knowing once again tie homecare workers to their proper place as carers? This is an unresolved tension in the project at present.

There is also an issue raised by Tronto (2013) in terms of more democratic ways of thinking about care, which is that at times we will all be receivers *as well* as providers of care. None of us are autonomous. Thus, rather than thinking about care only from the perspective of the caregiver, which Tronto believes reinforces the notion of autonomy that underpins current thinking on democracy and freedom, it is essential that care recipients also be involved in decisions around care.

While the above questions are important to consider and incorporate as the research progresses, I propose that a feminist aesthetics of care, where care is conceptualized in terms of sensory dimensions, is a useful starting place in terms of reimagining care. This includes moving beyond the conceptual constraints of Western philosophical thinking and the privileging of the white, male gaze in how we researchers of lifelong learning research and produce knowledge on embodied and sensory ways of knowing.

Notes

1 See project website at: http://www.bbk.ac.uk/research/centres/social-change-and-transformation-in-higher-education/projects
2 The Care Plans, which list the tasks that will be provided during the visit, are written by an Occupational Therapist after an initial visit and assessment with a prospective service user.
3 See https://www.youtube.com/watch?v=_iTuSah5RXo&feature=youtu.be
4 See https://www.bbk.ac.uk/news/homecare-a-community-engagement-event-1
5 See #BirkbeckInspires: How we might recognise the value of homecare provision [https://www.youtube.com/watch?v=F0PWKlZmDmM&list=PL2Fy-5oxIlb72tRO-O1XN1-Ahklep88D2&index=18]

References

BBC Panorama, (2019). Crisis in care. In A. Mason (Producer): BBC.

Boris, E., & Parreñas, R. S. (Eds.). (2010). *Intimate labors*. Stanford University Press.

Buse, C., Martin, D., & Nettleton, S. (2018). Conceptualising 'materialitites of care': Making visible mundane material culture in health and social care contexts. *Sociology of Health & Illness, 40*(2), 243–55.

Buse, C., & Twigg, J. (2018). Dressing disrupted: Negotiating care through the materiality of dress in the context of dementia. *Sociology of Health & Illness, 40*(2), 340–52.

Chanter, T. (2018). *Art, politics and Rancière: Broken perceptions*. Bloomsbury Academic.

Chatzidakis, A., Hakim, J., Littler, J., Rottenberg, C., & Segal, L. (2020). *The care manifesto: The politics of interdependence*. Verso.

Classen, C. (1998). *The color of angels: Cosmology, gender and the aesthetic imagination*. Routledge.

Classen, C. (Ed.). (2005). *The book of touch*. Berg.

Classen, C., Howes, D., & Synnott, A. (Eds.). (1994). *Aroma: The cultural history of smell*. Routledge.

Cuban, S. (2013). *Deskilling migrant women in the global care industry*. Palgrave Macmillan.

Datta, K., McIlwaine, C., Evans, Y., Herbert, J., May, J., & Wills, J. (2010). A migrant ethic of care? Negotiating care and caring among migrant workers in London's low-pay economy. *Feminist Review, 94*, 94–116.

Eichler, M., Albanese, P., Ferguson, S., Hyndman, N., Liu, L. W., & Matthews, A. (Eds.). (2010). *More than it seems: Learning through household work*. Women's Press of Canada.

English, L. M., & Irving, C. J. (Eds.). (2015). *Feminism in community: Adult education for transformation*. Sense.

Fenton, W., Polzin, G., Price, R., McCaffrey, R., & Fozzard, T. (2020). *The state of the adult social care sector and workforce in England*. Retrieved from Leeds: https://www.skillsforcare.org.uk/adult-social-care-workforce-data/Workforce-intelligence/documents/State-of-the-adult-social-care-sector/The-state-of-the-adult-social-care-sector-and-workforce-2020.pdf

Gardiner, L. (2015). *Care to pay? Meeting the challenge of paying the National Living Wage in social care*. Retrieved from London: http://www.resolutionfoundation.org/publications/care-to-pay-meeting-the-challenge-of-paying-the-national-living-wage-in-social-care/

Goodfellow, M. (2020, April 11). While 'low-skilled' migrants are saving us, the government is cracking down on them. *The Guardian*. Retrieved from https://www.theguardian.com/commentisfree/2020/apr/11/low-skilled-migrants-government-cracking-down

Gouthro, P. (2009). Neoliberalism, lifelong learning, and the homeplace: Problematizing the boundaries of 'public' and 'private' to explore women's learning experiences. *Studies in Continuing Education*, *31*(2), 157–72.

Harman, K. (2016). Examining work – education intersections: The production of learning reals in and through practice. *European Journal for Research on the Education and Learning of Adults*, *7*(1), 89–106.

Harman, K. (2019). Enacting equality: Rethinking emancipation and adult education with Jacque Rancière. In F. Finnegan & B. Grummell (Eds.), *Power and possibility: Adult education in a diverse and complex world* (pp. 107–16). Brill.

Harman, K. (2021). Sensory ways of knowing care – possibilities for reconfiguring 'the distribution of the sensible' in paid homecare work. *International Journal of Care and Caring*, 443–6. https://doi.org/https://doi.org/10.1332/239788220X16063169476758

Hayes, L. (2017). *Stories of care: A labour of law*. Palgrave.

Hayes, L., Johnson, E., & Tarrant, A. (2019). *Professionalisation at work in adult social care*. Retrieved from https://www.gmb.org.uk/sites/default/files/Professionalisation_at_Work_0309.pdf

Hein, H. (1998). Why not feminist aesthetic theory. *The Journal of Speculative Philosophy*, *12*(1), 20–34.

hooks, b. (1989). *Talking back: Thinking feminist, thinking black*. South End Press.

Korsmeyer, C. (2004). *Gender and aesthetics*. Routledge.

Lanoix, M. (2013). Labor as embodied practice: The lessons of care work. *Hypatia*, *28*(1), 85–100.

Latimer, J. (2018). Afterword: Materialities, care, 'ordinary affects', power and politics. *Sociology of Health & Illness*, *40*(2), 379–91.

Lawrence, R. L. (Ed.). (2012). *Bodies of knowledge: Embodied learning in adult education*. Jossey-Bass.

Mol, A. (2008). *The logic of care: Health and the problem of patient choice*. Routledge.

Moraga, C., & Anzaldua, G. (Eds.). (1983). *This bridge called my back: Writings by radical women of colour* (2nd ed.). Women of Color Press.

Pink, S., Morgan, J., & Dainty, A. (2014). The safe hand: Gels, water, gloves and the materiality of tactile knowing. *Journal of Material Culture*, *19*(4), 425–42.

Rancière, J. (1991). *The ignorant schoolmaster: Five lessons in intellectual emancipation*. Stanford University Press.

Rancière, J. (2004). *The politics of aesthetics: The distribution of the sensible*. Continuum.

Rancière, J. (2009a). The aesthetic dimension: Aesthetics, politics, knowledge. *Critical Inquiry, 36*(Autumn), 1–19.

Rancière, J. (2009b). The method of equality: An answer to some questions. In G. Rockhill & P. Watts (Eds.), *Jacques Rancière: History, politics, aesthetics*. Duke University Press.

Rancière, J. (2017). *Democracy, equality, emancipation in a changing world*. Retrieved from http://www.babylonia.gr/category/english/

Roy, C. (2016). Amplifying voices. In S. Butterwick & C. Roy (Eds.), *Working the margins of community based adult learning* (pp. 51–60). Sense.

Sedgwick, E. K. (2003). *Touching feeling: Affect, pedagogy, performativity*. Duke University Press.

Tronto, J. (1995). Care as a basis for radical political judgements. *Hypatia*, *10*(2), 141–9.

Tronto, J. C. (2013). *Caring democracy: Markets, equality, and justice.* New York University Press.

Twigg, J., Wolkowitz, C., Cohen, R. L., & Nettleton, S. (2011). Conceptualising body work in health and social care. *Sociology of Health & Illness, 33*(2), 171–88. doi: 10.1111/j.1467-9566.2010.01323.x

UNISON. (2016). *Suffering alone at home: A UNISON report on the lack of time in our homecare system.* Retrieved from London: https://www.unison.org.uk/content/uploads/2016/01/23574_Save_care_now_homecare_report-5.pdf

Weimar, C., & Harman, K. (2020). Caring about homecare. *Birkbeck Research.* http://blogs.bbk.ac.uk/research/2020/10/06/caring-about-homecare/

Whittome, N. (2020). I worked in the care sector – and I was sacked after speaking out about lack of PPE. *The Guardian.* Retrieved from https://www.theguardian.com/commentisfree/2020/may/07/i-worked-care-home-sacked-speaking-out-ppe-coronavirus

Wolkowitz, C. (2006). *Bodies at work.* Sage.

Chapter 15

Estrangement Pedagogy in Research-based Theatre about Madness

Lauren Spring

The opening act

(ANNA sits reading her history textbook, while WITCH speaks behind her)
WITCH
Accused women, despite denials, penance or detailed confessions, were hanged, burned, boiled, screwed, brutally slaughtered, drowned and stoned to death. There was a famous river torture test. If a woman was rumored to be sexing with the Devil, inquisitors would tie weights to her limbs and throw her in the nearest, deepest stream. If she truly was guilty she'd float back up to the top- if she did, of course- she'd promptly be stoned to death [The WITCH, as she speaks these words drops stones from her hands, *VILLAGER women enter with stones and scatter them around the stage. ANNA watches*] … If she was innocent however, and remained at the bottom of the river- well … There she'd wait for death. Waiting in the water- just wait, swallowing water.
ANNA
(focused)
8 bottles of water, 5,600 mls.
Medical expertise has nothing over me. I am in control.
In this colony of technology- of patriarchal institutions and rational conclusions …
There's still a *dis-ease* I feel-
witch, I have begun to embody.
So pretty, pretty, pretty please- Mechanize me!
Initiate my body into your world of numbers …
[Sound of fire crackling backstage]
23.5 carbohydrates per 48 gram serving,
5 grams of fat per 1 cup.
86 % of witches burned were women
98.3 % diagnosed with anorexia nervosa are female.
I will burn,

I will burn calories!
[ANNA gathers scattered stones and starts placing them in her underwear]
5:30 a.m. Run for 50 kilometers 7 days a week–
Rise before the sun and my mum knows where I am
1/4 a cup of 1% milk at 8:32 a.m.
Cut my bagel into halves, quarters, sixteenths
I will take 2 hours to eat the parts
I don't throw under the table.
I will fast
And run
Faster and faster until I reach that hunger high
so that I may fly above this world I never asked for.
Look what has become of your perfect little girl!
I will stand
and burn 130 calories an hour ... only 100 if I sit.
[ANNA throws hers arms out to the sides into a 'T' pose again while stepping on the scale to be weighed, ANNA realizes her position mirrors the WITCH at the stake].
3 times every 7 days, is judgment day- I am dragged to clinic
I step on the scale. I have been scheming since 2 this afternoon
I have shoved stones in my pockets and my panties, and swallowed 9 million
bottles of water, inside my bloated body ... My head foggy and floating.
Like I am drowning.

Theatre, research and learning

The above excerpt is from *Hourglass,* a play I wrote, acted in and staged in
Montreal in 2006. The main character Anna (age 16) has been diagnosed with
anorexia nervosa and is growing increasingly sceptical of the 'expert' medical
advice she is receiving from her doctors. This advice pathologizes her feelings
and behaviours, forces her into in-patient treatment against her will and seems
to do more harm than good. Out of loneliness, fear and a desperate need to be
understood, Anna embarks on a magic realist journey through time, summoning
key women throughout history along the way to help her make sense of her feelings
and experiences. Anna's hunger-induced hallucination transcends time and place
as she places herself in the company of iconic 'mad' women such as poet Sylvia
Plath, novelist Mary Shelley and an unnamed woman who was being accused of
witchcraft in 1575. These female allies serve as guides for Anna; their stories of
oppression overlap and weave poetically with her own lived reality and we see
through the play how this helps Anna to re-frame her own experience in ways that
enable her to transcend and resist the unsupportive bio-medical and psychiatric
approach being imposed upon her.

Inspired by my own traumatic experience of being diagnosed with and
forced into inpatient treatment for anorexia at age 16, *Hourglass* was written
primarily from a place of pain, shame and confusion. At the time, my feminist

consciousness was just beginning to develop and while I had graduated from theatre school and was working as a professional actor, I was not yet versed in the methodologies associated with research-informed theatre, feminist pedagogy or mad studies. Re-reading this script now, more than a decade after it was written and produced, I see how its central themes and ideas laid the groundwork for what I have recently come to develop as a 'feminist mad aesthetic' in research-based theatre.

Since writing and performing in *Hourglass*, I have gone on to pursue graduate-level research in adult education and have grown increasingly enchanted with critical feminist and arts-based approaches to framing and representing madness, broadly speaking. My feminist interest in gender – both femininity and masculinity – has expanded my initial focus on women and eating disorders to critiquing the diagnostic category of military-related PTSD and its associated 'treatment' approaches based in notions of masculinity and weakness. In addition, the feminist mad aesthetic I have developed over the years is critically linked to what I call 'estrangement pedagogy' that aims to upend gendered hegemonic framings of human distress and expectations through a theatre of storytelling.

Mad foundations: It's not just a problem with 'stigma'

Mad theory (and the recent academic discipline 'mad studies' it has inspired) is a critical alternative to biomedical approaches to 'naming and responding to emotional, spiritual, and neuro-diversity' as mental illness or disorders (Menzies, et al., 2014, p. 10). While mad theory is not in and of itself 'anti' psychiatry, nor does it reject the idea that some people might find the psychiatric system and pharmaceutical interventions helpful, mad activists and theorists tend to share the belief that the medical model is biologically reductionist (i.e. ignoring social forces that impact mental health and individual behaviours) and favours problematic capitalist ideals of conformity and productivity over exploring community-based approaches to helping those in distress.

There has been a trend in recent years, generally perceived as positive, to 'destigmatize' mental illness. From media soundbites to corporate de-stigmatization campaigns, to university policies implementing new 'models of care', the hegemonic idea that *if only* individuals weren't ashamed to admit their mental illnesses and/or disorders, *if only* diagnoses weren't stigmatized, *if only* access to professional care was available and accessible, much suffering could be averted and lives saved. Feminist and mad critics of this trend (Burstow, 2003; Morrow, 2014; Wipod, 2014) point out, however, that it is not actually 'stigma' but 'sanism' we should be working to dismantle. Gorman and LeFrancois (2017) put it succinctly:

> Sanism has the potential to account for both discrimination against those perceived as mad and for psychiatric violence, while 'stigma' only accounts for

the former. Indeed, in contemporary mental health campaigns, the 'problem' with stigma is that it causes delays in 'getting help' from what are, ultimately, oppressive systems.

(p. 110)

In underscoring the misogynist, ablest (and also colonial, racist, homophobic and classist) foundations of psychiatry, Mad studies is intrinsically linked to other social justice movements as it seeks to explore 'the agency and oppression of mad subjects' (Menzies et al., 2014, p. 1). My work critiques especially the misogyny at the core of psychiatry and for that reason focuses on eating disorders and military-related PTSD which are highly gendered diagnoses.

Patriarchal underpinnings of psychiatry

There have been abundant historical accounts of psychiatry's misogynist origins, but Burstow (2015) does a particularly thorough job tracing how the beginning of the professionalization of medicine was fundamentally linked to the witch hunts that started in the late sixteenth century in Europe as they largely sought to undermine the power women healers held in their communities. This trend continued throughout the early eighteenth and nineteenth centuries as psychiatry established itself as a distinct discipline and the age of the 'great confinement', when institutions to house the so-called mad became widespread, took hold. Burstow highlights how there was a troublesome focus on women's 'sexual and reproductive anatomy' that meant females were considered to have 'a biological propensity for madness' (p. 28). As a result, women were often removed from their families and committed to treatment facilities wherein they would be subjected to disempowering 'cures'. One of the most troubling and well-known examples of a gender-biased diagnosis was hysteria.[1]

In my own creative and academic work about troubled eating, I make the argument that given the cultural context in which we live, those suffering from what psychiatry classifies as eating disorders are pathologized for exhibiting 'normal' behaviour. For example, when it comes to body image, women are bombarded daily with messages that thinness is a measure of self-worth. Is it not then 'normal' that some might go to extremes to attempt to achieve such a physique or, at the very least, internalize this messaging? Gailey (2009) argues that women experiencing disordered eating – especially those who participate in pro-ana/mia online forums where they share weight-loss and exercise tips and tricks with other participants – should alternatively have their activities framed as edgework,[2] a phenomenon typically applied to males who engage in risky behaviours such as extreme sports that involve activity, skill and sensation. Gailey points out:

A woman who is rushed to the hospital because her major organs are shutting down from starvation is no different from a man who is near death from a motorcycle accident where he was 'screaming through an S-curve at 120 miles per hour' (Lyng 1998, p. 221). What does ultimately differ is the reaction by society, assuming they both live. The man will be treated and released; the woman will be sent to the psychiatric ward of the hospital until she gains 'enough' weight and has shown that she is 'recovered'.

(p. 105)

While (mostly male) online communities about extreme sports/racing are rarely, if ever, the target of moral panic, pro-online eating disorder websites are often considered threatening and dangerous to participants and society (Gailey, 2009; Schott & Langan, 2015). This subject, and public cries for these pro ana/mia sites to be shut down and/or censored, became the focus of a collaborative research project that began in 2014 that will be more fully explored in the coming pages.

Mad aesthetics in art

Studio artist, activist and mad-identified scholar, Jenna Reid (2019a) has reflected on and written a great deal about what a mad aesthetic might entail in the visual arts. She takes the stance that mad art is not simply any 'art by the mentally ill' but must be created 'within and alongside the Mad Movement' (p. 107). Reid also argues that a mad aesthetic should transcend 'personal experiences of madness … into a critique of systems, institutions, and dominant practices and beliefs' (p. 64). Though personal stories may not be inherently political, if they stress the social context of suffering instead of individual pathologization, they can help avoid the voyeurism and co-opting of narratives so often associated with mad storytelling (e.g. Costa et al., 2012).

Though space constraints prevent me from expanding on the numerous ways I believe the feminist and trauma-based magic-realist and expressionist work of artists like Frida Kahlo and Kathe Kollwitz provide particularly strong examples of what a mad aesthetic might consist of, both artists' deliberate disruption of the male gaze, representations of deeply embodied end emotional experiences, as well as their stated political objectives and desires for their works to provoke public debate, have deeply influenced my own process and aesthetics.

I have taken many cues from Reid's work as I've sought to apply a mad aesthetic to the research-based theatre work I've undertaken. The next section of this chapter will explore how my pedagogical and aesthetic objectives have impacted my playwriting by focusing on two specific plays I have written in recent years. I will incorporate specific examples to illustrate how what I have come to refer to as a 'feminist mad aesthetic' has developed in my work and theorizing over the years and why I believe that research-based theatre offers a unique pedagogical opportunity to 'make strange' and destabilize the patriarchal underpinnings of both psychiatry and traditional narrative structure.

Pro-Ana/Mia Embedded

In 2014 I began a collaboration with fellow PhD student Nicole Schott during which I worked with her to transform her Master of Arts research data on paternalistic censorship of online pro anorexia/pro-bulimia communities into a theatre script that could be used as a social justice tool. We have written in detail about the early stages of our collaboration (see Schott et al., 2016) where we highlight several deliberate aesthetic choices we made along the way to firstly, centre the focus of the play on the social context in which eating disorders occur (as opposed to psychiatry's centring on brain chemistry) and secondly, represent the blurring of online and offline spaces as this was central to Nicole's methodology.

Since 2016, the two of us went on to present aspects of this work at several conferences and I proceeded to write a full version of the play that was presented as a staged reading as part of Nicole's PhD project. The workshop presentation of the play provided an opportunity to lift the data off the page in new and critical ways. I called upon my good friend and trusted collaborator Clara McBride (a professional director, improviser, movement coach, actor and Course Instructor at Ryerson Theatre School) to direct. In the rehearsal room both Clara and I (and the actors involved) drew on our backgrounds in physical theatre to inform aesthetic decisions and extra-linguistic movement sequences so that the staging aligned with our ultimate objectives to share the 'diverse views and opinions … (which) are rarely represented in medical literature or by the mainstream media' (Schott et al., 2016, p. 110) and to offer a unique glimpse into the social contexts that impact the minds, bodies and feelings of those diagnosed with eating disorders.

For example, in the final scene of the play, Anna, who hasn't eaten all day, begins to feel dizzy and fear for her own well-being. She decides to go to the grocery store to purchase a snack as her doctor suggested. While this supermarket environment starts off realistically enough, Anna soon becomes overwhelmed by choice in the aisles and doesn't know what to do. In the rehearsal room, as Clara and I worked together to stage this sequence, I drew on my own memories of feeling similarly debilitated, fearful and foggy-headed in grocery aisles, knowing I had to eat *something*, but feeling completely overwhelmed by choice and product messaging with respect to what was 'good' for me (Schott 2015 has theorized about the impact of food marketing on disordered eating as well). With the actors, Clara and I established a surreal movement-based sequence to capture what the experience *felt* like for Anna. As she tried to steady herself and fill her shopping basket, the products (animated by actors) popped up aggressively from all sides until the abundance of choice became staggering. The various diet products then began to pulse around Anna in a way that mirrored her racing heart rate. Actors recited diet product tag lines and lists of righteous ingredients in loud, overly upbeat and commercial sounding voices that steadily overlapped and increased in volume. Eventually the voices of the actors that began as generic and faceless marketing messages transformed into those of people from Anna's life introduced earlier in the play. It therefore became more overwhelming for

Anna to decipher the conflicting marketing messages from pleas of those in her immediate circle, as food choices also became linked to pressure from her mother, doctor and friends. As Anna's distress grew more palpable, the social forces behind what might otherwise be viewed as an individual 'pathology' were revealed.

Though Clara, Nicole and I did not discuss or apply the label 'feminist mad aesthetic' to our work at the time, as I have gone on to develop similar devices in my own doctoral work and playwriting it has become clear to me that situating a protagonist in a real-life context that is familiar to audience members *before* allowing the narrative to veer off course into a realm that transcends expectations and blurs the lines between individual/culture/society and real/surreal is an effective device that allows for a pedagogy of estrangement I believe is vital to mad storytelling.

Adult education and theatre

Within the field of adult educators, there is an understanding that learning, especially the most powerful, paradigm-shifting sort, tends to be voluntary and self-directed (e.g., Taylor, 2008). Many consciousness-raising approaches to adult education such as feminist pedagogy and transformative learning theory are centred on the idea of what Mezirow called a 'disorienting dilemma' where something that occurs leads to a period of critical reflection and often a change in one's 'frame of reference' (see Taylor, 2008, p. 5).

The arts and the institutions that house them (museums, theatres, etc.) serve as some of the most vital semi-formal and informal settings for learning and have an important role to play in this critical reflection process. Sarah Lewis speaks about the power of 'aesthetic force' in art to help ignite disorienting dilemmas and mobilize and resist against injustice while also inspiring an 'ethics of care' (Popova, 2015). In conversation with playwright Ana Devere Smith who has used research-based theatre to achieve similar ends, Lewis says of aesthetic force:

> It leaves us changed – stunned, dazzled, knocked out. It can quicken the pulse, make us gape, even gasp with astonishment. Its importance is its animating trait – not what it is, but what it does to those who behold it in all its forms. Its seeming lightness can make us forget that it has weight, force enough to bring about a self-correction.
>
> (para 8)

Adult educators like me have long found theatre to be a particularly rich territory for adult learning. Their research has shown the potential of theatre to promote, for example, deep listening and community building (e.g. Butterwick & Selman, 2003). For Burstow (2008), 'mad' theatre is critical because it focuses on dialogue in the interests of humanization in ways that trouble audience members' assumptions and perspectives so they may 'view anew the self, others, and the world' (Kumagai & Wear, 2014, p. 973).

Masculinities and military trauma

As mentioned earlier, the research-based play I wrote for my own doctoral work focuses on aspects of masculinity and military trauma. Through theatre, I share my findings of veterans' complex stories in ways that uncover the gendered and morally injurious dimensions of their suffering that psychiatry and patriarchy overlook. Similar to eating disorders, diagnoses of military-related PTSD are therefore, highly gendered. The individuals (mostly men) who receive diagnoses of PTSD are often pathologized because their behaviours and feelings are associated with femininity and run contrary to the hyper-masculine cultural norm upon which the military apparatus is founded (e.g. Brown, 2008; Sheilds, 2016; Sheilds, Kuhl & Westwood, 2017; Whitworth, 2008). Soldiers are trained to embody this masculine ideal which emphasizes qualities such as emotional detachment and control, rationality, self-discipline, patriotism, loyalty, heterosexual competency, bravery and aggression (Gabriel, 1988; McLean, 2017; Whitworth, 2008).

In the pursuit of such an identity, those in the military are forced (subconsciously and/or via specific initiation and training practices) to squelch any feelings or behaviours within themselves that fall outside of the normative gender category and to obliterate the 'other' in the psyche of new recruits. Sheilds et al. (2017) refer to these renounced behaviours and feelings as 'abject identities' (p. 220). Whitworth (2008) argues that sexism, racism and homophobia underlie these 'abject identities' and that many of the insults thrown at those in the military are designed to stoke masculine anxieties.

Interestingly, during the First World War, what was referred to as shell shock at the time (the equivalent of PTSD today) was 'treated as a male form of female hysteria ... both the condition itself and soldiers who became victim of it were dismissed and denigrated through being feminized' (Whitworth, 2008, p. 110). Feminist critics of psychiatry who call attention to these gendered contingencies in diagnoses of military-related PTSD remind us that behaviours and experiences that the DSM classifies as 'symptoms' and that are often associated with the feminine such as deep emotions, nightmares and flashbacks ought to be re-framed as normal reactions to traumatic events. It was also feminists who first identified and called attention towards ideas of hegemonic masculinity that are rampant within military culture and impact the mental health of traumatized service members and veterans today.

Staging a military estrangement pedagogy

While space constraints prohibit me from sharing full scenes from this play, I highlight below a brief excerpt from one scene to illustrate how I apply a feminist mad aesthetic to a theatre script exploring the complexities of military trauma and moral injury that move us beyond the diagnostic category of PTSD. Let me first set the stage.

In one particular scene, we see a veteran being honoured at a Blue Jays baseball game in a large stadium in Toronto, Canada. The moment of public honouring begins innocently but then transcends recognizable reality and ventures into a deeply complex and problematic magic realist realm. At first, the crowd cheers for the veteran who is sat centre field in his wheelchair with one leg amputated beneath the knee. His face is shown smiling on the huge screen that is called a jumbotron. But rather than exiting the field when he is asked to so the game can begin, he remains. Slowly the crowd starts to turn on him, bombarding him with questions about war and his amputation they would never dare ask in reality. Equally, the veteran in turn tries to answer honestly about the complex 'masculinities' of war and military service that he never would in reality. The crowd eventually begins to boo him as they would a sports team they viewed as an adversary or more importantly, as losing and therefore, weak.

Over the jeering, we soon begin to hear a very different series of voices coming over a loudspeaker. These voices are offering veteran discounts and public service advice. At this point in the scene, it is unclear whether the voice is being played over the loudspeaker for all to hear or if it is inside the veteran's mind. This is the excerpt.

GENERIC PSA AD VOICE

Are you in distress? Considering suicide? Speak to a mental health professional right now. A confidential and free service available 24/7 to Veterans, their family members, and caregivers. Call 1-800-268-9944 and you will be immediately connected to an automated menu in French that asks you to type in your ID number and VAC298 third party consent form password. Sorry that number is not valid. Desolée, ce numero n'est pas valide. If you'd like to try again, press number sign. To return to the main menu press star of courage. To wait 30 years to be put on a waiting list that is five years long in order to see a professional a two hour drive away from where you live press seven. If your applicant statement was deemed incomplete press 17 U-N-F-I-T-F-O-R-D-U-T-Y. If your wife is about to leave you and take the kids for real this time, press number four, numero quatre. If you can't afford a lawyer and you know you would need to stop drinking before you could ask for custody rights, press 158 Canadian Armed Forces Members lost their lives in Afghanistan. Are you having trouble breathing? Tightness in your chest? Erectile dysfunction? Press a gun to your head. Did you know that our new mindfulness app is available on itunes and from the Google play store? Simply download, print, sin and submit your CF98 form via mail, email and fax before 21:00 three Fridays ago and we will issue you a seven-digit access key. If your matter is urgent, call 1800 Canadian soldiers have been wounded in Afghanistan. Unfortunately, we are experiencing a higher-than-normal volume of calls, and all our representatives are busy helping other killers. Please hang yourself or try again later.

Concluding remarks

In this chapter, I provided excerpts and descriptions of staging from plays I have written about what psychiatry would consider 'mental illnesses' to explore how a feminist mad aesthetic can help destabilize the patriarchal underpinnings of both psychiatry and traditional narrative structure. I have illustrated how the very constitution of sanity and 'mental illness' in late-twentieth-century society was 'anchored in the bedrock of male normativity' (Menzies et al., 2014, p. 6) and how this hegemonic, individualistic and biomedical framing persists today and may be powerfully disrupted using the arts and research-based theatre in particular. The feminist mad aesthetic I have developed over the years and the estrangement pedagogy at its core is based as much on Brechtian distancing devices (which are deeply entwined with adult learning objectives that 'estrange' audience members from their role as passive observers of a story unfolding on stage and transport them to a place of discomfort, critical engagement and political action) as it is on deeply personal, trauma-based magic-realist and expressionist renderings by artists such as Frida Kahlo and Kathe Kollwitz. This approach is proving particularly vital to the process of collecting, representing and sharing narratives of male veterans from the Canadian Armed Forces. It serves as an example of how feminist theoretical, methodological, aesthetic and creative frameworks can be equally as helpful when conducting research about the mental health of both female and male-identifying populations.

Notes

1   In the mid-nineteenth century French psychiatrist Jean-Martin Charcot, who specialized in treating so-called hysterical women, became famous for photographing and staging live demonstrations of his patients. His voyeuristic and erotic depictions both objectified and infantilize the women he 'treated' and serve as a stark reminder that what we consider 'mental illnesses' are historically and culturally contingent (White, 2017, p. 24).
2   A concept developed by Lyng (1990), edgework refers to activities that involve a 'clearly observable threat to one's physical or mental well being or one's sense of an ordered existence' and involve activity, skill and sensation' (p. 857). 'Edgework' drives those engaging in them to the 'edge' where they may test the limits 'between two physical or mental states, sanity versus insanity, consciousness versus unconsciousness, or an ordered environment versus a disordered environment' (Gailey, 2009, p. 95).

References

Andreasen, N. C. (1995). Posttraumatic stress disorder: Psychology, biology and the manichean warfare between false dichotomies. *American Journal of Psychiatry, 152,* 963–5.

Burstow, B. (2003). Towards a radical understanding of trauma and trauma work. *Violence against Women*, 9(11), 1293–317.

Burstow, B. (2008). Invisible theatre, ethics, and the adult educator. *International Journal of Lifelong Education*, 27(3), 273–88.

Burstow, B. (2014). A rose by any other name: Naming and the battle against psychiatry. In B. A. LeFrancois, R. Menzies, & G. Reaume (Eds.), *Mad matters: A critical reader in Mad Studies*. (pp. 79–90). Canadian Scholars Press.

Burstow, B. (2015). *Psychiatry and the business of madness; an ethical and epistemological accounting*. Palgrave.

Butterwick, S., & Selman, J. (2003). Deep listening in a feminist popular theatre project: Upsetting the position of audience in participatory education. *Adult Education Quarterly*, 54(1), 7–22.

Brown, L. S. (2008). *Cultural competence in trauma therapy: Beyond the flashback*. American Psychological Association.

Costa, L., Voronka, J., Landry, D., Reid, J., Mcfarlane, B., Reville, D., & Church, K. (2012). Recovering our stories: A small act of resistance. *Studies in Social Justice*, 6(1), 85–101.

Gabriel, R.A. (1988). *No more heroes: Madness and psychiatry in war*. Hill and Wang.

Gailey, J. (2009). Starving is the most fun a girl can have: The pro-ana subculture as edgework. *Critical Criminology*, 17(2), 93–108.

Gorman, R. (2013) Mad nation? thinking through race, class, and mad identity politics. In B. A. LeFrançois, R. Menzies, & G. Reaume (Eds.), *Mad matters: A critical reader in Canadian mad studies* (pp. 269–80). Canadian Scholars Press.

Gorman, R., & LeFrançois, B. (2017). Mad studies. In B. Cohen (Ed.), *Routledge international handbook of critical mental health* (pp. 107–14). Routledge.

Kumagai, A., & Wear, D. (2014). Making strange: A role for the humanities in medical education. *Academic Medicine*, 89(7), 973–7.

Lyng, S. (1990). Edgework: A social psychological analysis of voluntary risk-taking. *American Journal of Sociology*, 95, 851–86.

Lyng, S. (1998). Dangerous methods. Risk taking and the research process. In J. Ferrell & M. Hamm (Eds.), Ethnography at the edge. Crime, deviance, and field research (pp. 221–51). Northeastern University Press.

McLean, B. (2017). Contact! Unload. A narrative study and filmic exploration of veterans performing stories of war and transition. Unpublished Doctoral Thesis. University of British Columbia.

Menzies, R., LeFrancois, B., & Reaume, G. (2014). Introducing mad studies. In B. A. LeFrancois, R. Menzies, & G. Reaume (Eds.), *Mad matters: A critical reader in mad studies*, (pp. 1–22). Canadian Scholars Press.

Morgan, D. (1994). Theatre of war: Combat, the military, and masculinities. In H. Brod, & K. Kaufman (Eds.), *Theorizing masculinities* (pp. 166–82). Sage Publications Inc.

Morrow, M. (2014). Recovery: Progressive paradigm or neoliberal smokescreen? (Chapter 23). In B. A. LeFrancois, R. Menzies, & G. Reaume (Eds.), *Mad matters: A critical reader in mad studies* (pp. 323–33). Canadian Scholars Press.

Popova, M. (2015, April 8). The power of aesthetic force: Anna Deavere Smith and Sarah Lewis on beauty as a tool of justice and a catalyst for 'nonselfing'. *Brainpickings*. https://www.brainpickings.org/2015/04/08/anna-deavere-smith-sarah-lewis-nypl-beauty/

Reid, J. (2019a). Materializing a mad aesthetic through the making of politicized fibre art. Unpublished Doctoral Thesis. York University.

Reid, J. (2019b). Introducing Jenna Reid: DST's new limited term faculty. https://radssite. wordpress.com/2019/10/21/introducing-jenna-reid-dsts-new-limited-term-faculty/

Schott, N., & Langan, D. (2015). Pro-anorexia/bulimia censorship and public service announcements: The price of controlling women. *Media, Culture and Society, 37*(8), 1158–75.

Schott, N., Spring, L., & Langan, D. (2016). Neoliberalism, pro-ana/mia websites, and pathologizing women: Using performance ethnography to challenge psychocentrism. *Studies in Social Justice, 10*(1), 95–115.

Schott, N. (2015). Food marketing as a pedagogical act: Teaching women to consume 'Skinny'. *Journal of Social Justice, 5*, 1–23.

Spring, L. (2017). Beyond PTSD: How stories and artworks that 'make strange' can serve as signposts on new maps toward the communalization of mental health care. *Health Tomorrow: Interdisciplinarity and Internationality Journal, 4*, 88–122.

Spring, L. (2021). Beyond PTSD: Moving military trauma out of the realm of psychiatry and into an arts-based education and community-oriented framework. Unpublished PhD Thesis. University of Toronto.

Shields, D. M. (2016). Military masculinity, movies, and the DSM: Narratives of institutionally (en)gendered trauma. *Psychology of Men & Masculinity, 17*(1), 64–73.

Shields, D., Kuhl, D. K., & Westwood, M. J. (2017). Abject masculinity and military mental health: Theorizing a fulcrum of struggle and change. *Psychology of Men and Masculinity, 18*(3), 215–25.

Taylor, Edward. (2008). Transformative learning theory. *New Directions for Adult and Continuing Education, 119*, 5–15.

Whitworth, Sandra. (2008). Chapter 5: Militarized masculinity and posttraumatic stress disorder. In J. L. Parpart, & M. Zalewski (Eds.), *Rethinking the man question: Sex, gender and violence in international relations* (pp. 109–26). Zed Books.

Wipond, R. (2014). Pitching mad: News media and the psychiatric survivor perspective. In B. LeFrancois, R. Menzies, & G. Reaume (Eds.), *Mad matters: A critical reader in mad studies* (pp. 253–64). Canadian Scholars Press.

Chapter 16

Feminist Aesthetics and Mutual Learning in
Turbulent Times: The Politics of Listening
and Organization

Claudia Firth

> If listening were shown to be as important and as complex as talking, if it were
> shown to be equally valuable, there would be repercussions in all our social
> institutions.
>
> Dale Spender, 2001, p. 124

It is challenging to think about listening in a political climate so full of intractable
positions and shouting voices. However, it is vital if we are to take feminist writer
Dale Spender's challenge outlined in the quote above seriously. In this chapter,
I focus on listening in relation to the political, in a broad sense of the term, and
feminist aesthetics in terms of interconnection, perception and experience, and
examine what these might mean for organizing and organizations. In particular,
I am interested in what opportunities there might be for mutual learning within
groups, collectives and organizations if attention is paid to listening and ways
it can operate as a tool or method. In order to focus attention on listening, I
draw from *The Force of Listening* (2017), a collaborative book I co-authored on
listening in the intersection between art and activism, and some of the work I have
done with groups and organizations. Moving between the individual, the inter-
relational and organizational, I map listening in relation to institutional blockages
and obstructions, disagreement and care, and the reproductive labour needed to
maintain a group or organization. I do this with a feminist aesthetic in mind.

In thinking about organizations, I am taking a systemic perspective, with an
understanding that the personal, interpersonal, small group, organizational and
larger social and political contexts all affect each other. This is especially the case
if organizations are viewed as networks of meaning and communication that are
continually created and renewed, rather than being fixed entities (Campbell, 2000;
Miksitis, 2019). If this is the case, then listening, as a pre-requisite for dialogue and
good communication, is one element sorely needed for building social relations,
for creating social movements and for rethinking and reimagining new forms
of organization and democracy. Moreover, paying attention to listening has real
consequences for challenging contemporary conditions of neoliberalism and the
organizations and institutions which constitute it.

The way that listening and its corollaries, speech and voice, are regarded, approached and valued is heavily dependent on how the political is conceptualized. The current increase in polarizing and divisive discourse can be linked to a rise in populism which in itself has emerged as a result of contradictions inherent within the current neoliberal framework (Brown, 2019). Far from being simply a body of conceptual and theoretical arguments about the economy, neoliberalism is 'a complex social formation that involves many different elements' (Gilbert, 2013, p. 20). Politics is reduced to the implementation of market functioning, effectively evacuating the role of the social. Its model of governance depends on a range of tools and techniques that work in order to 'generate political inertia' and individualized impotence (p. 15). As social and political organization, neoliberalism operates on the basis that voice does not matter (Couldry, 2011). Voice as a process is denied and undermined, either directly or in more subtle ways, such as through a focus on speaking which doesn't expect to go anywhere or really to change anything. This is also reflected in the wider political context, in which freedom of speech has become particularly weaponized. Freedom of speech, in an extreme neoliberal context, signifies the right to say in public whatever one wants to say without constraint (which in itself raises ethical questions of accountability and responsibility) (Brown, 2019, p. 139). Yet, this only holds for certain subjects, while other voices are not only not privileged but positioned as being inaudible or only perceivable as noise (Bassel, 2018).

In thinking about how the political is defined, it is important to recognize that political activity takes place not only within the formal political system but also 'underneath, outside, against and beyond it' (Kioupkiolis, 2019, p. 124). This works against the narrow definition deployed by neoliberalism. For this chapter, I lean heavily on writing by feminist political theorist Susan Bickford (1996). Bickford draws on Arendt and other feminist thinkers to locate politics as being conflictual and contentious while also acknowledging interrelatedness as a fundamental condition. This is an ethical position which does not shy away from socio-economic inequality, conflict and diversity but also tries to grapple with the joint action needed to build bridges. There may seem to be an inherent contradiction between conflict and diversity and what is held in common; however, it can better be thought of as a tension that makes communicative interaction necessary. Politics can therefore be thought of as being the art both of living together well and of disagreement (Garver, 2011). I use the term 'art' here to mean a particular kind of knowledge or skill which includes the creative imagination. Following feminist thinking, not only is the personal political, but so is, and perhaps more importantly, the inter-personal. If we understand politics as the art of living together well and of disagreement, listening must be an essential part of this art if we are to realize the possibilities of change that Spender proposes.

Taking a feminist aesthetic pedagogical perspective is precisely to understand the political on this everyday level of living together based on interconnectedness as a fundamental condition of being. We can therefore think about the 'art' of listening through a feminist aesthetic that is committed to a sense of fundamental interconnection. A feminist sensibility here includes reciprocity, dialogue and an understanding of power relations, and is related to aesthetics through perception and experience (Farinati & Firth, 2017). As well as pertaining to art objects and the beautiful, aesthetics also refers to how things are perceived and experienced and it is this aspect of aesthetics that is most relevant here. In addition, aesthetic categories such as form, judgement, attitude and value can be applied to describe an artistic ethics of something, its art or craft. These categories can be used 'to ask how we perceive something, what the sensibilities are in that perception and how they change or are affected by other things' (Firth, 2019, p. 34). Our inter-relations with others, the way that we communicate, cooperate, disagree, care, and indeed, listen, can all be imbued with such an artistic ethics and this is the lens that I will use in this chapter.

My work with organizations

I will focus here on my work with groups and organizations. This can be traced as coming out of activist practices I have been involved with and my own artistic training. What is of specific relevance here are histories of dematerialized and social practice art in which there is not necessarily an art object or particular process of production. Social practice art instead focuses on engagement through human interaction and social discourse. It is also heavily influenced by feminist education theory (Helguera, 2012). Artists involved in this kind of work frequently set up encounters and interactions between people, social systems and the artist or artwork and there is often a relation to social activism. Suely Rolnik describes the move of artists towards more social kinds of practices as being in response to art's own political potential being blocked. This blockage is produced by the marketized and immaterial logic of cognitive and neoliberal capitalism which is embodied by the art world (Jelinek, 2013; Rolnik, 2007). Art per se, within an art world context at least, cannot therefore be taken for granted as a field of liberation.

My work with groups and organizations has come through activist practices that share a sensibility with social art practice in recognizing that social relations, social encounters and interactions are valuable and worth paying specific attention to. As a practice, this work is very much grounded in a feminist aesthetics, as an ethical 'art of doing', which includes attending to power relations, interdependence and relationality. I generally work with non-hierarchical groups, collectives and organizations across the arts, activist and community management sectors. With all the groups I work with, I aim to hold a space open for their voices using dialogic tools and speaking and listening practices. These can allow me to listen to the participants as a whole and to create safety for them to listen to each other, which in turn can produce reflection and analysis on both an individual and group or organizational level. The creation of this metaphorical 'space' is an intuitive process of building rapport, trust and psychological safety with the participants of the group. It involves attending to organizational structures as well as perceptions and experiences of power, influence and agency, and alienation and impotence on the part of the participants. Attention to stories that participants tell, and language, images and metaphors they use, are all important for understanding how the group or organization works and how it might change.

While I have not always thought of my work with organizations as being pedagogic, it is very clear that much education and learning takes place. Indeed, Butterwick and Selman (2020) argue, learning 'occurs beyond the walls of formal classrooms – in civil society, communities and workplaces and social movements' (p. 7). They also argue that dialogic activity engages people and provides them with plausible alternatives to the status quo, and in particular, alternatives to divisive and polarizing discourse. If feminist principles such as inter-relationality are applied to this kind of pedagogy, learning and knowledge have less to do with certainty and possession than with reciprocity and mutual learning, especially within a group or organization.

Hearing and listening

Before examining issues of listening in relation to organizations and organizing, it is worth drawing the distinction between hearing and listening. Although most often defined as being synonymous with hearing, listening is substantially different from hearing and it is important to state the distinction. Hearing is an involuntary physiological act whereas listening is a more conscious psychological activity of attentiveness (Barthes, 1992). Listening is intentional. We cannot close our ears, but we can choose whether and how to listen. Listening is an activity that consists of 'tension, intention and attention' (Nancy, 2007, p. 5). Effort is needed in order to be able to hear something in a way that will matter. Listening, in this sense, is therefore an activity to be trained and cultivated. As with anything that needs cultivating, there is an ethical aspect to the decision to cultivate it well, to listen with care and attention. A more profound or deep listening as opposed to giving something mere cursory consideration. Listening should be understood, in this instance, especially in the context of organizations, as being in relation to voice. If voice is understood as 'giving an account of one's self', paying attention to listening is to 'make voice really matter' (Couldry, 2011, p. 13). Listening is not only an integral part of the struggle to find voice but also of creating the conditions in order to render that voice meaningful and effective.

Obstructive listening in institutions and organizations

Within organizations, even when there are spaces for voice, voices can be heavily controlled and regulated. Hierarchical chains of command can mean that only certain kinds of communication can travel in particular directions or certain voices privileged over others. Mechanisms can be embedded through formal policies and procedures or through unwritten norms and behaviours. In particular, in institutions where norms and routinely reproduced patterns of behaviour are prevalent, the creation of the conditions that can make voice meaningful through mutual interchange is quite often closed off. Policies, procedures and practices can all work to be as non-performative as they can to be effective, not responding to, or even working against voices which challenge the functioning of the organization, such as those that make complaints (Ahmed, 2021).

If listening does take place in an institutional setting, often it cannot be allowed to have consequences. For *The Force of Listening* (2017), conversations were had with a number of arts-activist collectives, theorists and activists. The practitioners used listening in their practices in a range of ways, from more activist-based contexts and approaches to more artistic ones. Over and over again in our conversations, the institutional steps taken to make sure that things were not allowed to leak out of their designated boxes and affect that which was outside of them, were discussed. Invitations to voice seemed to operate in a similar way, as a kind of closed unit, a boundaried space in which speech circulates but does not have consequences.

One member of the activist collective the Precarious Workers Brigade, a collective that works on issues of precarity within the arts and education sectors, gave an example of the Dean of a university department who, in a meeting, came and stood on stage and proclaimed, 'I am here to listen … you can tell me anything', of course, not understanding the particular hierarchical and non-feminist institutional framework in which he was operating and that this gesture alone would not change anything (Farinati & Firth, 2017, p. 152). While there was potentially a space in which to speak, whether it would actually be heard by the institution and acted upon is a wholly different question. There was no real attempt to understand, change or create the conditions for listening. Another illustration within a more community-based context was situated in relation to structures of gentrification. In this context, there are complex apparatuses 'set up as platforms for listening to voices but actually using that moment of hearing as the justification for the next step' (p. 111). Consultation sessions are often set up in order to give people a chance to speak, only for a decision which has already been made to then be implemented. Ultra-red, a sound art and activist collective, describe these endeavours to foreclose conversations and their effects:

> The people working with us found this to be a double violence. There is this kind of management of freedom that is quite central to processes of neoliberalism and how institutions, politicians, corporations understand the voice. It's really not about censorship in that sense, and the mistake that many people make in over-emphasizing the voice is to say 'well we've spoken'. Or, 'at least we had a place to speak' and to not actually attend to what the conditions of speaking and listening are in the wider context i.e. whether the structural conditions of the situation: what is said to rupture or re-organise conditions.

For us, these are 'dynamics of speaking and listening that are habituated through experiences of neoliberalism, a kind of conditioning of the voice to speak constantly, but a total dearth of conditions that enable listening to take place' (p. 113).

Listening as a feminist tool for organizing

In opposition to these kinds of non-performative listening, it can be argued that listening has always been a very effective feminist practice. However, as with many academic disciplines, listening has not been focused on as much as the struggle to find voice (Bassel, 2018). Traditionally, listening has been devalued and perceived as more passive (and associated with the feminine), as opposed to voice which has been perceived as active and powerful. However, listening should be seen as being as important as speech, and in order to challenge silencing or obstructive mechanisms, it is imperative to understand how it can be utilized as a tool for organizing. Listening operates in parallel with speech, as part of an inter-relational, reciprocal practice which is fundamental to the basic building blocks of the women's movement. Speaking about their own conditions in consciousness-raising groups, women listened to each other's accounts of their lives and through this sharing process, realized that their personal issues were not purely individual, but part of the much bigger social situation created by patriarchy. This leads to a process of collective analysis which both developed solidarity between women and enabled the women's movement to produce political demands. Solidarity was produced in these groups through an inter-relational processes of resonance and recognition.

If something said resonates with others, it can lead to a mutual recognition of the participants' 'abilities to create a concrete contribution to a "material community"' (Farinati & Firth, 2017, p. 147; see also Honneth, 2014). The building of solidarity is a process by which an individual recognizes themselves in a collectively produced voice. However, it may be that the building of solidarity is not possible or even appropriate in some contexts. One of the issues the feminist movement struggled with at that time was in dealing with creating solidarity across differences such as race and class. The movement struggled to deal well with issues of intersectionality, and this played out within the consciousness-raising groups themselves. Their collectively produced voice did not always take difference into account. Learning from this, it is therefore necessary to find ways to build solidarity across difference. As feminist Ahmed (2000) has suggested, we need to find ways to put that space of difference 'to work' (p. 180). Indeed, in their article on deep listening in a recent feminist theatre project, Butterwick and Selman (2020) chart both the necessity and the difficulties of building solidarity within feminist coalitions. In one particularly poignant passage, they describe 'the practice of conflict' as 'an art which many women especially white middle-class women are poorly skilled' in (p. 10). This follows feminist hooks (1994) in her call for more documentation of 'the ways barriers are broken down, coalitions are formed and solidarity shared' (p. 110).

Political listening and care

Dealing with conflict and disagreement is, as we have seen, a necessity in the building of solidarity and coalition. This work needs to be done with care. However, the relationship of political listening to care is not as straightforward a relationship as it might first appear. Care is an emotive term with many connotations. Listening seems to align itself very easily as a form of care. However, Bickford (1996) suggests that 'political listening is not a primarily caring or amicable practice' (p. 2). This becomes even more pertinent in conditions in which solidarity or coalition building is complicated or problematic. For Bickford, political action occurs in the context of conflict and inequality, the space of politics (following Hannah Arendt), being a conflictual and contentious one, even in or even especially in, democratic societies. A very particular kind of listening is therefore required, one not necessarily based on care or friendship. Care is not the aim here, but more a means, with the aim, as I interpret it, of developing understanding or shifting power dynamics. That is not to dismiss care, but rather to differentiate it as an ethical position, not an end in itself. There is currently growing attention on care as a principle for rethinking or reorganizing society, with recent publications like the Care Manifesto (The Care Collective et al., 2020). In addition, sociologist Silvia Federici has argued that self-organized communities of care, the places where and how we can cooperate with each other, could be where any 'new world' might be created (Federici, 2020, p. 125). What is involved in that cooperation and how the listening as redolent of an inter-relational micro-politics might contribute to it is worth exploring further.

For solidarity and coalition building, it is clear from the previous section that there has to be space made for dissonance as well as for resonance. Moreover, if politics is understood as a field of inequality and disagreement, the practice of the art of disagreement or conflict becomes more pertinent. Indeed, as Bickford argues, it is exactly the presence of conflict and difference that makes communicative interaction necessary. Bickford argues instead for a specific kind of attention. On an inter-personal level, for political listening to be effective, she argues that the self should not be negated. She argues that while listening is often seen as a self-annulling process, political listening should not be grounded in an absence of self. Indeed, there can be a cost to the self if it is pushed to one side in the process. As Arlie Hochschild (2012) has documented, listening can play a substantial role in emotional and affective labour and care work, which has traditionally been gendered as female, undervalued and often involved side-lining the self, with sometimes quite negative consequences for the listener.

Political listening, for Bickford, 'requires self-involvement with others in action, where we do not "draw back" but actively engage with one another with direction and purpose' (1996, p. 146). Politics should be thought of much more as an interaction, a joint action. Bickford also looks to Merleau Ponty at this point and his ideas of figure and ground. This is very much in the realm of aesthetics that we are concerned with here, of perception and experience. In this case, an image is created with the self as the ground, while the other is focused on as the figure in the fore. The two exist simultaneously, but in a particular relationship to each other, with one as a distinct focal point and the other as background or scape. This works in order that 'I understand my perspective in the light of others and theirs in the light of mine' (p. 146). Listening in this context is very much active and creates possibility of a 'we' that acknowledges differences. The relationship is one of consultation and exchange. There must be an openness but also agency and situatedness.

This is not to say that it does not take care and attention to listen well, especially if it is to be an active kind of listening that will produce change. Rather, active listening enacts a form of care that does not polarize into either caring for someone and not the self, or vice versa. There are definite ethics involved in processes of active listening, as well as certain kinds of vulnerability. Listening is risky if we accept that what we hear might require change from us. Change can potentially be painful. The need for attention to others that does not erase or annul the self therefore involves a nuanced position of enabling a space for someone to speak, holding one's own space and allowing that speech to have consequences for the listener and beyond. In this sense, it is also something of an art. Bickford suggests that listening should be seen as a journey or bridge to travel on. The journey is a joint effort between listener and speaker, with the listener being expected to change as much as those who are being listened to. There is therefore a necessity to accept inter-subjectivity in a way that might change the self and this is precisely why a feminist perspective is useful. However, there may also be moments when engagement is not possible or desirable and is decided against. Consequently, therefore, care can be thought of as being both a possibility and a limit.

Attending to listening as reproduction or maintenance

In relation to organizations and organizing practices, I want to explore careful listening as part of the reproductive labour, that is, the labour necessary to reproduce an organization on an ongoing basis. The reproductive labour of maintaining interpersonal relations in any organization is vital. If organizations are understood as networks of communication, the maintenance and repair of these networks are as crucial as the maintenance and repair required to keep the buildings that house them in good shape. However, like all affective labour, this social maintenance tends to be invisible. In fact even the physical maintenance of buildings often isn't paid much attention to. Maintenance is treated with indifference by most architects. Nevertheless 'with the day-to-day wear and tear on surfaces, buildings eventually decay if left unkept. Labour is required through the form of maintenance to keep buildings looking new' (Sample, 2016, p. 1). Likewise, social relations in organizations need maintaining. Small gestures like saying hello to a neighbour or colleague in a lift can be significant for the ongoing history of social relations within an organization (Sewell, 2007). Even in more nebulous or informal organizations, such as social movements, the importance of the labour involved in interpersonal relations cannot be underestimated. Without face-to-face encounters, social movements are pretty likely to fail. Most of these social interactions are taken for granted because they are governed by a myriad of intricate forms of shared social knowledge, such as the rules governing reciprocity when one gives and receives gifts. There are whole sets of unwritten emotional rules through which people contribute to the relational whole of any given social situation. In this emotional gift economy, transactions pass back and forth between people, with expectations for both giver and receiver. The labour of managing these transactions, 'of creating and maintaining the emotional tone of social encounters' (Hochschild, 2012, p. 20), has traditionally been left to women and isn't always noticed. As Hochschild argues, often the places which require the most emotional labour recognize it the least.

Listening can play a role in building, repairing and keeping these social relations maintained on both an interpersonal level and an organizational level. This is a level of care and attention which becomes especially needed as things become more contested. In this sense, politics 'emerges when these forms of shared knowledgeability fray and become contestable, so that the risks of social interactions are no longer predictable' (Warren, 1996, p. 244). When the rules governing emotional transactions become shaky or break down, through disagreement or neglect, more attention is needed. Bickford's ideas outlined above for political listening become particularly important in these contexts.

Attention to reproductive labour and social maintenance can also create a different kind of temporality. Janna Graham from Ultra-red has characterized the group's debt to feminist organizing practices in terms of the importance of cups of tea in their practice and in community organizing in general. In one project, the group spent six weeks drinking tea with people who had experienced racism before they could begin to really have the conversations about it that were needed. Many micro encounters were necessary before they could sit in a room and talk about racism. For Ultra-red it is precisely 'the labour of the cups of tea, the decisions made in how these encounters are organised, and the affect created', as invisible affective elements of a project, that produce the conditions for listening and the possibilities of collective analysis and action that might follow (Farinati & Firth, 2017, p. 140). This is one way that Ultra-red attends to the micro-politics of listening, the particular roles of speakers and listeners, and in so doing, disrupts the dynamics of power and privilege.

Attending to the politics or micro-politics of listening becomes extremely complicated as organizations become larger, more stratified or established. There may need to be some reliance on the institution 'to hold voice, allow it to stay', and to have real consequences for change (Farinati & Firth, 2017, p. 104). Given that power is often embedded in structures through policies, procedures and unwritten norms and practices, there might need to be mechanisms for this to happen. However, it is also important to be wary of institutionalizing listening (Dobson, 2014). Stable, routine-reproduced patterns of behaviour can easily perform the empty non-performances of listening that were described above. More attention needs to be paid to how this happens and what might be done to mitigate this violence, and instead create truly dialogic organizations. In addition, we can educate ourselves in the arts of disagreement and the recognition of emotional labour. Arlie Hochschild uses the Hopi term *arofa* for the idea of the individual affective contribution to the collective or 'feelings-as-contribution-to-the-group' (2012, p. 18). If the transactions that take place within organizations were acknowledged, or we were able to educate ourselves to be aware of our and others' contributions as something that we all make, it might make a difference to the organizational systems of which we are a part.

Conclusions

I would like to come back to the quotation that began this chapter. Spender suggested that if listening were really valued and taken seriously it might change our social institutions. The question of whether it might be possible to have more dialogic organizations and institutions depends on how we can intervene on the multiple levels of communication that organizations function on, including both the interpersonal and the wider social and political contexts. We can learn to recognize our own contributions, and how they affect our relationships and wider groups we are a part of. We can also learn to recognize and interrogate obstructive institutionalization, challenge it and engage in political listening to build coalitions and shift power relations. On a wider political level, it is possible that neoliberalism as we have known it is coming to some kind of end. Challenges to it and tensions within it have been surfacing for a number of years now. With the retreat of the Covid-19 pandemic in sight, there is perhaps an opportunity to rethink what new worlds we might want or are able to co-create. This is where a feminist aesthetics which includes a deep ethical awareness of our interdependence and connection and an understanding of the ways in which power can operate on both a micro and structural level is crucial. A creative imagination that takes these aspects into account is vital if we are to imagine new possible worlds and work towards them. And while not underestimating the challenge that this poses there is always the possibility of co-creating new worlds that put listening with humility and ethical care in the service of challenging and changing power relations and inequality.

References

Ahmed, S. (2000). *Strange encounters: Embodied others in post-coloniality*. Routledge.

Ahmed, S. (2021). *Complaint*. Duke University Press.

Barthes. (1992). *The responsibility of forms: Critical essays on music, art and representation* (New ed.). University of California Press.

Bassel, L. (2018). *Politics of listening: Possibilities and challenges for democratic life*. Palgrave Pivot.

Bickford, S. (1996). *The dissonance of democracy: Listening, conflict, and citizenship*. Cornell University Press.

Brown, W. (2019). *In the ruins of neoliberalism: The rise of antidemocratic politics in the west*. Columbia University Press.

Butterwick, S., & Selman, J. (2020). Community-based art making: Creating spaces for changing the story. *New directions for adult and continuing education*, 35–47.

Campbell, D. (2000). *The socially constructed organization*. Karnac.

Collective, T. C., Chatzidakis, A., Hakim, J., Littler, J., Rottenberg, C., & Segal, L. (2020). *The care manifesto: The politics of interdependence: The politics of compassion*. Verso.

Couldry, N. (2011). *Why voice matters: Culture and politics after neoliberalism*. Sage.

Dobson, A. (2014). *Listening for democracy: Recognition, representation, reconciliation*. Oxford University Press.

Farinati, L., & Firth, C. (2017). *The force of listening*. Errant Bodies Press.

Federici, S. (2020). *Revolution at point zero: Housework, reproduction, and feminist struggle*. PM PR.

Firth, C. (2019). Reading the collective subject, three moments of crisis, aftermath and the aesthetics of resistance. Unpublished PhD manuscript, Birkbeck, University of London.

Garver, E. (2011). *Aristotle's politics: Living well and living together*. University of Chicago Press.

Gilbert, J. (2013). What kind of a thing is neoliberalism? *New Formations, 80*(81), 7–15.

Helguera, P. (2012). *Education for socially engaged art*. Jorge Pinto Books.

Hochschild, A. R. (2012). *The managed Heart: Commercialization of human feeling*. University of California Press.

hooks, b. (1994). *Teaching to transgress: Education as the practice of freedom*. Routledge.

Honneth, A. (2014). *Disrespect: The normative foundations of critical theory*. Wiley.

Jelinek, A. (2013). *This is not art. Activism and other 'not-art'*. I.B. Tauris.

Kioupkiolis, A. (2019). *The common and counter-hegemonic politics: Re-thinking social change*. Edinburgh University Press.

Miksits, M. (2019). Systemic practice for work with teams and organisations. In A. Novacovic & D. Vincent (Eds.), *Group analysis: Working with staff, teams and organisations* (pp. 24–36). Karnac.

Nancy, J. L. (2007). *Listening* (C. Mandell. Trans. Annotated ed.). Fordham University Press.

Rolnik, S. (2007). The body's contagious memory. Lygia Clark's return to the museum. http://eipcp.net/transversal/0507/rolnik/en

Sample, H. (2016). *Maintenance architecture*. MIT Press.

Sewell, W. H. (2007). *Logics of history: Social theory and social transformation*. University of Chicago Press.

Spender, D. (2001). *Man made language*. Pandora.

Warren, M. E. (1996). What should we expect from more democracy?: Radically democratic responses to politics. *Political Theory, 24*(2), 241–70.

Chapter 17

On Fostering Feminist Friendships for Resistance and Respite: Love-letter-making

Kathleen (Kaye) A. Hare and Amber Moore

Co-author Kaye once texted to co-author Amber, 'You are like a diary who writes back'. As late-stage PhD candidates, we experience our doctoral programme through a generative and generous partnership grounded in a shared research interest in feminist approaches to sexuality, sexual trauma and witnessing, a mutual obligation to advancing anti-oppressive and anti-racist ways of knowing, and an intense investment in one another's happiness and success through friendship. As we enter the final stages of our dissertations, this transition period creates room for reflection about how we contribute to each other's academic growth, particularly how we use arts-based, critical and embodied forms of enquiry to help reconfigure conditions that perpetuate femme-based inequities in academic institutions.

This chapter is inspired by the work of the *Survivor Love Letter Project*, an activist and artistic undertaking founded by Tani Ikeda on Valentine's Day in 2012. The original undertaking reimagines the traditional love letter genre by recasting writing as explicitly resistant, launching a love letter writing campaign in support of victim-survivors of sexual violence. These letters communicate how experiences of violence are believed, heard and loved. Inspired by this and with the goal of contributing to the understudied field of love letters (VanHaitsma, 2014), we engage in an epistolary writing project to expound our critical, feminist friendship. In doing so, we play with the romantic aesthetics of love letters by bending genre conventions to both extend the tradition of celebrating our partnership and take up contemporary traditions of reimaging love letters as a place for feminist resistance, persistence and respite. In this chapter, we explore how our love-letter-making challenges patriarchal, heteronormative understandings of affection, care and support in neoliberal professional settings and beyond. Because love letters are traditionally written to someone to whom the writer is (or hopes to be) romantically entangled, we also endeavour to construct creative *counter* letters as we cherish one another but are not romantically connected. Said another way, we use this project to, in part, disrupt the hierarchizing of romantic relationships in order to centre the triumphs of feminist friendship(s) in academia.

Academic critical and feminist friendships

When we began this project, we were surprised to learn that academic friendships remain underexplored (Gallagher, 2018; Webster & Boyd, 2018). However, considerable literature does attend to the importance of 'critical friends' (i.e. Costa & Kallick, 1993; Storey & Wang, 2017; Swaffield, 2008). A critical friend (CF) is 'someone who provides both support and challenge within a relationship that may be one-to-one or involve a CF working with a group of people' (Storey & Wang, 2016, p. 107). It can entail practices such as advocacy, community building, confidentiality, encouragement, provocations, validations, sharing and so forth. Essentially, a CF has a comprehensive appreciation for, investment in, and understanding of their colleague's work, aims and context. Such friendships are important coalitions for combatting neoliberalism, which prioritizes abstract, rationalized knowledge and produces what Enslin et al. (2019) refer to as 'dark times' for scholars by centring competition, individualism, managerial politics, market-determined practices and many demands in academic life. Friendship in higher education offers respite from and resistance to this current regime by embracing care, community, criticality and creation of space for navigation.

More specifically, academic feminist friendships are 'relationships that enable continuous evolution of our beings and mindsets, of our values and visions in conversation with one another without feeling threatened by one another' (Nagar et al., 2016, p. 508), representing rich sites of knowledge as places to re-make subversively the world (McGregor, 2018). Because critical friendship is congruent with feminism stances (Appleton, 2011), we understand feminist friends to be kinds of CFs but with a more explicitly aligned sense of care practices and politics. For example, Fernández, Hisatake and Nguyen (2020) explore how decolonial feminist friendships amongst Women of Colour in academia can be built through reflexive individual storytelling vignettes threaded together, enmeshing experiences for coalition building. Other feminist scholars are now investigating the power and possibility of such academic collaborations and friendships (i.e. Breeze & Taylor, 2018; Gibbs Grey & Williams-Ferrier, 2017; Godbee & Novanty, 2013; Nagar et al., 2016; Webster & Boyd, 2018). We contribute to this growing body of literature with this project.

Friends and letters

We consider ourselves to be not only feminists but feminist killjoys. While the term killjoy can be seen as derogatory, Ahmed (2017) uses it quite differently. Killjoys are women who speak out against injustice, even when it is uncomfortable to do so. They are feminist accomplices and allies, therefore, who speak truth to power in all situations, even when it 'kills the joy'. Feminist killjoys push back against patriarchal culture(s), resist actions that are 'too soft, too safe' (p. 239) to make a difference by doing the unappealing work of being the one who openly challenges sexism, exposes violence or racism over and over. Killjoys are courageous because they are willing to get into trouble for what they believe. We two as feminist kill joys embody what Wunker (2016) refers to as 'that irreverent figure who lights a match and joyfully flicks it into the dry hull of patriarchal culture' (p. 15). However, feminist killjoys need friends and friendship 'is a radical act' (Wunker, 2016, p. 29), which we evidence in this chapter.

Drawing further from Ahmed (2012), we attend to her contention that what guides enquiries in neoliberal higher education institutions is no longer '"Is it [a knowledge claim] true?" but rather, "What use is it"' (p. 84). Ahmed takes up this contention in the context of the various documents produced in academic institutions, describing how power relations surface through understandings of what various documents are doing (e.g., strategy, policy, scholarly and/or evidentiary); and accordingly, 'we need to follow them around – considering how they circulate within organisations, creating vertical and horizontal lines of communication' (p. 85). We take heed of noticing that we are discussing a topic that is not typically captured in these document paper trails – doctoral student friendship consisting of personal connections, digital exchanges and acts of service that exist outside of formal institutional processes, even while centred and dependent on such processes. We therefore see our letters as functioning as a kind of subversive feminist form of documentation by turning the oft-disregarded experience of academic friendship into the institutionally recognized asset of a scholarly publication. In the process, we can hear what such letters have to say about academic institutions.

Love-letter-making

Our enquiry is methodologically situated with an emergent body of literature that explores the inner workings of academia from first person, experiential perspectives (i.e. Breeze & Taylor, 2018; Gibbs Grey & Williams-Farrier, 2017). In particular, we find methodological alignment with studies that take up academic subjectivities within larger trajectories of feminist methodologies and epistemologies that prioritize experiential ways of knowing. Rich contributions to these trajectories have come through feminist academics surfacing the power of/in intersectional personal accounts of the academy (Baker-Bell, 2017; Henry, 2015), embodying and inhabiting accounts of race and academia (Ahmed, 2012; Overstreet, 2019), and attending to the co-constitutive nature of institutional life with identity (Gonzales & Terosky, 2020; Webster & Boyd, 2018).

Through such feminist projects, the epistemological status of experience has been problematized. Like Gannon et al. (2015) and Mason (2002), we understand that our accounts of experience cannot be taken uncritically as expressions of 'truth' or as self-evident empirical data; experience is mediated and rendered intelligible in multiple ways. We view the knowledge creation outlined in this chapter as an expression of our shared realities that have been constituted through historical and cultural conditions of our existence, including gender. The collective feminist method we employ in love-letter-making is particularly appropriate to our feminist aims, enabling consideration of subjectivity as part of the constitutive process of experience. A collective method also enables 'collaging individual stories to undermine the notion of narratives as individual' to create new understandings' (Brookes et al., 2020, p. 282). For feminists whose work combines investigations into resistance to rape culture and sexual/gender equity and producing 'data' with advocacy work, this notion of collaging to produce documents that are simultaneously academic and resistant holds much appeal.

Feminist academic collaborations, especially ones that employ shared forms of composition, can also be methods of enquiry themselves. Collaborative writing is an embodied process that has been used with success to explore feminists' career trajectories (e.g., Breeze & Taylor, 2018; Gibbs Grey & Williams-Farrier, 2017), including the 'relational complexities of academic work' (Gannon et al., 2015, p. 190). Feminist collaborations can also be a tool for deploying an ethic of care. That is, we seek to meet each other's particular needs, for the purposes of 'procuring a semblance of safety' (Whitehead, 2020, n.p.) that can allow for open, vulnerable reflections for change. In addition to being an intellectual project, our love letters are an ethical and political endeavour.

By both drawing on and veering off from romantic aesthetic strategies such as confessional tone (Takolander, 2017), restrained rhetoric (VanHaitsma, 2014), mutual vulnerability (Gunaratnam, 2007) and the pleasure of possibility (Knapp & Knapp, 2017) in our letters, we are not focused on producing letters that are valuable for their writerly conceits but rather seek to illuminate how unabashed, brazen and experiential composition can help produce an ethic of critical friendship. We story our separate and intertwined professional identities – challenges, hopes, possibilities and victories – to advance acting and being with each other (Ziarek, 2014), while also undertaking academic reflection that can provide emotionally textured theory on the uneasy art of learning to be a feminist scholar.

Our love letters

To help contextualize our letters, we offer here a brief introduction to the feminist story of our feminist friendship. We met at the start of our dissertation programme in Language and Literacy Education department at the University of British Columbia. We were immediately drawn to each other due to aligned research interests: Amber's doctoral work explores the pedagogical potential of teaching sexual assault narratives to enact resistances against rape culture (see Moore, 2020a, 2020b), while Kaye investigates novice educators' embodied experiences of sexual health education (Hare, 2021). Our fledgling relationship was solidified through early collaborations that confirmed our shared feminist values, mutual inability to not speak up against oppression/discrimination and our tendency to have too much fun while doing academic work. We have different strengths that help us work as feminist partners and a deep respect for each other that underlies our friendship inside and outside of academia. Our hobbies include documenting ideas for shared academic papers, finding funny Twitter threads and encouraging the other person to take much-deserved breaks from teaching/writing/servicing/ working.

In writing our love letters to document our feminist, critical friendship, we set deliberately loose parameters: Write a love letter as part of an academic book chapter and share the letter once completed.

Love Letter 1

My Dearest Amber,

I often think fondly about the first time that we met at a funding workshop for doctoral students. I have a vivid memory of you sitting at a table, hair bouncing, clutching a paper copy of your application. When we started talking about the application, you mentioned that you were a bit over the page limit. I remember looking at your paper copy and noticing that you had not realized the application had non-standard margins; by adjusting them you would gain precious cm of space. I am embarrassed to admit my first instinct was to wonder 'should I tell her? We are directly competing for this funding'. I remember thinking 'she seems kind' and 'don't knowingly let her stumble on a technicality', before the clincher of 'be better than that way of thinking'.

You immediately looked grateful and sent me a follow-up thank you email. I had no way of knowing that by giving you a cm, I would be making a friend whose gifts to me cannot be measured. I also did not yet know that you were just reaping what you sow, because you are incredibly intellectually generous people. You would unhesitatingly tell a fellow applicant that their margins were too big. You always have time to support others, give feedback, suggest references and smile encouragingly. You are above all else, a teacher, a doctor (and by the time this is published that title will be official). Many people are drawn to your particular mix of intellect and ethic of care, and I often feel sheepishly lucky that you have picked me to be your academic partner.

I have learnt intellectual bravery from you and the skills necessary to be academically brave. You have a transcendental ability to identify multiple applications of any text. You joyously read scholarship, connecting ideas in bold, innovative ways. Whenever I unleash some marginal little nugget of an idea, your response is normally three articles that can help me develop that nugget into an implementable project. With your influence, I have transitioned to a scholar who tells small stories, designs workshops on digital screaming, and writes academic love letters. It is my greatest wish that our side projects can one day move to central components of our scholarship. I see so many extensions and possibilities, even from this project. Having the embodied act of expressing love (via a 'menu of options') be what participants do and gain out of research, as well as being able to care-fully using love in academic feminist resistance, is the type of academic future that I want for us.

Speaking of 'care-ful', I think it goes without saying that I deeply value the support you provide for me as a human being. The PhD has been challenging. It is hard to be a fully adult person with fully adult problems but confined to the role and resources of a student. You get it, and don't need to hear the explanation to know the explanation. I am so very grateful for getting to leave words unspoken with you. On the flipside, as femme-forward youngish white women in the academy, we have talked many times about how to navigate being a femme-forward, youngish, white women in the academy. I have learnt much from your insights in those conversations, and now act with a more nuanced understanding of my positionalities.

But what I value the most is that in a situation where we are forced into competition for funding, awards and recognitions, we think differently about getting ahead. The benefit of our friendship is getting ahead. Another head to think expansively, question deeply, attend precisely, spot non-standard margins and metissage with vigour. And I think we and our work are much better for it. It doesn't mean that the circumstances beyond our control cease to exist, but it does mean that the way of managing them shifts from individual stress to collective will. And isn't that exactly what we are trying to do with our research anyway? We are just aligning theory with method with researcher. And who knows, if the stars come into alignment too, we might just get academic jobs.

In Academic Trust,

Kaye

Love Letter 2

KAYE,

I had to start this with all caps because this is often how I greet you via text, virtually 'screaming' in excited anticipation to share something: a compelling call for papers, a meme, a rant about the Kardashians, or a likely innocuous email that you will, as always, patiently read as I overreact, typing it all out in a burst of messages that could have been captured in a single one. I am always in a rush to connect with you. In fact, here's a brief list of what want to share after finishing this letter:

A recipe for grain-free tahini and coconut granola (for your 'tender tummy')
- *A Teen Vogue article about sex education (sending you things to read is my love language)*
- *Homemade honey and eucalyptus lip scrub (this will be post-pandemic but is well worth the wait. My lips are downright pillowy)*

Treats for Tika from the cat cafe two blocks away

Although I can't remember if this was before or after you gifted me with an Aaron Carter valentine, I feel like I first really got to know you when we were partnered for a grad school class presentation and you quickly and brilliantly smashed two of our interests together for a perfect project. I was terrified but you patiently guided me. This experience quickly cemented for me that I needed to barnacle myself to you – my grad school buoy.

Now, I save screenshots of advice you've offered, and my family asks for updates on how school is going for you too. I think of you when I see all-dressed chips in the grocery store, hear something about Edmonton, or discover a paper with really dynamic methods. Connecting with you is my safe place, my dumping ground, where I celebrate the wins, mourn failures, work through difficult decisions, and ask questions I'm too afraid to ask anyone else. You are considerate, sharply insightful and intelligent, quick to laugh, inspiring, loyal and ferocious in all the ways that matter. At this very moment, in my fridge, I still have leftover vegan cashew cheese from the care package you left on my doorstep weeks ago, filled with the ingredients – including homemade jam – for an apple grilled cheese sandwich I literally dreamed about and off-handedly mentioned. This is the considerate person that you are – a rare breed. I am so lucky and I often worry about whether or not I'm doing and saying enough to be reciprocal and deserving of your friendship.

If we chat in person, on the phone, or on Zoom, at the end, we always wryly laugh instead of offering goodbyes; rather, we say something akin to 'Okay, I'm sure we'll text like, within the hour' and so I feel compelled to do the same here. I know I will soon share this draft and send it to you with some excited emojis and several panicky 'I hope you like it~!?' messages because I know this isn't enough to celebrate your beautiful spirit. You've taught me that perhaps this might be understood as emotional litter (Hare, 2020).

However, what gives me immense joy and a true sense of ease is that I am confident that our friendship will only continue to deepen and strengthen, especially as we soon move on to the next phase of our academic careers. Thinking ahead to the possible postdocs, jobs, sessional teaching – whatever comes 'next' for us – is far less scary when I think about how we will not only see one another through these stages but celebrate each one together. I am damn lucky I am to have you as my dear friend. Thank you endlessly for everything.

In gratitude,
Amber

Lingering on love

We find that fostering critical feminist relationships can be a balm for the chaffs of research that often asks us to attend to the challenging parts of intimate relationships with rigorous criticality, as well as secure a shared space for us to find respite and 'respair'. Feminist respair is defined by Kay & Benet-Weisler (2019, p. 607) as 'fresh hope; a recovery from despair' and, returning to our conceptual frame of the killjoy – a figure who needs friends. Together, we build feminist killjoy survival kits to 'keep one's hope alive [because after all] 'we need each other to survive; we need to be a part of each other's survival' (p. 235). Our letters represent a hopeful source of feminist respair in the form of a survival strategy as we engage in unguarded self-expression that communicates an effusion of feeling toward one another through these fragments. Our letters are evidence of a larger experience of love between us that we regularly feed to stay 'alive' and thrive while navigating the neoliberal university and all the spidery ways in which academia impacts us.

While we do harness love letter genre conventions – indeed, 'pillowy lips' are mentioned – from the outset, we defy a central one because we are not courting one another (VanHaitsma, 2014). Rather, as we anticipate soon concluding our

PhD journeys, we express loving gratitude for help with reaching this point. Unbeknownst to one another, we went on to similarly invoke and play with particular conventions including tender salutations and valedictions, thoughtful anecdotes and confessional tones. To begin with, Amber launches into her letter with an all-caps 'shouting' to 'KAYE', demonstrating both a casual tone and sense of urgency. This rhetorical cannonballing into the letter disrupts the typical restrained pacing of a love letter; manuals for epistolary prose used to instruct writing in accordance with how a couple might sensibly pace a relationship (VanHaitsma, 2014). Kaye's salutation is also filled with meaning as she immediately claims Amber as hers similarly rushing forward in her writing by fore-fronting intimacy with the use of the personal pronoun 'my' – which Heath Wellman (2000) alleges has a kind of special 'magic' – and using the affectionate term, 'dearest'.

We then quickly launch into anecdotes about first connecting as feminist friends; Kaye offered Amber assistance with grant writing, while Amber reflected on our first collective project. The anecdote is a powerful genre nested within our love letters because it is a mainstay in feminist storytelling, teaching and knowledge production with its power to 'cut through' (Donegan, 2017, n.p.). Depending on how it is used, it can sometimes be an idiosyncratic technique for challenging detached intellectual discourse (Gregg, 2004), which certainly is a goal of this project. We begin with anecdotes to reflect on specific significant instances that can then be unpacked. Hopefully, these anecdotes facilitate shared knowledge with not only one another, but also, our audience so that we might, as McGregor (2019) argues, both 'open out our worlds' and do 'radical knowledge work' (p. 7). Although, as Gregg (2004) might say, our anecdotes are seemingly mundane, they offer illustrations of how academics-in-training often rely on one another for guidance rather than on sustained support from the university. Our anecdotes are 'at one and the same time literary and real' (Gallop, 2002, p. 3). Though both anecdotes represent fond friendship memories, anxiety is palpable in each, and yet they demonstrate triumph as our feminist friendship becomes the place where we can nurture our academic identities in tandem.

Lastly, each of our letters also carries distinct confessional tones. Confession represents a relevant way of knowing, and especially for our purposes, it can be politically enabling (hooks, 1994; hooks & Hall, 2018) and a place for feminist respair. For example, Kaye speaks to how the PhD is challenging because she is often infantilized despite being in her mid-thirties with an already successful professional life behind her. This is just one example of how Kaye demonstrates resistance by genre bending in her letter: infusing it with reflections on the politics of graduate school. Ahmed (2017) takes up the issue of complaint in the academy, particularly about institutionalized sexual harassment and racism, and how feminist killjoys can counter. Moving through formal university procedures for complaint is difficult because the complainer is usually treated as 'potential damage' (Ahmed, 2017, p. 515) and so, although Kaye is not complaining about a particular incident, her politicized rhetoric is sharply strategic because she nests her confessional complaining within a love letter – a kind of hiding in plain sight as it is published within an academic text. Amber takes on a particular confessional tone when she muses about whether she enacts adequate reciprocity, questioning if she is 'deserving' of this friendship. Reflecting on this particularly gave us pause as we realized that Amber might be making the common mistake of confusing gratitude with indebtedness (Mullin, 2011) and so revisiting her letter while writing this chapter allowed for her to trouble her confession. Reading Kaye's letter further helped her to see herself anew as someone who 'carefully uses love' in this feminist friendship.

Parting words

Love-letter-making allowed us to thread together our individual stories, challenging overly simplified understandings as feminist collaborations-as-resistance. From the beginning, our letters are places where we acknowledge 'the need for care, for mutual support' and to commit to 'repair[ing] collectively' (Kay & Benet-Weilser, 2019, p. 608) to complete the challenging work we undertake as a duo in our academic journeys. We talk of a hopeful shared future with planned projects, wherein we can enact feminist resistance through possibilities for continued work. Simultaneously, we acknowledge that such possibilities come with impossibilities, and that the increasingly neoliberalized academic institution wherein the numbers of available, secure academic jobs are shrinking renders such resistances tenuous.

With feminist love in our survival kits, we have helped each other navigate the academic terrain to this point. Perhaps the most radical knowledge work we can do now is to keep our hopes alive by thinking carefully and generativity about the implications of the closing note of both letters. In capturing relationality, Kaye's 'in academic trust' and Amber's 'in gratitude' speak to defying the mobilities of individual logics. There is significance in not only being feminists who love, but also are doing feminist love in academia. As educators, we thus also find it worthwhile to gesture towards the pedagogical possibilities inherent in feminist love-letter-making; for example, consider Hogan's (2014) gender studies course project where she assigns her students to write letters of gratitude to historical feminists as a way of diffusing anxiety and hostility. We believe that not only is love-letter-making a significant practice for fostering feminist friendships, but further, such partnerships might particularly begin in feminist classrooms. They are also a feminist aesthetic.

Finally, facing our collective uncertain future, we also 'do' by returning to Ikeda's (2021) love-letter project that inspired this work. We conclude by sharing an activist love letter from the project that we consider now and moving forward:

You are not alone. Take your hands
And cup your face gently
Close your eyes
Can you smell the night sky?
What you thought was loneliness
Is just the quiet pink space
between darkness and dawn.

References

Ahmed, S. (2012). *On being included: Racism and diversity in institutional life*. Duke University Press.

Ahmed, S. (2017). *Living a feminist life*. Duke University Press.

Appleton, C. (2011). 'Critical friends', feminism and integrity: A reflection on the use of critical friends as a research tool to support researcher integrity and reflexivity in qualitative research studies. *Women in Welfare Education, 10*, 1–13.

Baker-Bell, A. (2017). For Loretta: A Black woman literacy scholar's journey to prioritizing self-preservation and Black feminist-womanist storytelling. *Journal of Literacy Research, 49*(4), 526–43. https://doi.org/10.1177/1086296X17733092

Blunt, A. and Dowling, R. (2006). *Home*. Routledge.

Brookes, S. D., Dean, A. S. Franklin-Phipps, A., Mathis, E., Rath, C. L., Raza, N., Smothers, L. E., & Sunderstrom, K. (2020). Becoming-academic in the neoliberal university: A collective biography. *Gender and Education, 32*(3), 281–300. https://doi.org/10.1080/09540253.2017.1332341

Breeze, M., & Taylor, Y. (2020). Feminist collaborations in higher education: Stretched across career stages. *Gender & Education, 32*(3), 412–28. https://doi.org/10.1080/09540253.2018.1471197

Costa, A. L., & Kallick, B. (1993). Through the lens of a critical friend. *Educational Leadership, 51*(2), 49–51.

Donegan, M. (2017, April 5). Rebecca Solnit's faith in feminist storytelling. *The New Yorker*. Retrieved from https://www.newyorker.com/books/page-turner/rebecca-solnits-faith-in-feminist-storytelling

Enslin, P., & Hedge, N. (2019). Academic friendship in dark times. *Ethics & Education, 14*(4), 383–98. https://doi.org/10.1080/17449642.2019.1660457

Fernández, J. S., Hisatake, K., & Nguyen, A. (2020). Decolonial feminism as reflexive praxis: Lugoness's 'world'-travelling as stories of friendship in academia. *Frontiers, 41*(1), 12–34. https://muse.jhu.edu/article/755338

Gallagher, K. (2018). *The methodological dilemma revisited*. Routledge.

Gallop, J. (2002). *Anecdotal theory*. Duke University Press.

Gannon, S., Kligyte, G., McLean, J., Perrier, M., Swan, E., Vanni, I., & van Rijswijk, H. (2015). Uneven relationalities, collective biography, and sisterly affect in neoliberal universities. *Feminist Formation, 27*(3), 189–216. https://doi.org/10.1353/ff.2016.0007

Gibbs Grey, T., & Williams-Ferrier, B. J. (2017). #SippingTea: Two Black female literacy scholars sharing counter-stories to redefine our roles in the academy. *Journal of Literacy Research, 49*(4), 503–25. https://doi.org/10.1177/1086296X17733091

Godbee, B., & Novanty, J. C. (2013). Asserting the right to belong: Feminist co-mentoring among graduate student women. *Feminist Teacher, 23*(3), 177–95. https://doi.org/10.5406/femteacher.23.3.0177

Gonzales, L., & LaPointe Terosky, A. (2020). On their own terms: Women's pathways into and through academe. *Journal of Diversity in Higher Education, 13*(3), 274–87. https://doi.org/10.1037/dhe0000128

Gregg, M. (2004). A mundane voice. *Cultural Studies, 18*(2–3), 363–83. https://doi.org/10.1080/0950238042000020563

Gunaratnam, Y. (2007). where is the love? art, aesthetics and research. *Journal of Social Work Practice, 21*(3), 271–87. https://doi.org/10.1080/02650530701553518

Hare, K. (2021). Institutionalized states of information abstinence: Cut-up inquiry of sex educators' erasure poems. *Arts/Research International: A Transdisciplinary Journal, 6*(2), 415–41. https://doi.org/10.18432/ari29540

Hare, K. (2020). Collecting sensorial litter: Ethnographic reflexive grappling with corporeal complexity. *International Journal of Qualitative Methods, 19*, 1–12. https://doi.org/10.1177/1609406920958600

Heath Wellman, C. (2000). Relational facts in liberal political theory: Is there magic in the pronoun 'my'? *Ethics, 110*(3), 537–62. https://doi.org/10.1086/233323

Henry, A. (2015). 'We especially welcome applications from members of visible minority groups': Reflections on race, gender and life at three universities. *Race, Ethnicity and Education, 18*(5), 589–610. https://doi.org/10.1080/13613324.2015.1023787

Hogan, K. (2014). Come closer to feminism: Gratitude as activist encounter in women's and gender studies 101. *Feminist Teacher, 24*(3), 229–33. https://doi.org/10.5406/femteacher.24.3.0229

hooks, b. (1994). *Teaching to transgress: Education as the practice of freedom*. Routledge.

hooks, b., & Hall, S. (2018). *Uncut funk: A contemplative dialogue*. Routledge.

Ikeda, T. (2021). Survivor love letter. Retrieved October 20, 2021, from https://www.survivorloveletter.com/home

Kay, J. B., & Benet-Weilser, S. (2019). Feminist anger and feminist respair. *Feminist Media Studies, 19*(4), 603–9. https://doi.org/10.1080/14680777.2019.1609231

Knapp, J. F., & Knapp, P. A. (2017). *Medieval romance: The aesthetics of possibility*. University of Toronto Press.

Mason, G. (2002). *The spectacle of violence*. Routledge.

McGregor, H. (2018, January 26). *Law school & feminist friendship with Kendra Marks & Sylvie Vigneux – Secret Feminist Agenda* [audio podcast]. Retrieved from: https://secretfeministagenda.files.wordpress.com/2018/11/episode-2-2-law-school-_-feminist-friendship-with-kendra-marks-and-sylvie-vigneux.pdf

McGregor, H. (2019, May 10). *Feminist anecdotes – Secret feminist agenda* [audio podcast]. Retrieved from: https://secretfeministagenda.files.wordpress.com/2020/01/episode-3.29-feminist-anecdotes.pdf

Moore, A. (2020a). Pulping as poetic inquiry: On upcycling 'upset' to reckon anew with rape culture, rejection, and (re)turning to trauma texts. *Cultural Studies ↔ Critical Methodologies, 20*(6), 588–95. https://doi.org/10.1177/1532708620912802

Moore, A. (2020b). 'Why don't we always see her face?': The significance of gallery walks as an engagement strategy in teaching trauma literature. *English Practice, 61*(1), 43–7. https://bctela.ca/wp-content/uploads/2020/10/2020-BCTELA-English-Practice.pdf

Mullin, A. (2011). Gratitude and caring labor. *Ethics & Social Welfare, 5*(2), 110–22. https://doi.org/10.1080/17496535.2011.571061

Nagar, R., Aslan, O., Hasan, N. Z., Rahemtullah, O. S., Upadhyay, N., & Uzun, B. (2016). Feminisms, collaborations, friendships: A conversation. *Feminist Studies, 42*(2), 502–19. https://doi.org/10.15767/feministstudies.42.2.0502

Overstreet, M. (2019). My first year in academia or the mythical black woman superhero takes on the ivory tower. *Journal of Women and Gender in Higher Education, 12*(1), 18–34. https://doi.org/10.1080/19407882.2018.1540993

Ross, L. (2009). From the 'f' word to Indigenous/feminisms. *Wicazo Sa Review, 24*(2), 39–52. 10.1353/wic.0.0041

Storey, V. A., & Wang, V. C. X. (2017). Critical friends protocol: Andragogy and learning in a graduate classroom. *Adult Learning, 28*(3), 107–14. https://doi.org/10.1177/1045159516674705

Swaffield, S. (2008). Critical friendship, dialogue and learning, in the context of leadership for learning. *School Leadership & Management, 28*(4), 323–36. https://doi.org/10.1080/13632430802292191

Takolander, M. (2017). Confessional poetry and the materialisation of an autobiographical self. *Life Writing, 14*(3), 371–83. https://doi.org/10.1080/14484528.2017.1337502

VanHaitsma, P. (2014). Queering the language of the heart: Romantic letters, genre instruction, and rhetorical practice. *Rhetoric Society Quarterly, 44*(1), 6–24. https://doi.org/10.1080/02773945.2013.861009

Webster, N., & Boyd, M. (2018). Exploring the importance of inter-departmental women's friendship in geography as resistance in the neoliberal academy. *Geografiska Annaler: Series B, Human Geography, 101*(1), 44–55. https://doi.org/10.1080/04353684.2018.1507612

Whitehead, J. [@JWhitehead204]. (2020, April 17). *It's important, I think, to caretake for others passionately right now. Staying caring is a means of procuring a semblance of safety* [Tweet]. Twitter. https://twitter.com/i/status/1251318915621249024

Wunker, E. (2016). *Notes from a feminist killjoy: Essays on everyday life*. BookThug.

Ziarek, E. P. (2014). Feminist aesthetics: Transformative practice, neoliberalism, and the violence of formalism. *Differences, 25*(2), 101–15. https://doi.org/10.1215/10407391-2773445

INDEX

9 781350 231085